DEFINING MOMENTS
THE GREAT MIGRATION NORTH, 1910-1970

DEFINING MOMENTS
THE GREAT MIGRATION NORTH, 1910-1970

Laurie Lanzen Harris

Omnigraphics

155 W. Congress, Suite 200
Detroit, MI 48226

Omnigraphics, Inc.

Kevin Hillstrom, *Series Editor*
Cherie D. Abbey, *Managing Editor*

Peter E. Ruffner, *Publisher*
Matthew P. Barbour, *Senior Vice President*

Elizabeth Collins, *Research and
Permissions Coordinator*
Kevin M. Hayes, *Operations Manager*

Allison A. Beckett and Mary Butler, *Research Staff*
Cherry Edwards, *Permissions Assistant*
Shirley Amore, Martha Johns, and Kirk Kauffmann,
Administrative Staff

Copyright © 2012 Omnigraphics, Inc.
ISBN 978-0-7808-1186-7

Library of Congress Cataloging-in-Publication Data

Harris, Laurie Lanzen.
  The great migration north, 1910-1970 / by Laurie Lanzen Harris.
    p. cm. -- (Defining moments)
  Includes bibliographical references and index.
  Summary: "Provides a comprehensive overview of the movement of millions of African Americans out of the South during the twentieth century, including the political, social, and economic factors that drove their migration. Includes a narrative overview, biographies, primary sources, chronology, glossary, bibliography, and index"--Provided by publisher.
  ISBN 978-0-7808-1186-7 (hardcover : alk. paper) 1. African Americans--Migrations--History--20th century. 2. Rural-urban migration--United States--History--20th century. I. Title.
  E185.6.H27 2011
  307.2'40973--dc23   2011033540

The information in this publication was compiled from sources cited and from sources considered reliable. While every possible effort has been made to ensure reliability, the publisher will not assume liability for damages caused by inaccuracies in the data, and makes no warranty, express or implied, on the accuracy of the information contained herein.

This book is printed on acid-free paper meeting the ANSI Z39.48 Standard. The infinity symbol that appears above indicates that the paper in this book meets that standard.

Printed in the United States of America

TABLE OF CONTENTS

NARRATIVE OVERVIEW

BIOGRAPHIES

PRIMARY SOURCES

PREFACE

Throughout the course of America's existence, its people, culture, and institutions have been periodically challenged—and in many cases transformed—by profound historical events. Some of these momentous events, such as women's suffrage, the Civil Rights Movement, and U.S. involvement in World War II, invigorated the nation and strengthened American confidence and capabilities. Others, such as the Great Depression, the Vietnam War, and Watergate, have prompted troubled assessments and heated debates about the country's core beliefs and character.

Some of these defining moments in American history were years or even decades in the making. The Harlem Renaissance and the New Deal, for example, unfurled over the span of several years, while the American labor movement and the Cold War evolved over the course of decades. Other defining moments, such as the Cuban missile crisis and the Japanese attack on Pearl Harbor, transpired over a matter of days or weeks.

But although significant differences exist among these events in terms of their duration and their place in the timeline of American history, all share the same basic characteristic: they transformed the United States' political, cultural, and social landscape for future generations of Americans.

Taking heed of this fundamental reality, American citizens, schools, and other institutions are increasingly emphasizing the importance of understanding our nation's history. Omnigraphics' *Defining Moments* series was created for the express purpose of meeting this growing appetite for authoritative, useful historical resources. This series will be of enduring value to anyone interested in learning more about America's past—and in understanding how those historical events continue to reverberate in the twenty-first century.

Each individual volume of *Defining Moments* provides a valuable resource for readers interested in learning about the most profound events in our nation's history. Each volume is organized into three distinct sections—Narrative Overview, Biographies, and Primary Sources.

- The **Narrative Overview** provides readers with a detailed, factual account of the origins and progression of the "defining moment" being examined. It also explores the event's lasting impact on America's political and cultural landscape.

- The **Biographies** section provides valuable biographical background on leading figures associated with the event in question. Each biography concludes with a list of sources for further information on the profiled individual.

- The **Primary Sources** section collects a wide variety of pertinent primary source materials from the era under discussion, including official documents, papers and resolutions, letters, oral histories, memoirs, editorials, and other important works.

Individually, each of these sections is a rich resource for users. Together, they comprise an authoritative, balanced, and absorbing examination of some of the most significant events in U.S. history.

Other notable features contained within each volume in the series include a glossary of important individuals, places, and terms; a detailed chronology featuring page references to relevant sections of the narrative; an annotated bibliography of sources for further study; an extensive general bibliography that reflects the wide range of historical sources consulted by the author; and a subject index.

New Feature—Research Topics for Student Reports

Each volume in the *Defining Moments* series now includes a list of research topics, detailing some of the important topics that recur throughout the volume and providing a valuable starting point for research. Students working on essays and reports will find this feature especially useful as they try to narrow down their research interests.

These research topics are covered throughout the different sections of the book: the narrative overview, the biographies, the primary sources, the chronology, and the important people, places, and terms section. This wide coverage allows readers to view the topic through a variety of different approaches.

Students using *Defining Moments: The Great Migration North, 1910-1970,* will find information on a wide range of topics suitable for conducting historical research and writing reports.

Acknowledgements

This series was developed in consultation with a distinguished Advisory Board comprised of public librarians, school librarians, and educators. They evaluated the series as it developed, and their comments and suggestions were invaluable throughout the production process. Any errors in this and other volumes in the series are ours alone. Following is a list of board members who contributed to the *Defining Moments* series:

Gail Beaver, M.A., M.A.L.S.
Adjunct Lecturer, University of Michigan
Ann Arbor, MI

Melissa C. Bergin, L.M.S., NBCT
Library Media Specialist
Niskayuna High School
Niskayuna, NY

Rose Davenport, M.S.L.S., Ed.Specialist
Library Media Specialist
Pershing High School Library
Detroit, MI

Karen Imarisio, A.M.L.S.
Assistant Head of Adult Services
Bloomfield Twp. Public Library
Bloomfield Hills, MI

Nancy Larsen, M.L.S., M.S. Ed.
Library Media Specialist
Clarkston High School
Clarkston, MI

Marilyn Mast, M.I.L.S.
Kingswood Campus Librarian
Cranbrook Kingswood Upper School
Bloomfield Hills, MI

Rosemary Orlando, M.L.I.S.
Library Director
St. Clair Shores Public Library
St. Clair Shores, MI

Comments and Suggestions

We welcome your comments on *Defining Moments: The Great Migration North, 1910-1970,* and suggestions for other events in U.S. history that warrant treatment in the *Defining Moments* series. Correspondence should be addressed to:

Editor, *Defining Moments*
Omnigraphics, Inc.
155 W. Congress, Suite 200
Detroit, MI 48226
E-mail: editorial@omnigraphics.com

HOW TO USE THIS BOOK

*D*efining Moments: The Great Migration North, 1910-1970, provides a comprehensive overview of the movement of millions of African Americans out of the South during the twentieth century, including the political, social, and economic factors that drove their migration.

Defining Moments: The Great Migration North is divided into three primary sections. The first of these sections, the **Narrative Overview**, provides a broad overview of the Migration and its aftermath. It outlines the history of slavery in the United States, recounts the establishment of Jim Crow segregationist laws in the South, describes the two major migrations of African Americans out of the South that took place in the twentieth century, discusses how the Great Migration contributed to the Civil Rights Movement, and examines the economic, political, and cultural legacy of the migrations.

The second section, **Biographies**, provides valuable biographical background on major historical figures associated with the Great Migration, including *Chicago Defender* publisher Robert S. Abbott, black nationalist Marcus Garvey, NAACP founder and intellectual W. E. B. Du Bois, civil rights leader Martin Luther King Jr., Harlem Renaissance poet Langston Hughes, and labor leader A. Philip Randolph. Each biography concludes with a list of sources for further information on the profiled individual.

The third section, **Primary Sources**, collects essential and illuminating documents related to the Great Migration. Selections include works that help readers understand the historical context of the Migration, including a 1916 excerpt from the *Chicago Defender* documenting the reasons blacks left the South; newspaper reports of anti-migration race riots in St. Louis and Chicago; an interview with an African-American migrant who found peace and prosperity in the North; and an essay from writer Maya Angelou exploring the reasons behind the so-called "reverse migration" of African Americans to the South in the latter part of the twentieth century.

Other features in *Defining Moments: The Great Migration North* include the following:

- A list of Research Topics that provide students with starting points for research.

- Attribution and referencing of primary sources and other quoted material to help guide users to other valuable historical research resources.

- Glossary of Important People, Places, and Terms.

- Detailed Chronology of events with a *see reference* feature. Under this arrangement, events listed in the chronology include a reference to page numbers within the Narrative Overview wherein users can find additional information on the event in question.

- Photographs of people, places, and events associated with the Great Migration.

- Sources for Further Study, an annotated list of noteworthy works about the Great Migration.

- Extensive bibliography of works consulted in the creation of this book, including books, periodicals, and Internet sites.

- A Subject Index.

RESEARCH TOPICS FOR
DEFINING MOMENTS: THE GREAT MIGRATION NORTH, 1910-1970

Starting a research paper can be a challenge, as students struggle to decide what area to study. Now, each book in the *Defining Moments* series includes a list of research topics, detailing some of the important topics that recur throughout the volume and providing a valuable starting point for research. Students working on essays and reports will find this feature especially useful as they try to narrow down their research interests.

These research topics are covered throughout the different sections of the book: the narrative overview, the biographies, the primary sources, the chronology, and the important people, places, and terms section. This wide coverage allows readers to view the topic through a variety of different approaches.

Students using *Defining Moments: The Great Migration North* will find information on a wide range of topics suitable for conducting historical research and writing reports:

- The economic, political, and social factors behind the Great Migration, including the "push" and "pull" factors that influence migration.

- Characteristics that differentiated migratory patterns in the first part of the twentieth century (the First Great Migration) from those of the post-World War II era (the Second Great Migration).

- The history of Jim Crow laws and their effect on the Great Migration.

- The development of the black middle class as a result of the Great Migration.

- The impact of the U.S. Supreme Court decision in *Brown v. Board of Education* on the Great Migration

- The Civil Rights Movement as an outgrowth of the Great Migration.

- Artistic responses to the Great Migration in literature, music, and the arts.

- The economic, political, and social factors behind the Return Migration.

- The political, demographic, social, and cultural legacies of the Great Migration.

NARRATIVE OVERVIEW

PROLOGUE

The history of Africans in America is a history of migrations. The first migration, from Africa to the New World, was a forced migration, in which more than half a million Africans were enslaved, shackled, and shipped across the Atlantic Ocean. After being torn from their families and ancestral roots and deposited on the shores of what would become the United States, these men, women, and children faced another forced migration. They were sold into slavery and sent to live with their new "masters" throughout the colonies. The majority of them ended up providing labor for the tobacco, rice, and cotton plantations of the South.

These first African Americans endured centuries of slavery so brutal, so inhumane, that it nearly tore the country apart. Yet even after the Civil War concluded and Congress passed a series of constitutional amendments that abolished slavery, granted African Americans citizenship, and gave black men the right to vote, newly freed blacks faced new humiliations from their white countrymen. This oppression was particularly stifling in the South. Under that region's notorious "Jim Crow" laws, African Americans were denied their most basic civil rights. Jim Crow smothered their right to vote, forced them to obey segregationist laws that limited their access to education, employment, home ownership, and travel, and bred intimidation from white terrorist organizations devoted to their continued suppression. After centuries of slavery on plantations, many free blacks had little choice but to become poor sharecroppers, often on the same lands they had worked as slaves. Working for white landowners who controlled every aspect of their lives, millions of African Americans in the South existed in a race-based class system that kept them in poverty and "in their place."

Then, history took a dramatic turn. In the second decade of the twentieth century, World War I began in Europe. The war stanched the flow of immigrants

3

from Europe that had fed the factories of the North for decades. As companies in the industrial North tried to keep up with orders for products to support the war, labor shortages became severe in many industrial cities of the North.

The economic upheaval gave African Americans in the South greater power to choose their work than ever before. And they chose to migrate. From 1910 to 1940, over 1.5 million African Americans left the South and moved to the North in what is called the First Great Migration. This exodus from the South was a watershed event in the country, and it marked the start of the largest internal migration in the nation's history. It established a pattern of relocation that continued from 1940 to 1970. This Second Great Migration carried more than 5 million additional African Americans to the major industrial cities of the North and West. These two Great Migrations led to a dramatic shift in all aspects of life for African Americans. They moved permanently from a rural to an urban environment, from agricultural work to employment in industry, and became, for the first time, a national presence.

The genesis of the idea that freedom and opportunity existed in the "Promised Land" to the North took place in the individual hearts and minds of millions of African Americans. But it also was championed by the *Chicago Defender*, an African-American newspaper founded in 1905 by publisher Robert S. Abbott. A tireless advocate for African-American rights and opportunities, Abbott put his newspaper to work to publicize and encourage the First Great Migration. He placed advertisements in the paper offering to help southern blacks find funding for their journeys, as well as assistance with finding jobs, housing, and other support once they arrived in Chicago.

The would-be migrants responded by sending letters to the *Defender* by the thousands, from all over the South. These notes are a testament to the depth of longing that so many African Americans felt for new work, a new community, and a new identity. Some of the letters were simple and straightforward. Some were well-written and eloquent. All of them, however, indicated that the authors yearned to fundamentally change their lives:

Winston-Salem, North Carolina
April 23, 1917

Dear Sir:

Colored people of this place who know you by note of your great paper and otherwise desire to get information from you of jobs of better opportunities for them and better advantages.

Beaumont, Texas
May 14, 1917
My Dear Sir:

Please write me particulars concerning emigration to the north. I am a skilled machinist and longshoreman.

Marcel, Mississippi
October 4, 1917

Dear Sir:

Although I am a stranger to you but I am a man of the so called colored race and can give you the very best of reference as to my character and ability by prominent citizens of my community both white and colored people that knows me although am native of Ohio whiles I am a northern descent were reared in this state of Mississippi. Now I am a reader of your paper the Chicago Defender. After reading your writing ever [week] I am compel & persuade to say that I know you are a real man of my color you have I know heard of the south land & I need not tell you any thing about it. I am going to ask you a favor and at the same time beg you for your kind and best advice. I wants to come to Chicago to live. I am a man of a family wife and 1 child I can do just any kind of work in the line of common labor & I have for the present sufficient means to support us till I can obtain a position. Now should I come to your town, would you please to assist me in getting a position I am willing to pay whatever you charge I dont want you to loan me 1 cent but *help* me to find an occupation there in your town. now please give me your best advice on this subject. I enclose stamp for reply.[1]

And so, in search of opportunity and freedom they had long been denied, the first African-American migrants made their way to the North. Their journeys marked the beginning of a movement that would transform the country, as blacks became a national force in politics, society, and industry. The African-American migration would also force individual Americans and the nation as a whole to examine their values and challenge them to define and defend those "self-evident" truths outlined in the Declaration of Independence: "that all men are created equal."

Notes

[1] "Letters of Negro Migrants of 1916-1918." *The Journal of Negro History*, October 1919, pp. 291, 293.

Chapter One

BECOMING
AFRICAN AMERICAN

<hr>

The spiritual strivings of the freedmen's sons is the travail of souls whose burden is almost beyond the measure of their strength, but who bear it in the name of an historic race, in the name of this the land of their fathers' fathers, and in the name of human opportunity.

—W. E. B. Du Bois, *The Souls of Black Folk*, 1903

In May 1607, a group of 105 settlers landed on Jamestown Island, some 60 miles from the mouth of Chesapeake Bay. They represented a group of merchants called the Virginia Company, who had been granted a charter from King James I of England to establish a colony in the New World. Their instructions were to bring "human Civility" to the "Infidels and Savages" in North America, but also to "dig, mine, and search for all Manner of Mines of Gold, Silver and Copper."[1]

This event, the founding of Jamestown, is widely celebrated as the first permanent English settlement in what would become the United States of America. By 1619, the settlers of Jamestown and other areas that would become Virginia had created the House of Burgesses, the first legislative assembly and the first system of representative government in the English colonies. That same year, however, a more sinister "first" also took place when the colony received its first African slaves. Over the ensuing 250 years, an estimated 500,000 Africans were torn from their homelands and forced to cross the Atlantic Ocean in slave ships so overcrowded and teeming with disease and misery that many perished before arriving in the New World. The survivors, meanwhile, were herded into a slave system that quickly became a major element in the economic prosperity of the early colonies.

The Evolution of Slavery in the United States

The institution of slavery in North America evolved with the passage of time. In the early days of Colonial America, Africans were sometimes considered "indentured servants" rather than slaves. These individuals were bound to provide labor to their masters for a specific period of time (usually seven years), and they often worked side-by-side with white indentured servants. At the end of their service, they were freed and sometimes given a piece of their own land. This practice produced a small number of freed blacks who lived throughout the colonies. But the vast majority of Africans were brought to the colonies in helpless bondage, where they would remain for the rest of their lives. This denial of rights became encoded in the laws of the colonies, and these laws remained in place when the colonies became states.

The first law regarding slavery in the New World was passed in the Massachusetts Bay Colony in 1641. Other colonies developed laws and customs that allowed for an increasingly brutal and restrictive form of bondage for African-American slaves. As early as 1662, the Virginia Assembly determined that all children born to a slave mother in the colony would also be slaves. Thus, Virginian slaveholders were able to secure generations of slave labor for their plantations. In 1705, a Virginia act declared that "all Negro, mulatto, and Indian slaves within this dominion shall be held to be real estate."[2] As the property of their owners, individual slaves could be sold off for any reason, and countless slave families were ripped apart so that owners could pay debts or increase their "wealth." In many regions, in fact, the wealth of an individual was frequently measured by the number of slaves he owned.

By the time of the Revolutionary War in 1776, slavery existed in every colony, and African-American slaves made up 20 percent of the five million people living in the new United States. There were some slaves in the northern colonies, where they worked on farms or in urban centers as skilled tradesmen in shipbuilding and other industries. The slave population, however, was concentrated in the southern colonies. In the tobacco-growing Chesapeake region, enslaved blacks made up 50 to 60 percent of the population. Further down the Atlantic coast, in South Carolina, they made up almost 80 percent of the population. After the Revolutionary War ended in 1781 and cotton overtook tobacco as the main cash crop of the South, many slaves were uprooted once again. Slaves by the thousands were sold to cotton plantation owners in Alabama and Mississippi, where the valuable crop could be easily grown and harvested.

Sept. 27, 1856.]   THE ILLUSTRATED LONDON NEWS   315

SLAVE AUCTION AT RICHMOND, VIRGINIA.

Wood engraving of an African-American woman being sold at a slave auction in Richmond, Virginia.

By the end of the eighteenth century, slavery had become firmly entrenched in the South as the foundation of economic power and individual wealth. By law and by custom, every aspect of a slave's life was controlled by the slave owner. Slaves had none of the rights outlined in the new U.S. Constitution: they could not freely speak, assemble, marry, own property, be educated, or vote. State legislatures, meanwhile, passed laws that gave slave owners the right to subject African Americans to cruel forms of physical punishment—and even take their lives—for almost any reason. Southern whites rationalized the system they had created by telling themselves that blacks were inherently inferior to whites. Many whites, in fact, insisted that the slave system enabled them to act as guardians over blacks, who were dismissed as too childlike and dumb to fend for themselves.

The Abolitionist Movement

While most white Southerners defended slavery and called it essential to their way of life, there were many people throughout the country—and espe-

The 1845 publication of Frederick Douglass's autobiography was a landmark in the history of the American abolitionist movement.

cially in the Northern states—who were strongly opposed to it and wanted to "abolish" the practice throughout America. This so-called abolition or abolitionist movement began in the United States and in Europe in the 1780s, just as the Revolutionary War was ending. Abolitionists sought to end both the institution of slavery and the trans-Atlantic slave trade, which had become a major source of income for the English, the Dutch, and the Americans.

Many American abolitionists were Christians who saw slavery as a moral outrage against their faith. Some of the most prominent opponents were members of the Society of Friends, a group more commonly known as the Quakers. In the 1820s and 1830s two major Quaker leaders, Lucretia and James Mott, joined with William Lloyd Garrison in promoting the cause of abolition in the United States and around the world. Garrison began publishing his famous anti-slavery newspaper *The Liberator* in 1831, and it quickly became the primary voice for the American Anti-Slavery Society, the biggest and most influential of the abolitionist organizations. As abolitionist fervor grew, Garrison was joined by another powerful voice in the struggle against slavery. Frederick Douglass was a former slave who had escaped to freedom in the North. In 1845 he published *Narrative of the Life of Frederick Douglass: An American Slave*. This important book, which detailed the horrors and inhumanity of slave life and also demonstrated the intellectual capacities of African Americans, made a deep impression on many white readers.

The escalating furor in the North over slavery also stemmed from the fact that the two regions were parting ways economically. The South remained firmly rooted in agriculture, but the North was swiftly transitioning to an industry-based economy during the 1840s and 1850s. Northern factories needed huge numbers of workers. But they did not need slaves, because the cities of the North were swollen with millions of European immigrants who were desperate for work. This state of affairs made Northerners even more critical of the South, which they increasingly described as an economically, politically, and morally "backward" region.

The Fugitive Slave Law and *Dred Scott*

Many Northerners who opposed slavery still felt that Garrison's approach was too radical, because he believed that pro-slavery and anti-slavery states could never exist as one country, and that separation was inevitable. That sentiment was shaken in 1850, when Congress passed the Fugitive Slave Law. This measure required law enforcement officials in the North to arrest any black person, whether free or slave, who was accused of being a runaway slave. The law not only sent numerous fugitive slaves back into bondage in the South, it also resulted in the conscription of many free blacks into slavery, since African Americans accused of being runaways had no legal right to defend themselves against such accusations in court.

In addition, the law included provisions that legally obligated any citizen to assist in the capture of a runaway slave or risk imprisonment and/or a steep fine. These penalties were explicitly aimed at participants in the so-called Underground Railroad, a network of people who helped slaves escape to the North and into Canada through the use of secret routes and "safe houses." The Fugitive Slave Law was greeted with outrage across much of the North, and the nation became even more deeply divided about race.

The rift between North and South over slavery widened even further in 1856, when the U.S. Supreme Court issued its infamous *Dred Scott* decision. The case had been brought by Dred Scott, a slave who had been taken by his owner from a Southern state into a Northern state, where slavery was banned. Scott sued for his freedom, claiming that he had become a citizen of a free state. But the Court disagreed. The justices ruled instead that as a black man, Scott had no rights as a citizen, and so he remained the property of his owner. Frederick Douglass summed up the Court's stance by writing that "Negroes are deemed to have no rights which white men are bound to respect."[3]

The Court ruled further that the Missouri Compromise, a law passed by Congress in 1820 that banned slavery in territories north and west of Missouri, was unconstitutional. This decision tore down one of the main agreements that had kept slavery from completely rupturing the fragile ties between North and South. It also made the abolitionist movement even more determined to stop the foul practice. As Douglass noted, "From 1856 to 1860, the whole land rocked with this great controversy."[4]

The South, though, remained unmoved by the rising chorus of condemnation from the North. Fully dependent on the free labor of slaves to keep their agriculture-based economy afloat, Southerners continued to defend slavery as a "natural" state of affairs, given, in their view, the inherent inferiority of African Americans.

The Civil War and the Emancipation Proclamation

As the debate over slavery raged, new political parties devoted to abolition developed in the Northern states. One of these new parties, the Free-Soil Party, eventually joined forces with other similar-minded groups to form the new Republican Party. In 1860 the Republican Party's first national candidate for president, Abraham Lincoln, was elected on the strength of support in the North. But the South saw the election of Lincoln, who shared the strong anti-slavery beliefs of his party, as clear evidence that the two regions could no longer co-exist under a single flag. In a firm rebuke to Lincoln and his abolitionist beliefs, the Southern states seceded and formed their own nation, the Confederate States of America. The remaining Northern states became known as the Union. Lincoln warned the South that its defiance was unacceptable, but to no avail. The Civil War between North and South erupted on April 12, 1861, when Confederate soldiers attacked a Union garrison at Fort Sumter, South Carolina.

In 1863 President Abraham Lincoln issued the Emancipation Proclamation, freeing all slaves in the Confederate states.

The Civil War, which raged from 1861 to 1865, pitted Northern troops who fought for the preservation of the Union and the abolition of slavery against Southern forces determined to preserve their "way of life," which included slavery. The death toll was enormous: over the four years of the war, some 300,000 Americans lost their lives. Midway through the conflict, on January 1, 1863, Lincoln issued the Emancipation Proclamation, which stated that all slaves living in the Confederate states were free. This historic declaration prompted an exodus of African-American slaves to the North, where some eventually took up arms for the Union. The war came to an end on April 9, 1865, when the battered Army of the Confederacy surrendered to Union forces.

Northern euphoria over the military victory was short-lived, however. On April 15 President Lincoln was assassinated by a Southern sympathizer named John Wilkes Booth. Andrew Johnson thus became the next president of the United States.

Reconstruction in the South

After the war, the period known as Reconstruction began in the South. The term encompasses the years 1865 to 1877, when the North aided the South in rebuilding the cities, roads, railroads, and farmlands that had been ruined during the Civil War. But it also refers to the federal policies and laws that reestablished civil governments in the Southern states and guaranteed the rights and roles of the newly freed African Americans living in the South.

At the beginning of Reconstruction, President Andrew Johnson appointed provisional governors who oversaw the creation of new legislatures in each state. The legislatures were supposed to elect new officials and ratify the Thirteenth Amendment, an amendment to the U.S. Constitution passed by Congress in January 1865 that abolished slavery throughout the United States. Though the ratification process was contentious, the amendment was ratified on December 6, 1865.

After the war was over, the Republicans still held a firm majority in Congress. But the Southern lawmakers refused to cooperate with their efforts to extend basic civil rights to African Americans. Instead, they created and passed "black codes," which were designed to limit the freedom and rights of African Americans and ensure that they remained in a social condition very similar to slavery. The codes restricted blacks from owning property or working as free laborers, and it denied them many other basic civil rights.

Many Northern citizens—and especially members of the Republican Party—were furious about this rebellion. The Republican majority in the U.S. Congress responded by passing the Civil Rights Act of 1866, a law specifically written to protect the rights of black Americans in the South. The Republicans knew that Johnson, a Southerner, would veto the Civil Rights Act after it had passed the Congress. With this in mind, they also crafted a Fourteenth Amendment to the Constitution guaranteeing the rights of full citizenship to all Americans, regardless of race. This amendment was passed by Congress on June 13, 1866.

The passage of the Fourteenth Amendment angered whites across the South, many of whom vowed that they would never ratify or honor such a law. Congress countered in 1867 by drafting the Reconstruction Act, which was intended to force the Southern states into compliance by demanding that they pass the Fourteenth Amendment. The act gave the federal government sweeping powers in the South: it divided the states into five military regions, each governed by a military commander, with federal troops installed in each state to keep the peace and implement the changes. One by one the Southern states reluctantly ratified the amendment, which became law on July 9, 1868. Ratification led to the election of the first black legislators from the South, though their tenure was short-lived.

Rise of the Ku Klux Klan

In 1868, another Republican, Civil War hero Ulysses S. Grant, was elected president of the United States. The election of the man who had defeated the Confederate Army was another bitter pill for Southern whites to swallow. This event, combined with the federal laws that granted blacks equal rights and the continued presence of federal troops in their territories, led growing numbers of whites to lash out in increasingly violent ways. They formed vigilante groups such as the notorious Ku Klux Klan, a terrorist organization devoted to "white supremacy."

Initially founded in 1866 by Confederate veterans of the Civil War, the Ku Klux Klan quickly rose to become the best-known and most violent white supremacist organization in the South. Members routinely used lynching—the killing of someone outside of any legal process, usually by hanging—to intimidate blacks. Other standard practices included setting fire to blacks' homes, schools, and churches; humiliating verbal attacks against African-

New Constitutional Amendments Give African Americans Hope

During the last months of the Civil War and the early years of Reconstruction, Congress crafted three amendments to the U.S. Constitution that gave essential civil rights to African Americans. Following are key excerpts from those amendments.

AMENDMENT XIII
Passed by Congress January 31, 1865. Ratified December 6, 1865.

Section 1.
Neither slavery nor involuntary servitude, except as a punishment for crime whereof the party shall have been duly convicted, shall exist within the United States, or any place subject to their jurisdiction.

AMENDMENT XIV
Passed by Congress June 13, 1866. Ratified July 9, 1868.

Section 1.
All persons born or naturalized in the United States, and subject to the jurisdiction thereof, are citizens of the United States and of the State wherein they reside. No State shall make or enforce any law which shall abridge the privileges or immunities of citizens of the United States; nor shall any State deprive any person of life, liberty, or property, without due process of law; nor deny to any person within its jurisdiction the equal protection of the laws.

AMENDMENT XV
Passed by Congress February 26, 1869. Ratified February 3, 1870.

Section 1.
The right of citizens of the United States to vote shall not be denied or abridged by the United States or by any State on account of race, color, or previous condition of servitude.

American members of their communities; and beatings of black men, women, and children. The Klan also sometimes targeted whites who were brave enough to challenge their racist views and criminal acts. The Klan met little resistance throughout the South, and its crimes went unpunished, either because law officers, judges, and political leaders agreed with the Klan's aims, or because they were afraid of becoming Klan targets themselves.

In 1870 Congress passed the Fifteenth Amendment, which guaranteed African-American men the right to vote. The South erupted in new spasms of violence against blacks. African Americans were harassed wherever they tried to vote, and black legislators were actually run out of office in Virginia, North Carolina, Tennessee, and Georgia. Throughout the South, white citizens elected all-white governments. And as they had done under slavery and under the "black codes," Southern states passed new sets of laws that discriminated against African Americans in every aspect of life. These laws dictated where blacks could live, work, and be educated, among other restrictions.

Once again the U.S. government intervened to protect the African Americans of the South and guarantee their rights. Congress passed laws to make violence by terrorist organizations like the Klan a federal offense, with offenders charged, tried, and punished through the federal court system. This intervention curtailed—but did not end—the violence and intimidation of blacks.

By the mid-1870s Northern support for the policies of Reconstruction began to wane. Weary of the continued violence and turmoil, many people in the North became more receptive to the idea of letting the South handle its own affairs if it would end the violence. Democrats in the South took this to be a sign of indifference to their racial politics, and in 1874 emboldened Southern Democrats carried out extensive voter intimidation campaigns against African Americans. This suppression of the black vote in the South helped Democrats win back the U.S. House of Representatives in the 1874 national elections.

Two years later, Republican Rutherford B. Hayes won the presidency in one of the most hotly contested elections in the nation's history. Its outcome was in many ways a referendum on the policies of Reconstruction and the state of the South. Hayes's opponent, Democrat Samuel Tilden, had won a mix of Southern and Northern states to win the popular vote. But Tilden was unable to clinch the required number of electoral votes after the results in Oregon, South Carolina, Louisiana, and Florida became clouded in dispute.

This drawing from an 1872 issue of Harper's Weekly depicts two murderous Ku Klux Klan members lurking in the doorway of an African-American family's home.

(Under America's electoral college system, the citizens of each state vote for president, and the winner of each state's election receives a number of electoral votes. The candidate who receives a majority of all available electoral votes wins the election.)

The final outcome of the presidential election was determined by a special electoral commission made up of eight Republicans and seven Democrats. The two parties worked out a compromise in which Democrats would agree to recognize Hayes as the winner—but only if all federal troops in the South were removed. When Hayes and the Republican Party agreed, Reconstruction came to an end.

The North Looks Away: The Age of Jim Crow

When federal troops were withdrawn from the South, post-Reconstruction scrutiny of the South's treatment of African Americans vanished. The federal government and Northerners in general turned away from the South and refocused their energies on other issues. The South once again became a place with nearly complete separation of the races, and it implemented laws and customs designed to entrench the race-based class system that had existed during slavery. "In the late 1880s Mississippi and the other Southern states, emboldened by Washington's post-Reconstruction hands-off attitude toward the South, began to pass the 'Jim Crow' laws that officially made blacks second-class citizens," wrote historian Nicholas Lemann. "The Mississippi constitution of 1890, which effectively made it impossible for blacks to vote, was a model for the rest of the South. After its passage, the new political order of legal segregation was fully in place."[5]

By the early 1890s, the ugly and pernicious system known as Jim Crow became the law of the land in the South. No one is sure of the origin of the name; it most likely came from a minstrel show popular among whites in the late nineteenth century that featured a character named Jim Crow played by a white actor in black makeup. But its meaning was unmistakable, to blacks and whites alike. Blacks lived under the constant threat of violence, imprisonment, and even death if they did not obey the rules of segregation. They were forced to live in a world with separate facilities for everything, including public transportation, restaurants, stores, schools, neighborhoods, and even sidewalks.

Jim Crow laws were also imposed to keep blacks out of the voting booth. The most common of these voting suppression measures were poll taxes and literacy tests, both of which were rigged against African Americans. "An invisible hand ruled the lives of all the colored people" in the Jim Crow South, summarized scholar Isabel Wilkerson. "It wasn't one thing; it was everything. The hand had determined that white people were in charge and colored people were under them and had to obey them like a child in those days had to obey a parent, except there was no love between the two parties as there is between a parent and child. Instead there was mostly fear and dependence—and hatred of that dependence—on both sides."[6]

The Plight of the Sharecropper

As conditions worsened for African Americans after Reconstruction, a small group of former slaves took part in the first major migration from the South. In 1879 about 6,000 blacks left the southern states of Mississippi, Louisiana, and Texas and settled in rural Kansas and Oklahoma. Called the

Black sharecroppers working in a cotton field, circa 1907.

"Exodusters," these migrants created the first all-black towns of the Great Plains, becoming homesteaders and settling on tracts of land made available by the Homestead Act of 1862.

Yet most African Americans remained in the South in the post-Reconstruction era, despite extreme poverty and the political and social oppression of segregation. They did so for the simple reason that they felt they had no other choice. Most blacks who lived in the South were agricultural workers who had formerly lived as slaves on plantations. Most of them had virtually no education or money, and they could not afford to buy land or farm equipment and supplies.

Instead, they became "sharecroppers," the term used for laborers who raised crops in fields that were the property of white landowners. Sharecroppers supported themselves with revenue from the sale of the crops they raised. But these earnings were shared with the landowner, with the landowner taking the lion's share of the money. Most sharecroppers, whether white or black, eventually became indebted to the landowner under this arrangement. The sharecroppers rented their homes, seed, plows, and even their small family gardens from the landowner. The landowner in turn kept track of how much they "borrowed" for those necessities. After the harvest, the landowner paid sharecropping families what he claimed they were owed from the sale of their crops, after subtracting the money they owed him for rent, seeds, and so on. In many cases, though, the landowner informed share-croppers that *they owed him* money.

> "Negroes are deemed to have no rights which white men are bound to respect," wrote Frederick Douglass.

Many landowners cheated their tenants outrageously. Yet the black sharecroppers were not allowed to question the accounting of the landowner, on pain of physical punishment or death. In addition, if crops were destroyed by insect infestations or floods, or if there was a decline in prices for a crop, the sharecroppers fell even deeper in debt to the landowners. They had to borrow against the proceeds they would receive from the next year's crop just to provide their families with basic staples like food (often at the landowner's store). This situation trapped tens of thousands of sharecropping families into a cycle of grinding poverty.

Plessy v. Ferguson Decision Adds to Despair

The second-class status of African Americans became even more firmly entrenched after the *Plessy v. Ferguson* decision by the U.S. Supreme Court in 1896. The case originated in Louisiana, which in 1890 had passed a statute called the Separate Car Act. It declared that all railroad companies carrying passengers in the state had to provide separate cars for blacks and whites, under penalty of fine or imprisonment. Homer Plessy was a resident who was one-eighth black. At that time in the South, anyone who had any African-American blood was deemed "colored" by law. So when Plessy bought a first-class ticket and sat in the car designated for whites only, he was arrested.

Plessy's attorneys argued in court that the Louisiana law violated his Thirteenth and Fourteenth Amendment rights. He lost the case in two lower courts, then took his case to the Supreme Court. The Court upheld the lower court rulings, declaring that racial segregation was constitutional because it was possible for segregated facilities to be equal. Therefore, according to the Court, the Louisiana law did not violate the rights of African Americans outlined in the Fourteenth Amendment.

The majority decision in *Plessy v. Ferguson* prompted an important dissent from Supreme Court justice John Marshall Harlan. He scolded his colleagues on the Court, stating that the Constitution was "color-blind" and that "in respect to civil rights, all citizens are equal before the law." He also predicted that the ruling, which he described as a clear violation of the spirit of the Fourteenth Amendment, would damage the nation by perpetuating the "race hatred" at the core of segregation laws.

Harlan was outvoted, though, and the *Plessy v. Ferguson* judgment became the basis for the "separate but equal" concept that governed segregation for the next half century. The ruling codified the Jim Crow segregationist laws throughout the South and further encouraged the creation of separate facilities for whites and "coloreds"—in trains, buses, restaurants, theaters, restrooms, and schools. Under the idea of "separate but equal," the Southern states could legally create a system that kept African Americans in perpetual second-class status and denied them rights available to their white fellow citizens. "The South began acting in outright defiance of the Fourteenth Amendment," wrote Wilkerson. "One by one, each license or freedom accorded [African Americans] was stripped away. The world got smaller, narrower, more confined with each new court ruling and ordinance," and the South set its course for "nearly a century of apartheid, pogroms, and mob executions."[7]

The reality of "separate but equal" facilities was that those created for African Americans were always inferior to those established for whites. For example, schools built for blacks often only went to the sixth grade; in much of the South, no black high schools even existed. Schools for blacks were often poorly constructed, overcrowded, and had few if any books. Black schoolteachers could be paid, by law, half of what white teachers were paid. Black students were forbidden to go to a white school, even if it was the school closest to where they lived.

In some states, the desire to separate the races went to absurd extremes. In many states, blacks had to step off the sidewalk into the street if a white person was approaching. In North Carolina, the courts kept two Bibles, one for whites and one for blacks, so that members of each race would not touch the same Bible when they were sworn in.

In Search of a Better Life

By the end of the nineteenth century, the South was engulfed in violence against blacks that was sanctioned and even encouraged by elected officials. "If it is necessary, every Negro in the state will be lynched," promised Missis-

Ida B. Wells was a Memphis-based civil rights pioneer who frequently wrote about the horrors of lynching.

sippi governor and later U.S. senator James K. Vardaman.[8] Between 1889 and 1929, a person was either hanged or burned alive every four days across the South. The vast majority of these victims of mob violence were black.

Lynchings became public spectacles, much like witch burnings in the sixteenth and seventeenth centuries. People were tortured, mutilated, and killed in front of huge crowds of men, women, and children. Blacks risked death for such alleged crimes as not paying a debt, stealing hogs, trying to act like a white person, or testifying in court.

These horrible events outraged Ida B. Wells, an African-American woman who co-owned and edited the anti-segregationist Memphis newspaper *Free Speech and Headlight*. Wells became one of the first African Americans to advocate for blacks to leave the South for the North. After two black shop owners were lynched in Memphis in 1892, she wrote:

> The city of Memphis has demonstrated that neither character nor standing avails the Negro if he dares to protect himself against the white man or become his rival. There is only one thing left to do. Save our money and leave a town which will neither protect our lives and property, nor give us a fair trial in the courts, but takes us and murders us in cold blood when accused by white persons.[9]

Wells (who changed her name to Wells-Barnett in 1895 after marrying Ferdinand Barnett) helped plant the early seeds of what became the First Great Migration. She herself eventually left the South and migrated to Chicago. But the concept had its detractors. The most influential African-American leader of the time, Booker T. Washington, urged blacks to remain in the South, where he insisted that they could continue to rise economically, politically, and socially through education and hard work. He promoted an ideal of racial harmony for whites and blacks that did not criticize segregation. "In all things purely social we can be as separate fingers, yet one as the hand in all things essential to mutual progress," he wrote.[10] In the South's atmosphere of daily violence and injustice, however, many blacks began to turn away from Washington's assurances. His words were of little comfort to tens of thousands of African Americans who just wanted the freedom to live, work, and raise their children in peace.

In 1910 the cotton industry collapsed in the South. Prices fell worldwide for the biggest cash crop in the region, and thousands of African-American sharecroppers lost their jobs and moved to southern cities looking for work. But work was scarce in the cities of the South, so desperate black workers began to look to the North. And they were excited by what they saw.

World War I, which began in 1914, created a huge demand for products manufactured in the factories of the industrialized cities of the North. Those same factories had in the past employed immigrant workers who made their way to America looking for a better life for themselves and their families. But the war and a wave of anti-immigrant sentiment reduced the level of immigration and left many jobs vacant. Desperate to replenish their workforces, northern companies began to actively recruit African-American workers. The First Great Migration was underway.

Notes

[1] First Charter of Virginia (1606). From *American Historical Documents, 1000–1904*. Vol. XLIII. *The Harvard Classics,* edited by Charles W. Elliot. New York: P. F. Collier & Son, 1909–14, p. 9.

[2] The Virginia Act of 1705 on the Status of Slaves. Reprinted in Schneider, Dorothy, and Carl J. Schneider, *Slavery in America*. New York: Facts on File, 2007, pp. 400-01.

[3] Douglass, Frederick. *Autobiographies*. New York: Library of America, 1994, p. 735.

[4] Douglass, p. 746.

[5] Lemann, Nicholas. *The Promised Land: The Great Black Migration and How it Changed America*. New York: Random House, 1991, p. 14.

[6] Wilkerson, Isabel. *The Warmth of Other Suns: The Epic Story of America's Great Migration*. New York: Random House, 2010, p. 31.

[7] Wilkerson, p. 38

[8] Wilkerson, p. 39.

[9] Wells-Barnett, Ida. From *The Free Speech*, 1892, quoted in Brands, H. W. *American Colossus: The Triumph of Capitalism, 1865-1900*. New York: Doubleday, 2010, p. 398.

[10] Washington, Booker T. "Address of Booker T. Washington, principal of the Tuskegee Normal and Industrial Institute, Tuskegee, Alabama, delivered at the opening of the Cotton States and International Exposition, at Atlanta, Ga., September 18, 1895." Washington, DC: African American Perspectives: Pamphlets from the Daniel A. P. Murray Collection, 1818-1907.

Chapter Two
THE FIRST GREAT MIGRATION

⋘∫⋙

There is no mistaking what is now going on. It is a REGULAR EXODUS. It is without head, tail, or leadership. Its greatest factor is MOMENTUM, and this is increasing, despite amazing efforts on the part of white southerners to stop it. People are leaving their homes and everything about them, under cover of night, as though they were going on a day's journey—leaving forever.

—"'Spring Drive' Is On in Exodus of Race
from All Over the South,"
Cleveland Advocate, April 28, 1917

In 1910 there were eight million African Americans living in the United States; seven million of them lived in the South. That same year, a migration of blacks began that would change the nation. Over the next thirty years, this trickle of migrating blacks became a flood of humanity. By 1940 1.5 million African Americans had migrated from the South to the North in the greatest internal migration in the nation's history. Determined to find better jobs, nicer homes, and increased educational opportunities for their children, African Americans left the corrosive segregationist policies of the Jim Crow South behind and journeyed north to claim their right to the American dream.

Northern Industries Cry Out for Workers

When World War I began in Europe in 1914, immigration from Europe to the United States fell considerably. This decline was due in part to the impact that the conflict had on ocean transportation and the large number of European men who entered military service. But the downturn also stemmed from a wave of anti-immigrant sentiment in the United States that had been building for a number of years. These feelings led Congress to pass laws that reduced the flow of immigrants onto American shores.

These developments posed a growing problem in the North, which was the home of many industries that supplied the armies of Europe. Left without an adequate supply of workers, many manufacturers looked to replenish their workforces by luring some of the vast numbers of African Americans who were toiling away on the farms and in the cities of the Deep South.

Labor agents for a wide range of companies, led by railroads desperate for employees to help transport war materials, began to visit the South. Factory owners offered free train tickets to the North, focusing most of their attention on healthy black males. The Pennsylvania Railroad was one of the first companies to actively recruit African Americans. Its agents sometimes stood on the corners of southern cities, giving their sales pitches to eager audiences.

The main routes of the First Great Migration thus followed America's train lines from specific points in the South to specific industrial centers in the North. In 1916, the Penn Railroad hired 16,000 southern African Americans, taking them mainly to the Pittsburgh area. The Illinois Central Railroad was another main route and source of transportation for migrants from Louisiana, Mississippi, Tennessee, and Arkansas. Thousands used this route to reach Chicago and other bustling Great Lakes cities, including Detroit and Cleveland. On the East Coast, the Seaboard Line took migrants from Florida, Georgia, North and South Carolina, and Virginia to New York, Boston, Philadelphia, and Washington, D.C.

Making the Decision to Leave

As black newspaper *The Cleveland Advocate* noted, the First Great Migration was an essentially leaderless phenomenon. It was made up of individual African Americans who weighed the possibilities outlined by the labor agents and the reports of family members and friends who sent letters back home after settling in the North themselves. African Americans also thought long and hard about their future prospects if they stayed in the South. They all knew the reality of life for blacks in the region. The Jim Crow laws limited every aspect of their lives: where they lived and worked, their incomes, the

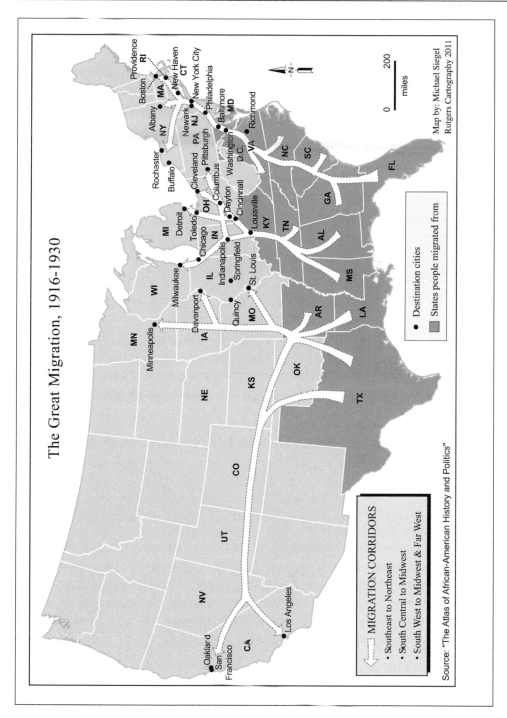

The Great Migration, 1916-1930

Providence
RI
Boston
MA
New Haven
CT
New York City
Albany
NY
Newark
NJ
Philadelphia
PA
Baltimore
MD
Rochester
Buffalo
Pittsburgh
Washington, D.C.
Richmond
VA
Cleveland
Columbus
OH
Dayton
Cincinnati
Louisville
KY
NC
SC
FL
GA
TN
AL
MS
Detroit
MI
Toledo
Chicago
Indianapolis
IN
Springfield
IL
St. Louis
Milwaukee
WI
Davenport
Quincy
MO
AR
LA
Minneapolis
MN
IA
NE
KS
OK
TX
CO
UT
NV
CA
Los Angeles
Oakland
San Francisco

N

0   200
miles

Map by: Michael Siegel
Rutgers Cartography 2011

• Destination cities

States people migrated from

MIGRATION CORRIDORS
• Southeast to Northeast
• South Central to Midwest
• South West to Midwest & Far West

Source: "The Atlas of African-American History and Politics"

This map shows the major migration corridors of the peak years of the First Great Migration.

education available to them and their children, their ability to vote, and the personal safety of their families.

Social scientists often write about "push" and "pull" aspects of migrating populations—the factors that influence a group of people to move from one area to another. For African Americans in the South, the intolerable social and political situation under Jim Crow provided the "push," while the prospect held out by the North of better employment, better schools, the protection of voting, and other basic civil rights provided the "pull." As historian Isabel Wilkerson observed, the Great Migration was thus very similar to "the vast movements of refugees from famine, war, and genocide in other parts of the world, where oppressed people, whether fleeing twenty-first century Darfur or nineteenth-century Ireland, go great distances, journey across rivers, deserts, and oceans or as far as it takes to reach safety with the hope that life will be better wherever they land."[1]

Once African Americans decided to migrate, they had to work out the particulars. Some individuals and families traveled by bus, boat, or truck. The most popular method of travel, however, was the train. Train routes took migrants directly to where the jobs were. The Illinois Central Railroad, for instance, delivered African Americans to the center of Chicago. In addition, in the early days of the Great Migration, the railroad companies themselves paid the fare of migrants taking jobs in some northern cities.

Once the railroads stopped covering the fares, however, it became very expensive to travel by train from the South to the North. Many African Americans struggled to come up with the ticket fare, especially after the railroads increased prices to take advantage of growing demand. In 1915, it cost an average of 2 cents a mile to travel by train; by 1918, the cost had soared to 24 cents a mile.[2] As a result, families often could afford to send only one member at a time. They would save for the train fare, sometimes selling off their belongings, then send one person north. When that family member found work, he or she would begin sending money home for the rest of the family. Another strategy employed by some African-American families was to travel north together in stages, stopping periodically along the way to find work and raise money to continue their journey.

African Americans who chose to migrate often did so in secret. Fearing reprisals from the white southerners in their communities, they would "slip away" at night. This caution was well-founded. Most whites in the region

Union Terminal
Colored Waiting Room
Woodward

African-American migrants waiting in a segregated waiting room for their train to arrive at a rail depot in Jacksonville, Florida, circa 1920.

were taken completely by surprise by the size and scope of the migration, and they were furious at the loss of their cheap labor pool. City and business leaders, in fact, resorted to a variety of tactics to try to stop blacks from leaving. Migrating African Americans were pulled off trains and buses, beaten, and put in jail. Labor agents were fined, and local officials tried to keep them from going into the black communities. Whites also tried to convince African Americans to stay by painting a rosy picture of black life in the South. One headline from the *Commercial Appeal* of Memphis claimed:

SOUTH IS BETTER FOR NEGRO, SAY MISSISSIPPIANS

COLORED PEOPLE FOUND PROSPEROUS AND HAPPY

29

Such efforts indicated that white southerners recognized that the migration threatened their own livelihoods and the economic well-being of their communities. But these desperate moves also exposed their complete inability to understand how blacks in their communities truly felt about their circumstances.

The *Chicago Defender*

White southerners also tried to suppress the distribution of the *Chicago Defender*, the leading black newspaper of the era. The *Chicago Defender*, which journalist Isabel Wilkerson called "the agitator and unwitting chronicler"[3] of the Great Migration, was founded and published by Robert S. Abbott. A great advocate for the migration of African Americans to the North—and especially to Chicago—Abbott couched his advocacy in Biblical terms. Borrowing from the old Negro Spiritual songs that were popular in black communities, he likened the plight of African Americans in the South to the Jews held in bondage in ancient Egypt. He called Chicago "the Promised Land" and described the Great Migration as "the flight out of Egypt."

Not surprisingly, then, African-American churches frequently used the *Defender* to assure migrating blacks that they would be welcomed in the cities of the North. Large denominations like the African Methodist Episcopal (AME) Church and the Baptist Church placed advertisements offering assistance to northern-bound migrants. The churches also sponsored migration clubs in the South, where African Americans could get information on jobs, housing, and welcoming congregations in Chicago, and where letters from successful migrants were read to encourage others. The memberships of both the AME and Baptist churches soared during the First Great Migration on the steady influx of new arrivals.

The *Chicago Defender* was also one of the first black newspapers to describe the vicious atmosphere of racial hatred that existed in the South. On January 16, 1916, Abbott published an article, titled "Why They Leave the South," that outlined the number of lynchings that had happened during the previous year in individual southern states (see "The *Chicago Defender* Reports on Lynchings in the Jim Crow South," p. 169). In January 1917, a *Defender* headline announced "Millions to Leave the South. Northern Invasion Will Start in Spring—Bound for the Promised Land." The accompanying

The offices of the *Chicago Defender*, which played a leading role in publicizing opportunities for African Americans in the Northern cities.

story described the newspaper's efforts to make May 15, 1917, an epic day of mass migration, complete with reduced train fares to African Americans bound for the North. The grand event never took place, but blacks by the thousands wrote letters to the *Defender*, looking for more information about jobs, housing, and life in Chicago. The following letter, for example, reached the newspaper's offices from Dallas, Texas (dated April 23, 1917):

Dear Sir:

Having been informed through the *Chicago Defender* paper that I can secure information from you. I am a constant reader of the *Defender* and am contemplating on leaving here for some point north. Having your city in view I thought to inquire of you about conditions for work, housing, wages, and everything necessary.[4]

The *Chicago Defender*'s outspoken advocacy for black migration to the North so incensed white southern business owners and politicians that the newspaper had to be smuggled into the South. Police confiscated copies whenever they were found, and some regions banned the publication entirely. One Mississippi county even called it "German propaganda" in an effort to tie it to America's enemy in World War I. Often, black Pullman car porters on the Illinois Central railroad line delivered copies in secret to drop-off points throughout the South. The smuggling effort was extremely successful, and the *Defender* became the most-read and most-influential African-American newspaper in the country.

On the Move: The Migration Begins

The first African-American migrants made their way north beginning around 1910. By 1917, the number of migrants to the North had grown exponentially. Between 1917 and 1920, an estimated 700,000 to 1 million African Americans left the South. During the 1920s, another 800,000 to 1 million people made the move. The majority of them settled in the major industrial cities of the North, especially Chicago, Detroit, Cleveland, St. Louis, New York City, and Philadelphia. Their arrival and settlement changed the demographic character of those cities forever.

This massive migration might have had an even greater impact were it not for the Great Depression of 1929. The terrible economic downturn shuttered numerous factories and created record levels of unemployment across the country. With northern jobs in short supply, the black exodus from the South greatly slowed. During the entire decade of the 1930s, in fact, only about 350,000 black migrants headed north.

During the 1910s and 1920s, though, the black exodus from the South was an incredible phenomenon. In Chicago, the black population grew from 44,000 to 234,000—a fivefold increase—between 1910 and 1930. Detroit saw its African-American population grow by an astounding 1,900 percent

A 1922 photograph of a black family from the rural South shortly after its arrival in Chicago.

between 1915 and 1930, expanding from 6,000 to 120,000. In Cleveland, the black population grew from 8,500 in 1910 to 72,000 in 1930. During that same time period, St. Louis's black population more than doubled, from 45,000 to 94,000. New York saw its African-American population more than triple, from 100,000 to 328,000 from 1910 to 1930, while Philadelphia's grew nearly as much, from 84,500 to 220,600.[5]

As this migration intensified, certain patterns gradually emerged. African Americans from specific regions of the South tended to move to specific areas in the North. They settled in neighborhoods that were home to friends and family from their home region, much as ethnic immigrant populations who had come to the United States had done over the previous two centuries. Some blocks of Chicago, for instance, were populated almost entirely by people from the same southern town.

Finding Work and Housing in the North

Many African-American migrants found jobs easily in the North. Most of them were unskilled positions, but they often paid more than three times what the laborers had received in the South. In the North, industry jobs during World War I paid an average of $3 to $5 per day; in the South, agricultural workers (sharecroppers) averaged just 75 cents to $1 per day, and those working in southern factories averaged just $2.50 per day. Many African-American women worked as domestic household help in the North, just as they had done in the South. In the North, however, they earned about twice as much on average in daily wages as they had earned in their old jobs.[6]

In Chicago, African Americans found jobs in factories, slaughterhouses, meat-packing plants, and steel mills. In Detroit, Henry Ford hired more black assembly workers than any other automaker, and the number of African Americans working for Ford Motor Company grew from 100 in 1916 to 10,000 in 1926. In Cleveland and Pittsburgh, African-American men became a dominant force in steel mills, metal casting, mining, and other industries, especially those related to the manufacture of war materials.

The arrival of black workers from the South also changed the political environment in the North. One of the first steps many African Americans took after arriving in the North was to register to vote, a basic civil right that had been virtually impossible for them to exercise in the South. When elections came around they voted overwhelmingly for Republican candidates. Their allegiance to Republicans was partly due to the party's historic role in freeing them from slavery, but it also stemmed from the racist policies of the Democratic South. In 1915 a black man, Republican Oscar De Priest, was elected to the Chicago City Council for the first time. Thirteen years later, De Priest became the first African American elected to the U.S. House of Representatives in the twentieth century.

Unfortunately, the First Great Migration also triggered a housing shortage in nearly every urban center in the North. This crisis was even worse for blacks because of the existence of segregationist policies, written and unwritten, that determined where African Americans could live in the North. Although segregation in the northern states was not defined by laws, as it was

Black families from the rural South frequently struggled to find good and affordable housing in the industrial North.

in the Jim Crow South, anti-black sentiment and discrimination was commonplace. As African Americans poured into the North, angry groups of white citizens formed in Chicago, New York, and other major cities to lobby for laws that would prohibit landlords in their neighborhoods from renting to blacks. Another popular method for keeping blacks out of white residential areas was the "restrictive covenant," a clause in mortgage agreements that said a homeowner could not sell to specific minorities, including blacks. These covenants were a powerful force of racial discrimination throughout the country, and they endured in some states until the 1960s.

Housing shortages and discriminatory policies, combined with unofficial neighbor-on-neighbor pressure not to sell or rent to African Americans, left black families with few options for decent housing. With all other doors closed to them, they congregated in poor neighborhoods that had few city services. Many ended up in shoddy, overcrowded tenement buildings that sprouted up in all the major cities. Meanwhile, landlords frequently took full advantage of this housing shortage to charge exorbitant rents to the black migrants.

The steep cost of securing even the most basic lodging forced countless black families to share small apartments with friends and relatives. Some apartments became so overcrowded that migrants would even share beds, with one individual sleeping while another went to work. Social scientists believe that the housing crisis of the late 1910s and 1920s thus played a major factor in the formation of the first black ghettos in America's major cities.

Black Organizations Reach Out to the Migrants

In the early years of the First Great Migration, several African-American organizations were formed to aid black migrants in facing the challenges of the unfamiliar urban environment they had entered. These organizations helped them find work, housing, and a sense of belonging in their new surroundings.

According to Alain Locke, African Americans migrated north to pursue "a new vision of opportunity or social and economic freedom."

One of the most prominent of these groups was the National Association for the Advancement of Colored People (NAACP), which was founded in 1909 by W. E. B. Du Bois and others in response to the racial injustice in the nation. The NAACP offered legal and economic help to black migrants, and it used its magazine, *The Crisis*, to document—and crusade against—racism and racist policies in both the North and South. Another important group was the Urban League. It was founded in 1911 in New York City to fight racism and increase opportunity for African Americans, especially those moving to New York as part of the Great Migration. The league eventually established offices in most urban centers of the North, providing help with jobs, housing, and other adjustments related to relocation.

As they had done since the earliest days of the Migration, African-American churches also offered help to black individuals and families arriving in the North. The largest mainstream churches serving the black community were the AME and Baptist denominations, but a growing number of Pentacostal congregations in large urban areas also provided assistance and a sense of community to migrants. These small, evangelical denominations were often called "storefront" churches, because they frequently held services in vacant buildings in black neighborhoods.

Reaction from the White and Ethnic Communities

When African Americans arrived at their northern destinations, they often met with resistance and outright hostility from the immigrants who already lived in those cities. From 1870 to 1915, some 25 million European immigrants had settled in the United States, and by the time of the first Great Migration, they made up 25 percent of the nation's workers. Blacks often applied for jobs in industries that were dominated by immigrant workers, who accurately perceived African-American migrants as a potential threat to their livelihoods.

The two groups, migrant and immigrant, were in effect competing for the same jobs. In many cities, immigrants had been relegated to dirty, dangerous, and difficult jobs at the lowest rung of the economic ladder. Business owners quickly learned, however, that southern blacks were willing to work for even lower wages—a fact that undercut the earnings of some immigrants. As factory owners learned to play the two groups against each other for wage concessions, anger and resentment among the immigrant workers steadily increased.

Black migrants also were given the cold shoulder by labor unions. The major labor unions had accepted the immigrants into their membership, but many of them banned blacks from joining. This stance sometimes worked to the advantage of management. For example, African Americans who were excluded from unions were often hired to keep factories running during labor strikes. Their role as strikebreaking "scab workers" further contributed to tensions with native-born and immigrant white workers. With labor unions closed to them, African Americans sometimes formed their own unions. The Brotherhood of Sleeping Car Porters, one of the first black unions in the country, was the most prominent of these groups.

Race Riots in East St. Louis and Chicago

As the African-American population grew in the northern industrial cities, the migrants experienced intensifying racial discrimination in many aspects of life. As time went on, white anger and anxiety over the influx of blacks spilled over into violence with increasing frequency. From 1917 to 1927, twenty-six race riots erupted in northern cities. The best-known of these ugly events occurred in East St. Louis and Chicago, Illinois.

The East St. Louis riot broke out in July 1917 between unionized white workers carrying out a strike at an aluminum plant and African-American workers who had been hired to break their strike. The unionists went to the mayor, demanding that the migration of blacks to their city end. They warned that if the migration did not stop, they would use violence to stop it themselves. Before the mayor could even respond, the riot began. As the unionists left his office, a rumor began to circulate among the crowds of white labor protestors that a black man had shot a local white man. Another rumor circulated that a black man had insulted a white woman—a major offense in the North, just as it was in the Deep South.

These rumors further inflamed tensions in East St. Louis and chaos soon broke out, with mobs of whites attacking blacks. Whites drove through the city's black neighborhoods, shooting at black people and burning their homes. By the time the smoke cleared, 39 blacks and 8 whites were dead, and 6,000 African Americans had lost their homes. The city's all-white police force did nothing to contain the violence. Writing in *The Crisis*, W. E. B. Du Bois described "the massacre of East St. Louis" as another "foul and revolting page [in] the history of all the massacres of the world"[7] (see "The Massacre of East St. Louis," p. 171).

Two years later racial violence erupted in Chicago, where a post-World War I economic downturn had intensified the competition between working-class whites and blacks for jobs and housing. The incident that sparked the riot took place in the waters of Lake Michigan, at a public beach. Several black children swam into an area of the lake that was considered for whites only. Angry whites threw stones at the black children, and one drowned. When African Americans demanded that the white policeman called to the scene arrest the boys who had thrown the stones, he refused. Instead, he arrested a black man, because a white man had complained about him.

The tragedy triggered a race riot that raged for thirteen days across the south and southwest sides of Chicago, where the city's black population was concentrated. Whites attacked blacks; blacks attacked whites. Homes and businesses were burned. By the time the riots ended, 38 people (23 black and 15 white) had lost their lives and another 537 people had been injured. The fact that this horrible event took place in Chicago made the incident even

White rioters search for an African-American target during the Chicago race riot of 1919.

more depressing for African Americans, for the city had long been "famous for its remarkably fair attitude toward its colored citizens," according to the NAACP's Walter White.[8] But the racial violence that had erupted in its streets was, for many blacks, far too reminiscent of the South (see "The Chicago Race Riot of 1919," p. 174).

The Chicago Commission on Race Relations was formed to examine the issues behind the riot and make recommendations. Its massive report—some 818 pages in length—was published in 1922. *The Negro in Chicago* examined many aspects of black migrant life, including housing, employment, education, and recreational facilities. It also discussed the responsibilities of Chicago's citizens—white and black—to create peace and cooperation between the races. The authors recommended that race relations could be improved by ending segregation in housing and employment. Members also urged whites to make a greater effort to get to know blacks. The recommendations held no political or social force, but they accurately identified urban race relation problems that would continue to grow and fester for decades.

The report also disclosed the results of extensive interviews with African-American migrants. It found that despite the problems that prompted the riots, blacks in Chicago were overwhelmingly satisfied with their lives in the North. They were finding jobs and making more money, and some of them were advancing into the middle class for the first time in their lives. Respondents also indicated—even after the 1919 riots—that they felt much more freedom from white oppression in Chicago than they had ever felt in the Deep South. Most remained happy with their decision to leave the South and expressed optimism about their future in the North (see "African Americans Praise Life in the North," p. 181).

The report also exposed a rift within the black community, however. The small number of African Americans who had lived in the northern cities before the Great Migration had established themselves as a tiny but sturdy middle class, earning middle-class wages as postal workers, Pullman porters, servants, and similar positions. Many of them considered the new migrants to be socially and culturally inferior, just as middle-class whites did. Financially secure and established in their communities, these African Americans frequently viewed the migrants as a homogeneous group of poor, illiterate farm workers who needed to be educated by the northern blacks. To this end, they wrote pamphlets of "do's and don'ts" that were distributed through the African-American churches, the Urban League, and other organizations. Many migrants, though, viewed this assistance as condescending, and they sometimes accused middle-class blacks in the North of engaging in the same stereotyping of which whites were guilty.

The Harlem Renaissance

The First Great Migration also gave birth to the Harlem Renaissance, one of the most enduring and influential artistic movements of the twentieth century. New York City was one of the major destinations of the Great Migration, and African Americans in large numbers settled in the borough of Harlem. During the 1920s they worked together to create a vibrant and exciting community that filled African Americans with pride—and many whites with a blend of fascination and envy.

Artists from many different regions of the South gathered and shared their work in Harlem, including writers Langston Hughes, Countee Cullen, James Weldon Johnson, and Jean Toomer; musicians Louis Armstrong, Duke Ellington, and Bessie Smith; and painters Jacob Lawrence and Aaron Douglas. Though they used different methods to express themselves, each of these gifted individuals documented and celebrated the African-American experience in his or her art. They proved that the lives of blacks, and the experiences of slavery, segregation, and the Great Migration, could provide the inspiration and raw material for the creation of great art.

African-American author and critic Alain Locke wrote an essay titled "The New Negro" in 1925 that examined the First Great Migration and its

Children pose in front of their elementary school in Harlem, circa 1925.

effect on African-American life in general and the Harlem Renaissance in particular. Locke claimed that the migration was more than a response to the needs of northern industry, the collapse of the cotton industry, and the threat of violence from the Ku Klux Klan. He asserted that the Great Migration was driven by a new African American "vision of opportunity or social and economic freedom … [and] a spirit to seize, even in the face of an extortionist and heavy toil, a chance for the improvement of conditions." The Harlem Renaissance, he concluded, was a grand union of blacks from every part of the world: from Africa, the Caribbean, the South, the North, the city and the country. "In Harlem, Negro life is seizing upon its first chances for group expression and self-determination," he declared.[9]

Marcus Garvey and the Separatist Movement

The quest for self-determination noted by Locke also provided the foundation for the rise of Marcus Garvey and his movement for black nationalism

41

I Am a Negro—and Beautiful!

In 1926 poet Langston Hughes published a famous essay outlining the artistic and historical background of the Harlem Renaissance. In "The Negro Artist and the Racial Mountain," excerpted here, Hughes makes the case for art created by black artists that celebrates African-American life and themes:

> One of the most promising of the young Negro poets said to me once, "I want to be a poet—not a Negro poet," meaning, I believe, "I want to write like a white poet"; meaning subconsciously, "I would like to be a white poet"; meaning behind that, "I would like to be white." And I was sorry the young man said that, for no great poet has ever been afraid of being himself. And I doubted then that, with his desire to run away spiritually from his race, this boy would ever be a great poet. But this is the mountain standing in the way of any true Negro art in America—this urge within the race toward whiteness, the desire to pour racial individuality into the mold of American standardization, and to be as little Negro and as much American as possible....
>
> Most of my own poems are racial in theme and treatment, derived from the life I know. In many of them I try to grasp and hold some of the meanings and rhythms of jazz. I am sincere as I know how to be in these poems and yet after every reading I answer questions like these from my own people: Do you think Negroes should always write about Negroes? I wish you wouldn't read some of your poems to white folks. How do you find any thing interesting in a place like a cabaret? Why do you write about black people? You aren't black. What makes you do so many jazz poems?

But jazz to me is one of the inherent expressions of Negro life in America: the eternal tom-tom beating in the Negro soul— the tom-tom of revolt against weariness in a white world, a world of subway trains, and work, work, work; the tom-tom of joy and laughter, and pain swallowed in a smile.... [To] my mind, it is the duty of the younger Negro artist, if he accepts any duties at all from outsiders, to change through the force of his art that old whispering "I want to be white," hidden in the aspirations of his people, to "Why should I want to be white? I am a Negro—and beautiful!" ...

Let the blare of Negro jazz bands and the bellowing voice of Bessie Smith singing Blues penetrate the closed ears of the colored near-intellectuals until they listen and perhaps understand. Let Paul Robeson singing Water Boy, and Rudolph Fisher writing about the streets of Harlem, and Jean Toomer holding the heart of Georgia in his hands, and Aaron Douglas drawing strange black fantasies cause the smug Negro middle class to turn from their white, respectable, ordinary books and papers to catch a glimmer of their own beauty. We younger Negro artists who create now intend to express our individual dark-skinned selves without fear or shame. If white people are pleased we are glad. If they are not, it doesn't matter. We know we are beautiful. And ugly too. The tom-tom cries and the tom-tom laughs. If colored people are pleased we are glad. If they are not, their displeasure doesn't matter either. We build our temples for tomorrow, strong as we know how, and we stand on top of the mountain, free within ourselves.

Source

Hughes, Langston. "The Negro Artist and the Racial Mountain." *The Nation*, June 23, 1926. Available online at http://www.thenation.com/article/negro-artist-and-racial-mountain.

and separatism. Garvey was born in Jamaica, where he founded the Universal Negro Improvement Association (UNIA) in 1914. He moved to New York in 1916. During the early years of the Harlem Renaissance he devoted himself to reaching out to the African-American community with a message of racial pride, self-sufficiency, and entrepreneurship.

Unlike other black political leaders, Garvey did not believe that integration was an achievable goal; instead, he urged African Americans to join his organization and move back to Africa, where they would establish their own, all-black nation. He even created a black shipping company, the Black Star Line, to promote the return to Africa among his followers.

Garvey's message of pride in African-American cultural heritage was enormously popular, especially among poor, working-class blacks. During the early 1920s his UNIA attracted more than one million members. But Garvey also had influential critics within the black community. They included such important leaders as Du Bois and Abbott. They urged the U.S. Justice Department to look into Garvey's financial dealings regarding his Black Star Line, which led to his conviction and imprisonment on mail fraud in 1925. By 1927, when Garvey was deported to his native Jamaica, the UNIA had faded away. Garvey later moved to England, where he died in 1940. Although he never realized his goal of creating an African nation for black Americans, he did influence later movements in the black community, including the Nation of Islam and the Black Power movement of the 1960s.

African Americans and the New Deal

In 1929 the U.S. stock market crashed and the country swiftly descended into a terrible economic crisis known as the Great Depression. Millions lost their life savings and their homes, and one-quarter of the population lost their jobs. African Americans were especially hard hit by this crushing economic downturn. By 1932, 56 percent of the nation's African-American population was unemployed, compared with 28 percent of the white population.

When Democrat Franklin D. Roosevelt became president in March 1933, white and black Americans alike prayed that he would be able to deliver some measure of relief from the Depression. Their hopes were raised when Roosevelt moved decisively to address the massive unemployment that lay at the root of the country's economic problems. He developed a number of sweeping federal programs, known collectively as the New Deal, to help the

An African-American man working on construction of Douglas Dam in Tennessee, one of numerous Tennessee Valley Authority (TVA) projects. The TVA was one of the New Deal programs, which provided work to black and white laborers during the Great Depression.

country get back on its feet. Some of the most prominent of these programs were the Public Works Administration (PWA), the Works Progress Administration (WPA), the Tennessee Valley Authority (TVA), and the National Youth Administration (NYA).

The New Deal employment initiatives provided millions of workers for public construction projects that reached across the country. Enrollees in the PWA, TVA, WPA, and other federal programs built hospitals, schools, and housing projects, and improved the nation's infrastructure through the building of highways, harbors, waste treatment plants, and other public projects.

At the outset of the New Deal, African Americans frequently faced discrimination in hiring for the new jobs, especially in the South. One of the rural farming programs was created to employ sharecroppers, for example, but racist farm owners refused to hire black sharecroppers. When African Americans complained about these discriminatory practices directly to the administration, they were ignored.

In 1933 the NAACP, the National Urban League, and other civil rights organizations responded to the situation by forming the Joint Committee on National Recovery. African-American political leaders went to Roosevelt directly to demand equal treatment under the new programs, and their concerns were finally addressed. When Roosevelt signed the bill that created the WPA in 1935, he declared that all individuals who qualified for WPA positions "shall not be discriminated against on any grounds whatsoever." African Americans benefited to a much greater degree when a second wave of New Deal programs were instituted in the mid-1930s. From 1935 to 1939, millions of African Americans found work with the WPA, the NYA, the Civilian Conservation Corps (CCC), and other programs. They also occupied one-third of the public housing created by the New Deal.

Roosevelt also hired a group of outstanding African-American leaders to work in his administration, including educator Mary McLeod Bethune and economist Robert C. Weaver. These officials became unofficially known as Roosevelt's "Black Cabinet." In light of all these advances during Roosevelt's presidency, the political allegiance of black voters underwent a startling shift. By the late 1930s, African Americans who had once voted overwhelmingly for Abraham Lincoln's Republican Party had become one of Roosevelt's most reliable voting blocs.

Notes

[1] Wilkerson, Isabel. *The Warmth of Other Suns: The Epic Story of America's Great Migration.* New York: Random House, 2010, p. 179.

[2] "The Great Migration." Available online at: http://www.inmotionaame.org/migrations/topic.cfm ?migration=8&topic=4.

[3] Wilkerson, p. 36.

[4] "Letters of Negro Migrants of 1916-1918." *Journal of Negro History,* October 1919, p. 291.

[5] Trotter, Joe, Jr. "U.S. Migration/Population." In *Encyclopedia of African-American Culture and History,* edited by Colin Palmer. Vol. 4, 2nd ed. Detroit: Macmillan Reference USA, 2006, p. 1441.

[6] Trotter, p. 1443.

[7] Du Bois, W. E. B. "The Massacre of East St. Louis." *The Crisis,* September 1917, p. 219.

[8] White, Walter F. "Chicago and Its Eight Reasons." *The Crisis,* October 1919, p. 293.

[9] Locke, Alain. "The New Negro." Introduction to *The New Negro,* edited by Alain Locke. New York: Atheneum, 1968, pp. 3-16.

Chapter Three

THE SECOND
GREAT MIGRATION

⊰⊱

"So you're going north, hunh?"

"Yes, sir. My family's taking me with 'em."

"The North's no good for your people, boy."

"I'll try to get along, sir."

"Don't believe all the stories you hear about the North."

"No, sir. I don't."

"You'll come back here where your friends are."

"Well, sir. I don't know."

"How're you going to act up there?"

"Just like I act down here, sir."

"Would you speak to a white girl up there?"

"Oh, no, sir. I'll act there just like I act here."

"Aw, no, you won't. You'll change."

—Richard Wright, *Black Boy*, 1945

From 1940 to 1970, a Second Great Migration occurred in the United States. Five million African Americans moved from the South to the North and the West during those three decades, continuing an exodus that was already changing the shape and character of the nation. African-American populations expanded throughout much of the country, and black migrants climbed economic and social ladders to enter the middle class by the millions. They also became a potent political force during this period. Confronted by continued discrimination and racism, African Americans launched a national fight for freedom and equality that culminated with the Civil Rights Movement.

As was the case with the First Great Migration, the Second Migration was prompted by changing economic conditions and a world war. In 1939 Germany invaded Poland and declared war on England and France, catapulting the nations of Europe into World War II. Once again, the United States became a major supplier of war materials to the nations fighting Germany. As orders for their goods soared, American manufacturers in the industrial plants of the North and the shipbuilding and airplane manufacturing cities of the West struggled to find enough workers for their assembly lines. They promised southern blacks good jobs and a better life.

These efforts to lure African Americans became even more intense in late 1941, after the United States entered the war in response to the Japanese attack on Pearl Harbor. Direct American involvement in the war put virtually every manufacturing sector on a round-the-clock production schedule. Encouraged by the chance of new opportunities, millions of African Americans left their homes in the South to produce planes, tanks, munitions, and supplies for the war effort in the cities of the West and North.

The End of King Cotton

At the same time that the country was gearing up for war, the need for agricultural workers in the South's cotton fields dropped dramatically. During the Great Depression of the 1930s, cotton prices plummeted from 18 cents to 6 cents per pound. This decline brought great economic hardship to southern farmers and the sharecroppers who worked their land, most of whom were African American. To help the farm owners, the federal government developed a system of crop subsidies that paid farmers to reduce the total acreage of crops they planted. The government also agreed to purchase crop surpluses. The program aided landowners, but it did not help the sharecroppers, who suffered even greater poverty and hardship. By 1940, the United States was no longer the world's leading producer of cotton. Within another decade the South was not even the leading cotton-producing region in the country. It was supplanted by the West, where Arizona and California had developed new irrigation techniques to become major cotton producers.[1]

New technology was also transforming the cotton production that remained in the South. In 1941 the mechanical cotton picker was introduced to

A black man stands outside a segregated bus station in Durham, North Carolina, in 1940.

the vast plantations of the South. The introduction of this machine meant that landowners in Mississippi, Louisiana, Alabama, and other big cotton states no longer needed the millions of black sharecroppers who had made their meager livings planting and harvesting cotton by hand. The number of black share-croppers fell steeply, dropping by 50 percent between 1930 and 1950.[2]

Many of these farm workers first migrated to the cities of the South to look for work. Eventually, however, a large percentage of them pulled up stakes and headed to the cities of the North and West. In most instances, this decision was driven by the continued existence of Jim Crow laws across the South. These laws, which provided the foundation for enforced segregation of the races, were just as unfair and widespread in 1940 as they had been thirty years earlier, at the start of the First Great Migration.

Southern blacks still lived within a two-tier system that maintained unequal "white" and "colored" facilities in virtually every aspect of society, from schools and housing to restaurants and transportation. African Americans could not live, work, and educate their children where they chose. Restrictive rules denied them the right to vote, and the judicial system also denied them equality before the law. Incidents of lynching had decreased by the middle of the century, but African Americans in the South were still routinely threatened with violence and intimidated in public and private life. With Jim Crow "pushing" African Americans away and economic opportunity "pulling" them to the North and West, it is little wonder that the Second Great Migration became a mighty flood of humanity.

The Quest for a New Life

Most African Americans who left the South during the Second Great Migration moved to the same major urban centers in the North that had attracted previous generations of migrants. Blacks from North Carolina, South Carolina, Georgia, and Florida poured into New York, Boston, and Philadelphia. Migrants from those states also headed to Chicago and Detroit, where they were joined by large numbers of blacks from Mississippi and Arkansas. Detroit, in particular, saw a huge increase in its African-American population during World War II, as the city's huge automotive plants geared up to supply the nation's wartime "Arsenal of Democracy." As the war progressed, automobile plants in Detroit and other Michigan cities produced enormous volumes of war material for the U.S. military, including aircraft engines, B-24 bombers, jeeps and trucks, heavy artillery, armaments, and other supplies.

The Second Great Migration, however, also took a great many African-American individuals and families to the West, where major shipping and airplane manufacturing industries beckoned. In the aircraft industry alone, for example, employment jumped from 37,000 workers in 1940 to 475,000 in 1945.[3] Growing cities in California (Oakland, San Francisco, San Diego, and Los Angeles) and the Pacific Northwest (Seattle and Portland) all offered the promise of steady work, decent wages, and an escape from the humiliating shadow of Jim Crow. These migrants, who generally came from Louisiana, Texas, Arkansas, and Oklahoma, greatly swelled the black population in the West. In 1940, for example, the black population in all of California totaled only 124,000. This figure increased by 338,000 in the 1940s, by 340,000 in the 1950s, and by 250,000 in the 1960s. By 1970, more than one million African Americans were calling themselves Californians.[4]

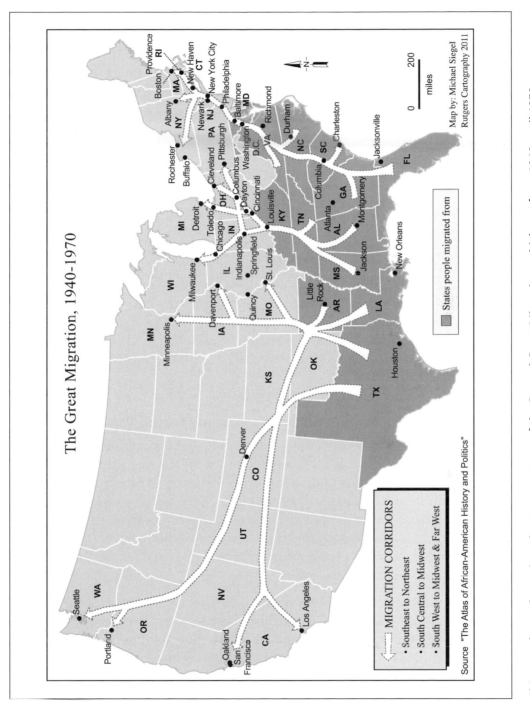

The Great Migration, 1940-1970

Map by: Michael Siegel
Rutgers Cartography 2011

0   200
miles

☐ States people migrated from

MIGRATION CORRIDORS
• Southeast to Northeast
• South Central to Midwest
• South West to Midwest & Far West

Source: "The Atlas of African-American History and Politics"

This map shows the major migratory patterns of the Second Great Migration, which ran from 1940 until 1970.

53

The African-American migrants usually started in entry-level, unskilled jobs. Some blacks, though, were experienced longshoremen and could begin work in the shipyards at higher levels of pay and responsibility. Others who had toiled for a few years in southern cities during their flight from the rural South came to the West and North with higher levels of vocational education and factory experience than their forbearers had possessed.

African-American women also benefited greatly from the increase in war-related employment opportunities. Prior to World War II, most African-American women had been relegated to work as domestic servants. As late as 1940, two-thirds of black women working in the North were domestics. Some managed to obtain steady work with a single employer, but others were forced to find temporary employment through so-called "slave markets." Under this system, which cropped up in New York, Chicago, and other major cities during the 1920s and 1930s, black women were forced to gather on specific street corners and wait for wealthy white women to stroll by and offer them work—usually for humiliatingly low wages. The rise of factory jobs in wartime gave African-American women another option. Some were able to enter the workforce as industrial laborers, where they frequently earned better pay and benefits. Others found rewarding work in business offices or service-oriented industries.

Discrimination in the Neighborhoods and on the Factory Floor

Housing shortages were commonplace in America's big cities during the 1940s and 1950s. African-American migrants suffered mightily from this situation due to the racism and discriminatory practices of landlords and home sellers. As in the First Great Migration, blacks were forced to seek housing in strictly segregated neighborhoods, where city services (like sanitation) or resources (like parks) were poor or nonexistent. But since housing options were so limited, landlords were able to charge high rental fees for filthy apartments in crime-ridden areas.

Recognizing that factory workers were an important element in the overall war effort, the federal government made some attempts to find adequate housing for the new migrants. These efforts were inadequate, however. In Detroit in 1941, for example, more than 9,000 black families applied for only 2,000 available apartments. Even the temporary federal housing built for defense workers was off limits to African Americans, because landlords

Three African-American women employed by Western Union Telegram pose in their uniforms, circa 1942.

refused to rent to them. Many African-American Detroiters had no choice but to live in homes without indoor plumbing, yet they were forced to pay monthly rent that was up to three times higher than the rents in white neighborhoods. Black defense workers also faced discrimination in the workplace. Some defense contractors refused to hire African Americans, and others gave blacks the most difficult, dangerous, and lowest-paying jobs.

The rampant discrimination that African Americans endured during wartime was made even more frustrating by the fact that blacks were serving in the U.S. armed forces during this same period (albeit in units that were segregated by race). As the war progressed, blacks channeled some of their frustrations about this situation into a "Double V" civil rights initiative. This campaign was initially launched in 1942 by the *Pittsburgh Courier,* a black newspaper, and quickly secured the support of the National Association for the Advancement of Colored People (NAACP), the country's oldest and largest organization devoted to securing the civil rights of black Americans. The "Double V" represented victory against Germany and Japan overseas, as well as victory over racial discrimination at home.

Many labor unions that represented factory workers closed their membership to African Americans as well. During the late 1930s and early 1940s, however, it became evident that racial attitudes within some sectors of the labor movement were undergoing significant change. The influential and fast-growing Congress of Industrial Organizations (CIO) actively recruited African Americans during this time. In addition, labor legend A. Philip Randolph spearheaded the passage of a new law aimed squarely at discriminatory employment practices in America.

A. Philip Randolph and the Fair Employment Act of 1941

Asa Philip Randolph was a nationally known labor leader who led the successful effort to unionize the country's most powerful labor union for African Americans, the Brotherhood of Sleeping Car Porters, in the 1920s and 1930s. Specifically, Randolph had negotiated a landmark labor agreement with the powerful Pullman Company, the nation's leading maker of luxury railroad sleeping cars. The 1937 agreement guaranteed that black porters, who were responsible for handling baggage and preparing sleeping cars for patrons, received decent wages, hours, and working conditions. It also made porters figures of particular prominence and influence in many African-American communities.

Even during his negotiations with Pullman, however, Randolph also kept an eye on the wider labor landscape. During the 1930s, for example, he became an outspoken critic of the segregationist practices of the American Federation of Labor (AFL), the largest labor organization in the United States. Alluding to Booker T. Washington's famous speech about separation of the races, Randolph told the AFL convention of 1936 that "white and black workers … cannot be organized separately as the fingers on my hand. They must be organized altogether, as the fingers on my hand when they are doubled up in the form of a fist.… If they are organized separately, they will not understand each other. They will fight each other, and if they fight each other, they will hate each other. And the employing class will profit from that condition."[5]

Race Riots in Detroit and Harlem During the War Years

When black migrants crowded into America's industrial cities during World War II, heightened competition between working-class whites and blacks for jobs and housing sometimes led to an escalation in racial tensions. Occasionally these tensions erupted into major episodes of violence. One of the most notorious of these World War II-era incidents took place in Detroit in June 1943. It began on Belle Isle, a popular, segregated park located on an island in the Detroit River. After a rumor circulated that a white man had thrown a black woman and her baby off the Belle Isle Bridge, the city dissolved into racial violence. Much of the ugliness came from roving bands of blacks and whites who engaged in shootings, beatings, arsons, looting, and other destruction. The Detroit police could not contain the violence—and in some cases officers engaged in lawless violence themselves. Federal troops were finally brought in, and by the time peace was restored, 34 people had been killed (25 black and 9 white) and another 700 injured, nearly 2,000 people had been arrested, and hundreds of stores had been looted and ruined (see "An Eyewitness Account of the 1943 Race Riot in Detroit," p. 191). Just two months later, a smaller race riot broke out in the Harlem section of New York. It left six dead and 300 injured.

In the aftermath of these two riots, American newspapers and magazines published a flood of essays, editorials, and reports that sought to understand the problem. Journalist Turner Catledge noted in the *New York Times Magazine*, for example, that "in the dissensions between whites and Negroes lie deep-rooted forces that grow in complexity." After listing the issues of inadequate jobs, housing, and continued discrimination, Catledge called for greater communication and understanding between the races: "Each group has first to cut through prejudices which have grown up on its side through the years in which the question has been badly handled, prejudices which now have become active and virulent."

Sources:

Catledge, Turner. "Behind Our Menacing Race Problem," *New York Times Magazine*, August 8, 1943.

Wilkerson, Isabel. *The Warmth of Other Suns: The Epic Story of America's Great Migration.* New York: Random House, 2010.

An African-American mechanic works on an army truck at Fort Knox, Kentucky, in 1942.

In 1941, Randolph took up the issue of discrimination against African Americans working in the defense industry. At that time, individual businesses with defense contracts could refuse to hire blacks based solely on their race. Randolph wanted the federal government to ban discrimination against blacks in any defense industry employment. He informed President Franklin D. Roosevelt that he was joining with the NAACP and black newspapers to organize a march of 100,000 African-American laborers in Washington on July 1, 1941, to bring attention to the problem. "We loyal Negro American citizens demand the right to work and fight for our country," Randolph declared.[6]

Roosevelt opposed the march, which would cast a spotlight on America's continued problems with racism and race relations to the country's wartime allies. He also wanted to appease those manufacturers supplying vital military armaments who did not want to be forced to integrate their workforces. On the other hand, Roosevelt wanted to keep the voting loyalty of African-American voters, and Randolph made it clear that he intended to press the issue. Finally, on June 25, 1941, Roosevelt signed Executive Order 8802, known as the Fair Employment Act (see "President Roosevelt Signs the Fair Employment Act," p. 189). According to this historic order, any company that possessed a work contract with the federal government could not discriminate against potential employees on the basis of race. The anti-discrimination law also extended to labor unions working in companies with federal contracts. Roosevelt also created a commission, called the Fair Employment Practice Committee (FEPC), to implement the law.

Randolph called off the march, and the FEPC began to investigate allegations of discrimination in the defense industry. But the committee proved to have little authority to enforce the Fair Employment Act. When confronted with a backlash from white business owners who refused to implement the new policies, the FEPC backed down. Although FEPC investigators held public hearings and issued orders to employers to stop discriminatory practices, the committee had little power to enforce its own orders. Despite the limited effectiveness of the Fair Employment Act and the FEPC, however, they marked important first steps on the part of the federal government to address the problem of racial discrimination. In addition, their very existence encouraged grassroots activists to continue waging their campaigns against discrimination.

The Post-war Job Market

When World War II ended in 1945, waves of veterans returned to the United States to resume their lives and take up their old jobs. Their return pushed out tens of thousands of African Americans who had been working in their place. In addition, the end of the war meant that the defense industry factories no longer had to operate night and day. As a result, many of these companies shed African-American workers who, as usual, were "last to be hired and first to be fired." The grim employment situation was especially hard on returning African-American soldiers. Forced into segregated battalions during the war, they had nonetheless served their country proudly. Yet after participating in the struggle to end tyranny in Europe and the Pacific, they still faced ugly discrimination when they returned home.

Post-war racial prejudice was particularly evident in major manufacturing centers like Detroit, home of the nation's powerful automobile industry. When skilled and experienced black workers tried to find jobs in the automobile plants after the war, they found most positions closed to them. "By all objective measures, white Detroiters citywide enjoyed preferential treatment at hiring gates, in personnel offices, in union halls, and in promotions to better positions,"[7] wrote historian Thomas Sugrue.

Blacks who *were* able to find work in the auto industry were often relegated to janitorial or other unskilled duties. Managers frequently based their hiring decisions on personal feelings of racial prejudice. But even those who did not harbor such views often avoided hiring African Americans out of a fear that white workers would not accept black workers as colleagues. Thus the racial perceptions of individual white workers, their managers, and the culture of individual businesses blended together to create a formidable employment barrier to blacks. Even during periods of labor shortages, some companies went out of state to hire white workers rather than consider black applicants from within the state.[8] For many years it was even legal for employers to specify a racial preference in help-wanted advertisements. In 1948, for example, 65 percent of the listings posted with the Michigan State Employment Services contained racial preferences for applicants. This practice was perfectly legal until Michigan passed the 1955 Fair Employment Practices Act, which outlawed many discriminatory hiring practices.

In the 1950s, the automobile industry was the largest business in Detroit, employing nearly one-third of the workforce. Henry Ford had been one of the first employers in the nation to hire African Americans in the early twentieth century, and by 1960 blacks accounted for 16 percent of the workforce for the entire industry. African-American auto workers who were members of the United Automobile Workers (UAW) union were among the best paid in the nation. Yet they still faced discriminatory treatment in a number of auto plants—some of which still employed very few blacks—and unequal and uneven representation from their own union. Some local chapters of the UAW engaged in blatant discrimination against African-American workers during the 1950s, yet other UAW locals emerged as strong supporters of civil rights during this same period. And when white members tried to organize strikes in response to black workplace gains, the UAW's national leadership supported the expulsion of members who organized or participated in the anti-black strikes.

An African-American neighborhood in Detroit in the 1950s.

Race-based discrimination also remained present in other industry sectors, such as skilled trades and construction jobs. Racial preferences, cultural habits, and the desire of some employee groups to preserve their high wages by excluding blacks and other "outsiders" from their work sites all combined to keep African Americans from lucrative work opportunities that were available to whites.[9]

The trends for blacks in post-war America were not entirely negative, however. The general economic expansion of the 1950s lifted many blacks just as it did whites (see "An African-American Migrant Builds a New Life in the North," p. 197). Good economic times gave blacks greater opportunities than ever before to find jobs that paid decent wages and allowed them to buy nice

Voices of the Second Migration: Literature and Music

The lives of the black migrants who settled in the North and West in the decades following World War II were chronicled in some of the finest literature and music of the twentieth century. Unlike the robust, life-affirming works of the Harlem Renaissance, however, much of the art inspired by the Second Great Migration gave voice to the despair and disappointment of the migrants. Among the best-known authors of the era are Richard Wright and Ralph Ellison. Wright's early life in the Jim Crow South and his later struggles to find freedom and peace in Chicago informed all of his work, including his famous novel *Native Son* (1940) and his autobiography, *Black Boy* (1945). These two works are unsparing in their depictions not only of the poverty, injustice, and misery of life for blacks in the South, but also of the disorientation and unhappiness African Americans frequently experienced in the North. Wright's quest for freedom eventually led him to move to France, where he lived in exile.

Ellison was born in Oklahoma and educated at the Tuskegee Institute, where he studied music. He moved to New York during the 1930s, where he met Wright and found work with the Federal Writers' Project, collecting

homes and move into the middle class. In addition, exposure to the wartime contributions of African Americans, both in the military and in the nation's factories, led growing numbers of whites to support their civil rights goals.

For many others, however, economic success remained out of reach. Most African Americans remained mired in low-paying jobs that offered little security, no benefits, and limited prospects for upward mobility. Indeed, these limitations increasingly isolated blacks in decaying inner cities, even as white families used their educational and economic advantages to build new middle-class communities in the suburbs.

Continued Violence and the Phenomenon of "White Flight"

The competition for jobs and housing during the late 1940s and 1950s led to spasms of racial violence in some northern cities. Some metropolitan areas such as Chicago were particularly hard-hit. As historian Arnold Hirsch

African-American folk tales. Jazz music and black folk tales inform his famous novel *Invisible Man* (1952), which is told in the first-person by a nameless character who leaves the segregated South to seek his identity and place in the world in New York City. After arriving, however, he fails to escape the soul-killing society that defines him by his race alone. Speaking of his migration north, the character muses, "What on earth was it that made us leave the warm, mild weather of home for all this cold, and never to return, if not for something worth hoping for?"

Most of the great musicians who created the singular sound of the Chicago blues were migrants, too. After years spent working on a plantation, Muddy Waters moved north to Chicago from Mississippi, bringing with him the classic sound of the Delta blues, which he refined and made his own in Chicago. He and other southern-born blues musicians, including B. B. King, frequently wrote about the conflicting emotions of migrants who departed from familiar roots for uncertain futures in the North.

Sources:

Ellison, Ralph. *Invisible Man*. New York: Random House, 1952.

Rowe, Mike. *Chicago Blues: The City and the Music*. Cambridge, MA: Da Capo Press, 1975.

---

wrote, "In the years immediately following World War II, Chicago endured a pattern of chronic guerrilla warfare that was related less to ideological currents than to the ebb and flow of populations."[10] Hirsch noted that as the African-American sections of the city grew more overcrowded, black families increasingly tried to move out of their neighborhoods to surrounding areas that had previously been restricted to white families. When a black family moved into a white neighborhood, however, the backlash was often severe. Whites frequently used arson and other acts of violence to drive out black "invaders," and "large housing riots—the mobbing of black homes by hundreds, if not thousands, of whites—broke out, thus revealing a form of resistance rarely seen outside the context of a large citywide disorder."[11]

The other dominant white response to the arrival of African-American families in their midst was to flee. The movement of even a single black family into a formerly all-white neighborhood would often set in motion a pattern called "white flight." If one black family moved in, neighboring white residents put their houses up for sale—often at bargain prices—because they were so anxious to sell their homes. This phenomenon caused property values to plunge, and as white residents left an area, it would become predominantly black.

Racial tensions extended to the use of public facilities as well. City parks became battlegrounds, as whites tried to restrict blacks from using playgrounds, ball fields, pools, and other public areas. Yet despite the regular incidence of racial violence, many residents had no idea about the dissension in their midst. In Chicago, for example, the Chicago Commission on Human Relations, which had been founded after the Detroit race riot of 1943 to deal with racial problems, reached an agreement with the region's major newspapers not to publicize incidents of racial violence. That goal was achieved for several years. But it fell apart in the wake of an ugly riot in Cicero, a suburb of Chicago.

An Ugly Episode in Cicero

In June 1951, the Clarks, an African-American middle-class family, attempted to move into a new apartment in the all-white suburb of Cicero, which borders southwest Chicago. It was a largely working-class community of immigrant families who were firm in their commitment to maintaining their city's traditional way of life—which did not include African Americans. A white mob met the Clarks at their new home as they were in the midst of unloading their furniture. The Clarks were told in threatening terms to get out of Cicero and not come back. The local police arrived, met the Clarks at the door of their new apartment, and blocked the entrance. The Clarks left that day, but they subsequently hired a lawyer and sued for the right to live in the apartment. When they tried to move in after winning their suit, they were once again met by a mob that mercilessly harassed them. The Clarks departed to get away from the abuse, whereupon the mob entered their apartment, destroyed their belongings, threw their furniture out the window, and set it on fire.

Later that day, the mob grew to 4,000 people. They set the entire apartment building on fire, then began a three-day rampage of looting and rioting. Governor Adlai Stevenson called in the National Guard to restore order; 118 men were eventually arrested, but not one was indicted in the incident. Instead, many residents blamed the Clarks for trying to move to an all-white enclave. The authorities sided with the white vandals as well. At one point

National Guardsmen hold back an angry white mob that had gathered to protest the arrival of a black family of renters in Cicero, Illinois, in July 1951.

the family was even indicted for inciting a riot, although these charges were later dropped.

Even as residents of Cicero tried to excuse their despicable actions, however, television coverage of the violence brought the reality of racial hatred in Cicero to viewers around the nation and the world. The rioters of Cicero were widely condemned, and U.S. attorney Otto Kerner represented the Clarks in a federal case accusing Cicero of denying them their civil rights. The grand jury refused to indict anyone in the case, however. This decision sparked another bout of widespread condemnation.

Despite the negative reaction to the Cicero riot, however, racial violence continued to erupt across the Chicago metropolitan area. Outbreaks were particularly common at public facilities in areas where black and white neighbor-hoods bordered each other. In July 1957, for example, a major riot broke out at Calumet Park. A crowd of more than 6,000 whites attacked some 100 blacks who were picnicking in an area that had previously been considered "whites only." The riot raged for two days, until 500 police finally restored order.

The First Stirrings of the Civil Rights Movement

Throughout the post-war era, African Americans sought to increase their meager political power by seeking representation in the Democratic Party at the local, state, and national levels. They took part in major voter registration efforts throughout the northern cities on a regular basis, and they worked to find common ground with other core Democratic constituencies, including Catholics, working-class immigrants, and labor unions. All of these efforts were undertaken for the purpose of advancing and defending their basic civil rights.

Black allegiance to the Democratic Party was strong because President Franklin D. Roosevelt and other members of that party had crafted the New Deal policies that had helped millions of African Americans survive the Great Depression. And it was further strengthened by events such as the bold 1948 decision by Democratic president Harry Truman to end segregation in the Armed Forces (see "President Truman Integrates the American Military," p. 195).

In the late 1940s and 1950s, however, the Democrats became divided over the issue of African-American civil rights. In 1948 the Democratic Party adopted a pro-civil rights position at its national convention, only to see several southern white members walk out in protest. This was the beginning of the "Dixiecrat" faction within the party, which rallied around an anti-civil rights position.

In the 1950s, the Democratic Party moved further to embrace civil rights as a major issue. As black populations grew in the urban centers, the first African-American city councilmen were elected in cities like Newark and Detroit. But powerful southern Democrats continued to resist black participation in their party—or in politics in general. They used gerrymandering and other unprincipled tactics to deny black nominees a fair shot in elections. (Gerrymandering is a practice in which election districts are divided by population in a way that minimizes the voting strength of opponents.) In some cities, for example, Democrats annexed big white suburbs to small, heavily black districts. Such districts favored white candidates over black ones and greatly reduced the political voice of African Americans.

African-American leaders increasingly looked to fight gerrymandering and other problems of racial discrimination in the courts. The NAACP, with future Supreme Court justice Thurgood Marshall as its head attorney, argued and won several major cases of national importance in the areas of voting rights, home ownership, and education in the early 1950s. It was Marshall who argued for the plaintiff in the landmark 1954 *Brown v. Board of Education* case. The U.S. Supreme Court declared in its decision that the concept of "separate but equal" facilities, originally outlined in the Court's 1896 *Plessy v. Ferguson* decision, was unconstitutional.

NAACP attorney Thurgood Marshall played a leading role in convincing the U.S. Supreme Court to end public school segregation with its 1954 *Brown v. Board of Education* decision.

This ruling was a momentous one in several respects. Most immediately, it meant that the Jim Crow laws that relegated blacks to second-class status in the South—and influenced racial attitudes nationwide—were no longer supported by law. But the *Brown v. Board of Education* ruling also signaled that despite the ugly outbursts in Cicero and other locations, racial discrimination and prejudice in America was being confronted more squarely and strongly than ever before. In both the South and the North, religious, political, and social leaders were uniting to end racial discrimination once and for all. And few corners of America were left untouched by this rising tide, for the First and Second Great Migrations had given African Americans a national presence they had never before enjoyed.

Notes

[1] "The Second Great Migration," from *In Motion: The African-American Migration Experience*. New York Public Library: The Schomburg Center for Research in Black Culture. Available online at http://www.inmotionaame.org/migrations/topic.cfm?migration=9&topic=1.

[2] "The Second Great Migration."

[3] "The Second Great Migration."

[4] "The Second Great Migration."

[5] Quoted in Hill, Norman. "Forging a Partnership between Blacks and Unions." *Monthly Labor Review*, August 1987, p. 38.

[6] Quoted in Arensen, Eric. "A Victory for Fair Employment?" *Footsteps*, January-February 2002, p. 36.

[7] Sugrue, Thomas. "'The Meanest and Dirtiest Jobs': The Structures of Employment Discrimination." In *The Origins of the Urban Crisis: Race and Inequality in Postwar Detroit.* Princeton, NJ: Princeton University Press, 1996, p. 92.

[8] Sugrue, p. 94.

[9] Sugrue, p. 119.

[10] Hirsch, Arnold. "An Era of Hidden Violence." In *Making the Second Ghetto: Race and Housing in Chicago, 1940-1960.* Chicago: University of Chicago Press, 1998, p. 41.

[11] Hirsch, pp. 65-67.

Chapter Four

THE CIVIL RIGHTS MOVEMENT

We've got some difficult days ahead…. But I want you to know tonight, that we, as a people, will get to the Promised Land.

—Martin Luther King Jr., April 3, 1968

The Second Great Migration revealed that racial discrimination was a national issue, not just one that afflicted America's southernmost reaches. As a result, the problem of racism moved to the forefront of the major political issues facing the nation. As Nicholas Lemann wrote,

> During the first half of the twentieth century, it was at least possible to think of race as a Southern issue. The South, and only the South, had to contend with the contradiction between the national creed of democracy and the local reality of a caste system; consequently the South lacked the optimism and confidence that characterized the country as a whole. The great black migration made race a national issue in the second half of the century—an integral part of the politics, the social thought, and the organization of ordinary life in the United States…. By the time the migration was over, the country had acquired a good measure of the tragic sense that had previously been confined to the South. Race relations stood out nearly everywhere as the one thing most plainly wrong in America, the flawed portion of the great tableau, the chief generator of doubt about how essentially noble the whole national enterprise was.[1]

At the same time that America confronted the many ways in which it was falling short of meeting its stated ideals of democracy and justice, African

69

Americans displayed increased confidence that they had an essential right, as American citizens, to demand the same civil rights that their white countrymen and countrywomen had always viewed as their birthright. Many of these early demands focused on education, a sector of American society that clearly reflected the nation's longstanding problems with racism.

Breaking Down Barriers in Education

The 1954 *Brown v. Board of Education* decision capped years of legal battles that had been undertaken by Thurgood Marshall and the NAACP Legal Defense Fund, the legal arm of the National Association for the Advancement of Colored People (NAACP). During the early 1950s Marshall and his allies crafted a legal strategy designed to force the U.S. Supreme Court to squarely confront the issue of racial segregation and African-American civil rights. Specifically, they mounted a direct challenge to the nation's continued acceptance of segregated education.

Three civil rights lawyers—George E. C. Hayes (left), Thurgood Marshall (center), and James M. Nabrit (right) celebrate outside the U.S. Supreme Court building on May 17, 1954, the day that the Court ruled that segregation in American public schools was unconstitutional.

During the 1950s, many states still maintained laws that either required or permitted segregation of schools and other facilities according to race. If the decision was left to individual school districts, they frequently chose to segregate black and white students. As a result, in community after community, black children went to schools that were inferior in their structure, curricula, supplies, and standards. The divide in quality between white and black schools in the South was particularly wide, and it victimized millions of African-American children whose families had remained in the South even as their neighbors moved on to the cities of the North and West.

In the *Brown* case, Marshall and the NAACP Legal Defend Fund represented plaintiffs in segregated public schools in Kansas, South Carolina, Virginia, and Delaware. Their lead plaintiff was Oliver Brown, an African American who had sued the Topeka (Kansas) Board of Education on behalf of his daughter, Linda, for maintaining segregated educational facilities that placed her at an educational disadvantage.

Topeka's segregated education system forced Linda, who was seven years old at the time the lawsuit was filed, to travel on foot and by bus for one hour and twenty minutes each day from her home to her segregated school, which was located twenty-one blocks away. In addition, this school assignment forced her to cross a dangerous railroad yard to get to the bus that took her to school. Meanwhile, a school for white students sat just seven blocks from her home. The NAACP suit claimed that Topeka's segregated system was unconstitutional because it violated the "equal protection" guarantees of the Fourteenth Amendment.

Momentous Ruling Sparks an Angry Backlash

The Supreme Court ruled in favor of Oliver Brown in a unanimous decision. Chief Justice Earl Warren authored the opinion in the ruling, which described public education as "perhaps the most important function of state and local government." Warren further explained that the Court found that "segregation of children in the public schools solely on the basis of race deprive[s] the children of the minority group of equal educational opportunity." Finally, Warren and his fellow justices obliterated the "separate but equal" excuse for segregation that the Supreme Court had handed down more than a half century earlier in *Plessy v. Ferguson*:

> We conclude that, in the field of public education, the doctrine of "separate but equal" has no place. Separate educational facilities are inherently unequal. Therefore, we hold that the plaintiffs and others similarly situated for whom the actions have been brought are, by reason of the segregation complained of, deprived of the equal protection of the laws guaranteed by the Fourteenth Amendment.

With the *Brown* decision, all forms of state-mandated and maintained racial segregation became unconstitutional. The ruling was a tremendous win for African Americans, but it met with immediate resistance. Hostility to *Brown* was particularly strong in southern white communities, where support for discriminatory Jim Crow laws remained very high.

Some southern communities implemented desegregation plans fairly quickly. Numerous other districts, however, moved slowly—or not at all—to comply with the desegregation requirements outlined by the Supreme Court in the *Brown* decision. A few communities, such as Little Rock, Arkansas, even adopted positions of outright defiance. In the fall of 1957 the head of the Little Rock chapter of the NAACP, Daisy Bates, arranged to enroll nine African-American students in the city's formerly all-white Central High School. But angry white mobs prevented the students from entering the school, and over the next several days Arkansas governor Orval Faubus used National Guard troops to keep the black students from entering. The crisis eventually forced President Dwight D. Eisenhower to send federal troops to Little Rock to control the violent white mobs outside the school and enforce the *Brown* ruling. The bravery of the black students known as the Little Rock Nine—who remained at Central High despite harassment and intimidation—served as an inspiration to the growing Civil Rights Movement.

Rosa Parks and the Montgomery Bus Boycott

At the same time that the walls of segregation in American schools were crumbling, African Americans in Montgomery, Alabama, launched one of the nation's first large-scale protests against segregation. This action—a boycott of the city's segregated bus system—was led by a young Baptist minister named Martin Luther King, Jr.

Montgomery's segregated buses reserved seating in the front for whites and relegated blacks to the back. If the white section was full, a white person could force any black person to give up his or her seat. On December 1, 1955, however, a mild-mannered seamstress and secretary of the local NAACP chapter named Rosa Parks was arrested for refusing to give up her seat to a white rider. Parks was asked by King and the NAACP if she would be willing to become part of a lawsuit against the Montgomery bus system to challenge its discriminatory policies. She agreed, and the NAACP called on the city's African-American community to boycott the buses. The protest action was a great hardship for many black workers, who had to carpool, catch rides with white employers, or walk great distances to their jobs. But the boycott, which involved an estimated 42,000 black residents, also took a toll on white-owned businesses in Montgomery, and it dramatically reduced the city's earnings from bus fares.

In 1956 Rev. Martin Luther King Jr. helped organize the Montgomery Bus Boycott to protest the city's segregated busing system. He is shown here speaking to a capacity crowd in a Montgomery church in the early months of the boycott.

The end of the Montgomery boycott finally came into sight when a federal circuit court issued a decision in *Browder v. Gayle*, a lawsuit that had been filed by black civil rights lawyers against the city. The circuit court agreed with the activists, who insisted that the *Brown* decision that desegregated public schools should apply to all forms of state-mandated segregation, including public transportation. The U.S. Supreme Court upheld the lower court's ruling on November 13, 1956, and the boycott ended when Montgomery city officials reluctantly obeyed the court order and desegregated the bus system on December 20.

The Montgomery showdown was a great victory for King, the NAACP, and their strategy of nonviolent protest. African Americans expressed renewed confidence in their quest for civil rights in the aftermath of Montgomery. They also felt pride about King, who had proven himself to be a charismatic and capable young leader. Soon, he was planning new challenges to the entrenched discrimination that still existed in the South.

New Groups Form to Fight for Civil Rights

In the wake of the success of the Montgomery Bus Boycott, King and sixty other African-American religious leaders formed the Southern Christian Leadership Conference (SCLC) in 1957. It became one of the most powerful groups within the Civil Rights Movement, in large measure because black churches were so integral to the spiritual and emotional well-being of black communities. Indeed, the support of black ministers was vital in defining the direction and purpose of the Civil Rights Movement in the South in much the same way that it had helped build momentum for the great African-American migrations earlier in the century. In both cases, the ministers encouraged black men and women to believe that a better life truly was within their grasp if they acted boldly and did not lose faith.

One of the first major campaigns of the SCLC was the Crusade for Citizenship, which began in 1958. This campaign was a direct challenge to the racist laws that had prevented African Americans from voting in the South for years. In most states, blacks were forced to take literacy tests, pay poll taxes, and withstand intimidation and threats of violence when seeking to vote. The SCLC was determined to bring an end to this disenfranchisement once and for all.

The SCLC's Crusade for Citizenship also inspired the creation of another important organization in the fight for civil rights: the Student Nonviolent Coordinating Committee (SNCC). Founded by Ella Baker and other civil rights activists in 1960, the SNCC was a student organization that coordinated civil rights demonstrations across the country. Among the most effective of these peaceful protest actions were "sit-ins"—nonviolent demonstrations in which African Americans occupied lunch counters and restaurants across the South that were designated as "white only." The most famous of these sit-ins occurred on February 1, 1960, when a group of four students in Greensboro, North Carolina, staged a sit-in at a Woolworth's lunch counter. The national publicity surrounding this event inspired many other students to stage similar protests throughout the segregated South, but the impact was felt all across the country. As northerners became more aware of the unfair policies

Student activists played a leading role in the early Civil Rights Movement. In this photo SNCC leader Diane Nash, who also coordinated sit-ins and freedom rides across the South, leads a group of peaceful demonstrators outside a Nashville police station in 1961.

that Woolworth's and other national retail chains maintained in the South, many people—both black and white—boycotted the stores in their own communities as a way to show their support for the students. This economic pressure eventually forced Woolworth's and other targeted businesses to integrate their stores and restaurants.

In addition to the sit-ins, the SNCC and another civil rights group called the Congress for Racial Equality (CORE) organized "freedom rides," in which black and white individuals rode together on public transportation throughout the South in defiance of traditional segregated seating arrangements. These groups, who began their rides in May 1961, sometimes encountered frightening displays of violence and hatred. Freedom Riders were beaten by angry white mobs in Birmingham and Montgomery, for example, and hundreds of Freedom Riders were arrested and thrown into local jails and state prisons. But civil rights activists refused to back down, and the publicity surrounding these assaults and misuses of police power forced President John F.

Kennedy to intervene. In September the Kennedy administration issued a formal order requiring the desegregation of all public transportation facilities. When the order took effect on November 1, 1961, segregation laws were struck down in all aspects of interstate travel, from buses and trains to facilities such as terminals, waiting rooms, restrooms, and lunch counters.

From Birmingham to Washington

In April 1963 Martin Luther King Jr. and leaders from the SCLC organized civil rights demonstrations in Birmingham, Alabama, a segregationist stronghold that was home to police chief Eugene "Bull" Connor, one of the most notorious racists in the entire South. The nonviolent protesters were attacked by the police, and King was arrested and put in jail. King used this time to compose one of his best known writings, entitled "Letter from a Birmingham Jail."

In this public letter, which was addressed to his fellow clergymen, King explained that "I am in Birmingham because injustice is here," and that "injustice anywhere is a threat to justice everywhere."[2] He also pondered the crisis of conscience that the violence in the South had instilled among Americans of all faiths, and he emphasized the importance of staying true to the course of civil rights.

King was eventually freed from his cell, but Birmingham remained in tumult. In May, Birmingham police sprayed fire hoses and released attack dogs on unarmed protesters. The scene was broadcast around the world on television. Most Americans, repulsed by the hatred and the violence they saw, demanded action on the part of the federal government. President Kennedy responded on June 11 with an address to the nation in which he urged Congress to create civil rights legislation that would end racist policies in public and private institutions. The importance of such legislation—and the larger struggle to stamp out racial hatred in America—was underscored one night later, when prominent NAACP activist Medgar Evers was murdered in the driveway of his home in Jackson, Mississippi.

The March on Washington

King and other civil rights leaders planned to bring attention to their cause and to the pending legislation by sponsoring a March on Washington on August 28, 1963. The march was another defining moment in the history

A scene from the historic March on Washington of August 28, 1963. Leaders of the march included NAACP president Roy Wilkins (lower left) and A. Philip Randolph of the Brotherhood of Sleeping Car Porters (lower center).

of the Civil Rights Movement, and it forever altered the course of the United States. The rally was attended by nearly 250,000 people, who came from widely diverse political, social, and religious backgrounds.

The historic March on Washington concluded in front of the Lincoln Memorial, and it was there that King gave one of the most famous speeches in modern history. King's "I Have a Dream" speech harkened back to the suffering and shameful legacy of slavery and Jim Crow laws, reminded listeners about the migrants who left the South in search of freedom and opportunity, and restated African-American claims to freedom and justice. King concluded his famous speech with a vision of a future America in which all Americans, of every color and background, are able to live at peace and in harmony.

King's ideal of peace was shattered just weeks after his landmark speech. On Sunday, September 15, 1963, a bomb exploded in the 16th Street Baptist Church in Birmingham, Alabama, during pre-service Sunday school classes, killing four African-American girls. The bombing, which was the work of terrorists from the Ku Klux Klan, rocked the nation. The 16th Street Baptist Church had been a gathering place for civil rights demonstrations, and the movement's leaders believed it was no accident that the church had been singled out for the attack. King gave the eulogy at the funeral for three of the girls. There were 8,000 mourners, but not one city official of Birmingham was present at the service.

Two months after the bombing in Birmingham, in November 1963, President John F. Kennedy was assassinated in Texas. His successor, Lyndon Baines Johnson, was a southerner. During a dozen years (1949-1961) in the U.S. Senate, however, Johnson had gradually emerged as a supporter of civil rights. After becoming president, he vowed to get Kennedy's civil rights legislation passed and enacted. This was a difficult task, given the strong opposition in Washington from southern lawmakers. But Johnson used his considerable abilities as a politician to keep the legislation alive through 70 days of public hearings and a 57-day Senate filibuster organized by opponents. (Procedural rules in the Senate allow members to extend the debate over a bill indefinitely by continuing to speak without interruption. As long as the members involved in a filibuster hold the floor—and the other members do not have enough votes to cut off debate—no other legislative business can be conducted.) Urged on by the Johnson White House, Senate leaders finally managed to gather enough votes to end the filibuster and pass the Civil Rights Act of 1964.

This historic legislation, which Johnson signed into law on July 2, 1964, prohibited discrimination in public facilities, education, and employment, ended federal aid to segregated institutions, and created a department of Equal Employment Opportunity. "The purpose of the law is simple," Johnson declared in an address to the nation. "It does not restrict the freedom of any American, so long as he respects the rights of others. It does not give special treatment to any citizen. It does say the only limit to a man's hope for happiness, and for the future of his children, shall be his own ability. It does say that those who are equal before God shall now also be equal in the polling booths, in the classrooms, in the factories."[3]

The Push for Voting Rights

Even with the passage of the Civil Rights Act, however, more work remained to be done to secure equal rights for African Americans. Next on

Praise for the Civil Rights Act of 1964

When President Lyndon B. Johnson signed the Civil Rights Act of 1964 into law on July 2, 1964, he also delivered an address to the American people explaining why the law was in keeping with the nation's proudest traditions and values:

> Americans of every race and color have died in battle to protect our freedom. Americans of every race and color have worked to build a nation of widening opportunities. Now our generation of Americans has been called on to continue the unending search for justice within our own borders.
>
> We believe that all men are created equal. Yet many are denied equal treatment. We believe that all men have certain unalienable rights. Yet many Americans do not enjoy those rights. We believe that all men are entitled to the blessings of liberty. Yet millions are being deprived of those blessings—not because of their own failures, but because of the color of their skin.
>
> The reasons are deeply imbedded in history and tradition and the nature of man. We can understand—without rancor or hatred—how this all happened. But it cannot continue. Our Constitution, the foundation of our Republic, forbids it.... My fellow citizens, we have come now to a time of testing. We must not fail. Let us close the springs of racial poison. Let us pray for wise and understanding hearts. Let us lay aside irrelevant differences and make our nation whole. Let us hasten that day when our unmeasured strength and our unbounded spirit will be free.

Source:

Johnson, Lyndon Baines. Address to the Nation on the Signing of the Civil Rights Act of 1964, July 2, 1964. Available online at http://www.lbjlib.utexas.edu/johnson/archives.hom/speeches.hom/640702.asp.

the civil rights agenda was the drive to end discrimination in voting. Even though the Civil Rights Act contained a clause that was supposed to enforce the right to vote for all people regardless of race, it did not eliminate literacy tests, poll taxes, or violence against nonwhite voters. Since African Americans had suffered these impediments to voting since the end of Reconstruction, civil rights leaders and Johnson knew that further legislation was needed to guarantee an end to voting rights violations.

The summer of 1964 became known as "Freedom Summer," as thousands of civil rights workers went to the South to carry out a voter registration campaign in African-American neighborhoods and communities. At that time, the segregationist laws that had long discouraged blacks from voting in the South had kept black voter registration levels extremely low. In Mississippi, for example, only 6.7 percent of adult black residents were registered to vote in 1962.[4]

The idealism of the Freedom Summer initiative was soon marred by murder. In August 1964, the remains of three young civil rights workers from the North—James Chaney, Andrew Goodman, and Michael Schwerner—were found near Philadelphia, Mississippi, buried in an earthen dam. They had been beaten and shot to death. The facts that eventually came out indicated that local police had arrested them for speeding, held them in custody until after dark, and then released them into the hands of the Ku Klux Klan.

The FBI arrested 18 men in connection with the murders in October 1964, but had trouble getting convictions. Some of the men were acquitted by all-white juries, and a few others received light sentences for conspiracy from a federal judge. For decades, it appeared that no one would ever be punished for the Freedom Summer murders. But thanks to the work of an investigative reporter in Jackson, Mississippi, the man who planned the murders, local KKK leader Edgar Ray Killen, was finally convicted of manslaughter on the 41st anniversary of the crime in 2005.

A Voting Rights March Turns Bloody

Despite such heartbreaking setbacks, the movement persevered. Although the voting rights initiative had a limited effect on the number of new voters it was able to register, it did lead to greater awareness on the part of Americans, who turned their attention to the South and to the continuing movement for civil rights.

In March 1965 leaders of the SNCC and SCLC organized a civil rights march from Selma to Montgomery, Alabama, to advocate for voting rights. On March 7 a group of 600 marchers led by civil rights leaders John Lewis and

In March 1965, Martin Luther King Jr. organized the second Selma-to-Montgomery march.

Hosea Williams tried to cross the Edmund Pettus Bridge to leave Selma (King was leading a church service in Atlanta that morning). They were stopped by Alabama state troopers and local policemen who beat them with clubs and cattle prods and sprayed them with tear gas. Once again, television cameras broadcast the scene throughout the world; once again, Americans were shocked at the outbursts of hatred and violence in their midst.

The reaction to "Bloody Sunday," as March 7 came to be known, was swift. King returned to Selma and organized a much larger civil rights demonstration. On March 21 another Selma-to-Montgomery march began with King at the helm. Marching under federal protection, the group swelled to include over 25,000 demonstrators by March 25, when it made a triumphant entrance into Montgomery.

President Johnson used the national outrage over the violence in Selma to promote another crucial piece of civil rights legislation, the Voting Rights Act of 1965. Signed by Johnson on August 6, 1965, the act prohibits the denial or abridgement of a person's right to vote based upon race or color. It also provides for federal oversight and intervention, if necessary, in the exercise of voting rights.

Black Muslims and Malcolm X

King and the NAACP were by far the most visible leaders of the Civil Rights Movement in the 1960s. But they were not the only option for blacks dissatisfied with segregation and discrimination in mid-twentieth-century America. The Nation of Islam, whose followers are commonly called the Black Muslims, had been founded in Detroit in 1930 by Wallace D. Fard, later known as Wali Fard Muhammad. The tenets of the faith, developed by Fard's successor, Elijah Muhammad, focused on the superiority of blacks over whites and the responsibility of whites for the economic and political inequality of blacks. The Nation of Islam also promoted a version of black nationalism similar to the one espoused by Marcus Garvey and his United Negro Improvement Association back in the 1920s. The Black Muslims promoted racial separatism, the development of black-owned businesses, and adherence to strict religious and dietary laws.

The Nation of Islam developed a significant following in many of the receiving cities of the Great Migration, especially Chicago, Detroit, and New

York. The religion became prominent in the mid-1950s, when Malcolm X emerged as one of its most powerful and charismatic leaders. His speeches denouncing white racism attracted large crowds, and he organized marches against discrimination in government policies and against police brutality. But he was also an immensely controversial figure because he openly challenged the approach to winning civil rights espoused by King. Malcolm X stated that racial equality and integration were foolish goals and that nonviolence was not the way for blacks to achieve justice. Instead, he argued that violence was an appropriate response when black civil rights were threatened.

Malcolm X gestures during a 1963 speech in Harlem, New York.

With the passage of time, however, Malcolm X changed his point of view. In 1964, he broke with Elijah Muhammad and the Nation of Islam and founded his own religion, the Muslim Mosque. He made a pilgrimage to Mecca, in Saudi Arabia, the holiest city of Islam. The experience brought an entirely new dimension to his Muslim faith. It led him to believe in the fellowship of all peoples, regardless of their race, and the possibility of peace.

Upon returning to the United States, Malcolm X sought out other religious and political leaders, including King, to work for human rights for all people. He also founded a new group, the Organization of Afro-American Unity, to promote his beliefs. But his message of reconciliation displeased his former allies in the Nation of Islam. Malcolm X was assassinated on February 21, 1965, at the age of 39; three members of the Black Muslims with close ties to Elijah Muhammad were eventually arrested, tried, and convicted for the crime.

Riots and Violence in the North and West

The assassination of Malcolm X was another indicator of the volatility in racial politics in the mid-1960s. Triumphs such as the Civil Rights Act and Voting Rights Act had torn down many discriminatory barriers in American society. In addition, the Johnson administration and Congress made huge new federal investments during the 1960s in education and anti-poverty programs, many of which were tailored to address problems in African-American families and communities.

Many of these programs had only limited effect in their opening months of existence, however, and African Americans expressed growing frustration with the pace of change in American society. They noted that ghettos persisted in every American city, and that these ghettos were largely populated by a black underclass (African Americans who could afford to do so generally fled the ghettos for better neighborhoods or the suburbs). Trapped in a cycle of poverty, meager educational opportunities, and violence, these residents felt a growing sense of hopelessness and isolation from the rest of the country.

This dynamic of "hypersegregation," as it came to be called, was a cruel development for the African-American migrants who had come north seeking opportunity and a chance at a life beyond Jim Crow's shadow. By the late 1960s, many of these migrants—and their children and grandchildren—existed in a world of almost complete separation of the races. Historian Isabel Wilkerson reported that the top ten "hypersegregated" cities "after the 1980 census (the last census after the close of the Great Migration, which statistical-

A national guardsman scans surrounding buildings for snipers during the Detroit riot of July 1967.

ly ended in 1970) were, in order of severity of racial isolation from most segregated to least: (1) Chicago, (2) Detroit, (3) Cleveland, (4) Milwaukee, (5) Newark, (6) Gary, Indiana, (7) Philadelphia, (8) Los Angeles, (9) Baltimore, and (10) St. Louis—all of them receiving stations of the Great Migration."[5]

The anger and frustration that simmered in some black communities manifested itself in a variety of ways. Stokely Carmichael, a former SNCC member and King associate, reached a breaking point in 1966. Once an advocate for nonviolent protest, he became a leader of the "Black Power" movement. Believers in this political philosophy promoted separatism, community organizing, and the right of blacks to arm themselves against the white threat. The Black Panthers, founded in 1966 by Huey P. Newton and Bobby Seale in the migration city of Oakland, represented a further radicalization of the struggle for civil rights. This organization promoted black separatism and increased educational and economic opportunities for African Americans, but

84

it also used violent and threatening "revolutionary" rhetoric that made it a lightning rod for criticism from whites as well as the mainstream Civil Rights Movement.

In 1967 racial tensions in America became even more volatile. During the course of that year the nation was wracked by 159 race riots. The worst of these events took place in the ghettos of Detroit, where 40 died and another 2,000 were injured, and Newark, New Jersey, where 26 died and 1,500 were injured. The riots cost both cities millions of dollars in property losses and pushed them into a downward economic spiral from which they have not yet recovered.

Continued Problems with Racial Inequality

The racial crisis in the northern cities in the mid-to-late 1960s caught mainstream America off guard. Politicians, intellectuals, and activists who had allied themselves with the civil rights cause were enormously troubled by the unrest. As journalist Nicholas Lemann explained, "The very notion that an enormous racial problem existed in the North caused the whole consensual vision of American society to crumble. Segregation in the South was a regional issue with deep historical roots.... Deep-seated racial conflict in the North was another story—it was not supposed to exist anymore."[6]

The Johnson administration and Congress undertook several efforts to analyze the situation and outline corrective action. One of the earliest and most controversial analyses of the era was a report issued by Senator Daniel Patrick Moynihan (D-NY) entitled *The Negro Family: The Case for National Action* (1965). This study, which came to be known as the Moynihan Report, asserted that the inner cities became riddled with severe social problems created by the migrants' arrival in neighborhoods that did not have the educational, economic, or housing resources to support them.[7] It also charged that some migrants were motivated to migrate to the North for welfare checks rather than opportunity. Moynihan also claimed that slavery had greatly weakened the institution of the family among African Americans, which in turn resulted in high rates of out-of-wedlock births and social instability in black communities.

The Moynihan Report was initially well-received by the *New York Times* and other influential mainstream voices. A backlash quickly developed, however, among reviewers who felt that Moynihan skirted coverage of white poli-

Martin Luther King Jr. (second from right) stands with fellow civil rights leaders Hosea Williams, Jesse Jackson, and Ralph Abernathy on the balcony of a motel in Memphis, Tennessee, on April 3, 1968—one day before he was assassinated while standing at almost precisely the same spot.

cies and attitudes that drove many of the problems facing poor black families. America's black community found many of his conclusions to be deeply insulting, and many reformers and sociologists—both black and white— attacked it as a deeply flawed document.

The riots of 1967 also prompted another federal analysis, the Kerner Report, published in 1968 (see "The Kerner Report Analyzes the Root Causes of Racial Tensions in America," p. 203). Its famous summary painted a bleak picture of America: "Our nation is moving toward two societies, one black, one white—separate and unequal."[8] The report proposed billions of dollars in new federal programs to fight poverty and unemployment in the black ghettos, but it did not receive the backing of Congress or the president. Johnson's so-called War on Poverty of the mid-1960s had already made inner-city issues a major focus. When the Kerner Commission described those efforts as ineffectual, Johnson reacted with angry defensiveness. In addition, the president was convinced that the sheer number and intensity of the riots had to be linked to some outside organizing force or conspiracy. Finally, the Kerner Report was released at a time when the Johnson administration was focusing much of its time and energy on the Vietnam War.

The Assassination of Martin Luther King Jr.

By 1968, the coalition that had developed mid-decade between the Civil Rights Movement and the Johnson administration was in tatters. Martin Luther King Jr. further distanced himself from Johnson when he became an active and vocal critic of the Vietnam War. The two political leaders who had worked effectively on civil rights legislation now found themselves on opposite sides of a polarizing issue. With a restive public calling for federal reforms and the end to an unpopular war, President Johnson decided to leave politics. To the great surprise of the nation and his party, he declared on March 31, 1968, that he would not seek re-election that November.

King, meanwhile, continued his civil rights work. He announced plans for a new initiative—a Poor Peoples Program—that aimed to address the plight of poor blacks and whites in America's urban slums. On April 4, 1968, however, he was shot and killed by a white assassin in Memphis, Tennessee. The country reeled from the death of King, the most visible and respected member of the nation's black community. Riots broke out in black neighborhoods in numerous cities when residents heard the news of his tragic death, and many Americans openly wondered whether whites and blacks would ever learn to live together in racial harmony.

Notes

[1] Lemann, Nicholas. *The Promised Land: The Great Black Migration and How It Changed America*. New York: Random House, 1991, pp. 6-7.

[2] King, Martin Luther Jr. "Letter from a Birmingham Jail," April 16, 1963. Available online at http://mlk-kpp01.stanford.edu/index.php/resources/article/annotated_letter_from_birmingham/.

[3] Johnson, Lyndon Baines. Address to the Nation on the Signing of the Civil Rights Act of 1964, July 2, 1964. Available online at http://www.lbjlib.utexas.edu/johnson/archives.hom/speeches.hom/640702.asp.

[4] "Voting Rights Act of 1965." *The Encyclopedia of Race and Racism*, Vol. 3. Edited by John Moore. Farmington Hills, MI: Macmillan Reference/Gale, 2008, pp. 205-08.

[5] Wilkerson, Isabel. *The Warmth of Other Suns: The Epic Story of America's Great Migration*. New York: Random House, 2010, p. 398.

[6] Lemann, p. 117.

[7] Moynihan, Daniel Patrick. *The Negro Family: The Case for National Action*. Washington, DC: Office of Policy Planning and Research, U.S. Department of Labor, March 1965. Available online at http://www.dol.gov/oasam/programs/history/webid-moynihan.htm.

[8] Kerner Commission. *Report of the National Advisory Commission on Civil Disorders*. Washington, DC: U.S. Government Printing Office, 1968. Available online at http://www.eisenhowerfoundation .org/docs/kerner.pdf.

Chapter Five
THE "RETURN" MIGRATION

⌐╼▥▯▥╾⌐

> We came north looking for jobs and freedom. We are going back south looking to find better jobs and better living conditions. When I left Greenville [South Carolina], there was not a single black working on Main Street—not one could work on Main Street. That's not true any more of the new South—those jobs didn't exist 30 years ago.
>
> —Jesse Jackson, 2005

Through much of the twentieth century millions of African Americans had made their way out of the South, where bigotry and racial discrimination shadowed every aspect of life. These migrants settled in the cities and towns of the North and West, far from Jim Crow and its many humiliations. Around 1970, however, a "reverse" migration took shape. Black Americans began returning to the South, which had been dramatically transformed by the Civil Rights Movement of the 1960s. African Americans were intrigued by the job opportunities that suddenly existed in the South, and they were heartened by reports that the racial animosity and distrust that had long defined the region were beginning to fade in intensity.

To be sure, the Civil Rights Movement's success in tearing down Jim Crow policies and attitudes in the 1950s and 1960s did not magically transform the American South—or the rest of the nation—into a land free of racial tensions and bigoted attitudes. Whites and blacks alike remained all too prone to viewing people of different ethnicities in stereotypical and hostile ways. But the victories of the Civil Rights Movement nonetheless ushered in a genuinely new era in race relations across the country, and across the South in particular.

The Growth of the "Sun Belt"

These wide societal changes were an important driver of the reverse migration, but African Americans also turned their gaze southward for other reasons. Some relocated in order to reconnect with family members who had remained in the South. Others headed south to reclaim the world of their forefathers as their own. Finally, many African Americans (and Americans of other ethnicities) headed south for the simple reason that the southern economy was booming at a time when many northern industries were struggling.

Throughout the 1970s and 1980s, the warm and sunny "Sun Belt"—essentially the southern and southwestern United States—emerged as a favorite destination for businesses. Manufacturers in particular were attracted by the region's lower labor costs, its more temperate climate (which meant lower energy costs), its abundance of inexpensive land, and the willingness of southern states and municipalities to extend tax breaks to companies that would bring good jobs to their communities. None of these assets were as widely available in the "Rust Belt"—the industrial states of the Northeast and Midwest. As a result, the South's share of the nation's total manufacturing output jumped from 21 percent in 1963 to 29 percent in 1989.[1]

> *"The South and the Southwest are frontiers of the new industrial America, where people can still reach the American dream," declared Houston mayor Fred Hofheinz.*

As Sun Belt populations jumped, jobs in government, banking, restaurants, and other industries also became more plentiful across the South. All told, the number of workers in the South surged by 22 percent between 1965 and 1975 alone.[2] "The South and the Southwest are frontiers of the new industrial America, where people can still reach the American dream," declared Houston mayor Fred Hofheinz in 1976. "This is the new Detroit, the new New York. This is where the action is."[3]

Patterns of Reverse Migration

The African Americans who returned to the South in the last decades of the twentieth century hailed from every socioeconomic background. Many working-class laborers moved to the South after recessionary economic conditions resulted in the widespread loss of industrial and manufacturing jobs in the North. Other migrants were middle-class and upper-class professionals

A black auto worker inspects a car on the assembly line at a manufacturing plant in Kentucky in 2008.

who moved in search of new opportunities in their fields. In fact, the largest demographic group to make this reverse migration consisted of college-educated individuals. Their relocation came to be known as a "brain gain" for the South—and a "brain drain" for the North.

According to a 2004 demographic study published by the Brookings Institution, blacks moved back to the South from all three major regions of the country—the Northeast, Midwest, and West—where they had settled during the Great Migrations. As one might expect, the major receiving cities of the First and Second Great Migrations experienced the greatest losses of black populations. From 1970 to 2000, New York lost more than 500,000 black residents to Southern migration. Other cities that had once been viewed by poor Southern blacks as promised lands suffered significant population losses as well, including Chicago (175,000 lost to Southern migration), Los Angeles (50,000), Detroit (40,000), and San Francisco (37,000).[4]

The return migration also gathered momentum after the early 1970s. The U.S. Census Bureau reported that from 1970 to 1990, 500,000 African Americans moved to the South in search of better lives. This trend greatly accelerated in the following decade; 368,000 blacks migrated from North to South between 1990 and 1995 alone, and a staggering 680,000 moved south between 1995 and 2000.[5] Many of these people ended up in big cities like Atlanta, which gained more than 215,000 black residents from 1970 to 2000, or Dallas, which absorbed 68,000 African-American migrants during the same time frame.[6]

The years between 2000 and 2009 saw even greater growth in African-American migration to the South. During that time span, some 1.7 million blacks moved from addresses in the North to such large southern cities as Atlanta, Dallas, Houston, Washington, Miami, Charleston, Orlando, Baltimore, Tampa, Norfolk, and Raleigh.[7]

Many of the return migrants settled in regions where they had been born or where their parents or grandparents had once lived. This pattern actually first became evident in the mid-1960s. From 1965 to 1970, in the years before the return migration officially began, some two-thirds of return migrants went back to the region where they had been born. Between 1975 and 1980, more than 40 percent of southern-bound black migrants returned to their families' places of origin.[8]

Among these migrants were the children and grandchildren of men and women who had moved north during the First and Second Great Migrations. Many of these migrants traveled the routes that their ancestors had taken—but this time they followed the path in reverse. Blacks who had settled in Ohio and Michigan returned to their roots in Alabama; those who had lived in Chicago returned to their ancestral roots in Mississippi; natives of New York, Philadelphia, and Baltimore returned to North and South Carolina, where their ancestors had once been slaves; and African-American families that had long lived in California chose to return to Texas, where their grandparents had once worked as sharecroppers.

The Declining Cities of the North and West

Reverse migration was not entirely due to positive aspects of life in the South, however. Some African Americans (and growing numbers of whites) packed their bags for southern destinations out of a sense of disillusionment

Unemployed workers in line at a Detroit soup kitchen in 1982.

with the North, which by the early 1970s was grappling with high levels of poverty, unemployment, crime, and pollution in its urban centers.

During this period, higher operating costs, rising overseas competition, and recessionary economic conditions took a heavy toll on large industrial companies all across the North and West. These manufacturers had attracted and employed African Americans by the millions during the First and Second Great Migrations, but the economic downturn forced them to shed large numbers of jobs or close their doors altogether. These trends had a brutal impact on white and African-American families that had always supported themselves through unskilled manufacturing jobs.

In some big cities of the industrial North, like St. Louis, Cleveland, Chicago, and Detroit, employment in the manufacturing sector fell by close to 20 percent over the course of the 1960s and 1970s. In industry-heavy states such as Michigan and Ohio, the loss of manufacturing jobs was staggering. In 1947 the city of Detroit supported 3,272 manufacturing firms, which employed approximately 338,400 people. Thirty years later, the number of manufacturing establishments in Detroit had dwindled to 1,954 firms employing 153,300 people.[9]

These losses further accelerated during the 1980s. The continued decline in jobs was due partly to automation of factory operations. But it also stemmed from the decision of some large automotive manufacturers, including Ford, General Motors, and Toyota, to open facilities in the South, where states and cities offered generous tax breaks. These new facilities frequently paid lower labor costs, since wages in the mostly non-union South were not as high as in the more heavily unionized North.

Around this same time, the promise of lower labor costs led growing numbers of American companies to relocate their manufacturing operations overseas and to Mexico. The decision of U.S. industries to "globalize" their production operations was keenly felt in the African-American community, where many workers had been able to reach the middle class from wages paid in manufacturing employment.

The black population in Atlanta doubled between 1990 and 2004, when Black Enterprise *magazine placed it atop its list of "Top Cities for African Americans."*

In the West, similar patterns of job loss occurred in the 1970s. In Los Angeles, the city's post-World War II economy restructured from an industrial aircraft production center to entertainment- and service-based industries.[10] As the manufacturing plants closed in Los Angeles, some 70,000 jobs were lost, most of them in the African-American and Hispanic communities. During the same decade, more than 200 Los Angeles-based firms, including Hughes Aircraft, Northrop, and Rockwell, opened new manufacturing facilities in Mexico.[11]

The rising rates of unemployment in the urban centers of the North and West led to even greater problems of poverty. In 1980 nearly 40 percent of the working-age African-American male population in Los Angeles were classified as either unemployed (10.3 percent) or "nonparticipants"—unemployed people who had stopped looking for work (31.4 percent). Nearly one-quarter of black households in the city lived below the poverty line. In Detroit in the same year, 35 percent of the black male population was either unemployed (19 percent) or nonparticipant (16 percent), and one-quarter of black households lived below the poverty line.

High rates of poverty and unemployment were cited by sociologists as a key factor in the rising instability and fracturing of black families. Impoverished black communities, for example, experienced significant growth in the number of households headed by unmarried females with young children.[12] As urban centers became more impoverished, violence and crime rates (much of it related to drugs) soared in these same neighborhoods. Meanwhile, the quality of inner-city public schools and public housing plummeted.

Not surprisingly, many black individuals and families that had the financial means to leave these grim surroundings did so. Some of them found homes in the surrounding suburbs, where their children could play and go to school in relative safety. Others looked to distant parts of the country—such as the South—to make a new start. The departures of these residents further weakened inner-city cores and made life even harder for the elderly and poverty-stricken people who remained behind.

The South's "Brain Gain"

College-educated African Americans marched at the forefront of the new migration to the South. This so-called "brain gain" further spurred economic growth across the region and also served as a catalyst for southern educational institutions to improve themselves. As scholars David R. Goldfield and Thomas E. Terrill wrote, "Universities expanded and the quality of curricula and faculties increased."[13] A cycle of growth thus took root in which growing educational communities attracted ever greater numbers of skilled and educated African Americans to their streets and campuses.

Traditional black colleges in the South—such as Fisk University in Nashville, Morehouse College and Spelman College in Atlanta, and Howard University in Washington, D.C.—benefited from these infusions of bright and ambitious students and young professionals. But so did state universities and entire metropolitan areas. In Atlanta, for example, the city's black population doubled between 1990 and 2004, when *Black Enterprise* magazine placed it atop its list of "Top Cities for African Americans." (The top eight cities on the list, in fact, were all located in the South: Atlanta, Washington, Dallas, Nashville, Houston, Charlotte, Birmingham, and Memphis.) According to the 2010 census, blacks made up 50 percent of the population of Atlanta, and 25 of the city's African-American residents had college degrees.

The South also emerged as a popular destination for African-American retirees over the last decades of the twentieth century. Older blacks chose the South for their later years for many of the same reasons younger African

A Call to Home

In her book *Call to Home: African Americans Reclaim the Rural South*, Carol Stack examines the motivations and consequences of the return migration among a community of blacks in rural North and South Carolina. Stack did not use the real names of the people she interviewed for her book or the place names of the communities they lived in. The names in the excerpt below are fictitious, meant to be representative of the rural South:

> [After] a century in which people have moved out and about, the roiling shifts of population have carried ideas and experiences from one American place to another. Most recently the tides have brought millions of northerners and Midwesterners, black and white, to the Sunbelt, where they have changed the face of the South. Even sparsely populated places far from the new crowds—even Powell and Chestnut counties—feel the changes, at least indirectly, as state governments reach directly into the global economy. Powell and Chestnut's own people are moving back, bringing home citified ways of thinking about things and doing things, reshaping country life in an urban image.
>
> The old rural-urban dichotomy is based on the nonsensical proposition that rural life—"traditional" society—proceeds outside of history, in a timeless realm of grace. You can't go home again because, like Adam and Eve, you can't get back to the Garden; the real world, the urban, modern world, ensnares you and sullies you.
>
> But people are going home again. And however large the distance between Burdy's Bend and the Bronx, that distance is nothing compared to the gap between Burdy's Bend and Eden.

Not a one of the people returning would ever confuse the two. No one is seeking timeless paradise; and no one, however nostalgic, is really seeking to turn back the clock, to return to the Burdy's Bend of segregation and starvation. What people are seeking is not so much the home they left behind as a place that they feel they can change, a place in which their lives and strivings will make a difference — a place in which to create a home.

Back home again, they will learn right away, if they don't know it already, that they'll need a lot of help to create much of anything out of Burdy's Bend. They'll need one another. In a small country community, people have always turned to one another, but in times past such neighborliness was often hostile to reform. People who have always lived close together, who have never lived among strangers or apart from their friends and family, find it excruciating to spurn that intimacy and maintain the emotional distance required to challenge old ways of doing things. In this regard the people coming home nowadays are more like strangers than homefolk; another way of putting it is that they are very much like migrants moving someplace new. The city may have been a school of hard knocks, but most people are not retreating from engagement, not running and hiding back home. Like new immigrants everywhere, they seek one another out, form organizations, build coalitions, and eventually start to shake things up.

You can definitely go home again, Eula Grant told me one afternoon on her porch in Burdy's Bend. *You can go back. But you don't start from where you left. To fit in, you have to create another place in that place you left behind*.

Source:

Stack, Carol. *Call to Home: African Americans Reclaim the Rural South*. New York: Basic Books, 1996.

Increased integration at work and school made the South more attractive to African Americans in the late twentieth century. In this 1997 photograph, black and white students at Central High School in Little Rock, Arkansas, gather together to honor the Little Rock Nine, who forty years earlier became the first black students to attend the school.

Americans did. The cost of living was lower than in the North, especially for housing. The warmer climate was also welcome to African Americans who had spent most of their winters in the snowy North. In addition, southern municipalities increasingly supported museums, concert halls, festivals, and other cultural attractions appreciated by retirees.

A Place of Family and Kinship

Perhaps most importantly, however, these retirees recognized that the South was the land of their ancestors. In returning home to the South, many of them sought to strengthen and replenish old family ties that had become frayed with the passage of time. "Over the years, stresses accumulate in families spread thin across the nation," observed anthropologist Carol Stack.

"After three or more northward-bound generations, a southern homeplace can loom large as a focus of family caregiving and commitment."[14]

Many of these retirees had grown up in the North hearing terrible stories of the South's Jim Crow rules and violence toward blacks. But many of these same youth had spent summers and vacations with family in the South, where they absorbed the cultural and familial traditions that united their southern and northern kin. Once the age of Jim Crow had passed and a "New South" had been born, they eagerly returned to their roots, where they could more fully explore their family histories, their cultural heritage, and the enduring contributions of blacks to America's growth and prosperity (see "Reasons for the 'Return Migration' to the South," p. 208).

Stack noted another important group that took part in the Return Migration. While the vast majority of return migrants moved to the flourishing metropolitan areas of the South, some chose to return to the rural areas of their southern homeland. Some of these areas were very poor, with little to offer the return migrants in terms of opportunity for jobs or financial gain. But the migrants returned nonetheless, for these rural outposts contained land that has belonged to their families for generations. Such soil, according to some migrants, offered them a sense of home and belonging that they never felt in the North.

Any relocation can be stressful, though, and some African Americans who returned to the South after extended absences confess that their new surroundings can be disorienting. For example, many recent arrivals in the South have admitted that although the towns they returned to were largely unchanged since they had been away, "*they* had changed, and the people they had become found the move back home jolting, confusing, exhausting, even paralyzing," according to Stack. "The process of readjustment, however, was not just a long unpleasantness—though it did seem long, sometimes unending. It was also exhilarating. When you have to fight old demons to make a place for yourself in your own home, you learn a lot about who you were and who you want to be."[15]

Notes

[1] "Return Migration to the South," from *In Motion: The African-American Migration Experience.* Schomburg Center for Research in Black Culture. Available online at http://www.inmotionaame .org/migrations/topic.cfm?migration=9&topic=1.

[2] Goldfield, David R., and Thomas E. Terrill. *The South for New Southerners*. Chapel Hill: University of North Carolina Press, 1991, p. 149.

[3] Goldfield and Terrill, p. 150.

[4] Frey, William H. *The New Great Migration: Black Americans' Return South, 1965-2000*. The Living Cities Census Series, Center on Urban and Metropolitan Policy. Washington, DC: Brookings Institution, May 2004, p. 5.

[5] Frey, p. 5.

[6] Frey, pp. 11-12.

[7] Dougherty, Conor. "South Draws U.S. Blacks," *Wall Street Journal*, January 10, 2011, p. A3.

[8] "Return Migration to the South."

[9] "Return Migration to the South."

[10] Johnson, James. "Recent African-American Migration Trends in the United States," *Urban League Review* 14, no. 1, 1990, p. 49.

[11] "Return Migration to the South."

[12] Johnson, pp. 51-52.

[13] Goldfield and Terrill, p. 151.

[14] Stack, Carol. *Call to Home: African Americans Reclaim the Rural South*. New York: Basic Books, 1996, pp. 198-99.

[15] Stack, p. 45.

Chapter Six

THE LEGACY OF
THE GREAT MIGRATION

—⟨⟨⟨⟨ʃ⟩⟩⟩⟩—

Tonight we proved once more that the true strength of our nation comes not from the might of our arms or the scale of our wealth, but from the enduring power of our ideals: democracy, liberty, opportunity and unyielding hope.

That's the true genius of America: that America can change.

—Barack Obama, upon winning the 2008 presidential election, November 5, 2008

During the six-decade-long span of the First and Second Great Migrations, more than six million African Americans moved from the South to villages, towns, and cities of the northern and western United States. When these mighty streams of humanity arrived in the Northeast, the Great Lakes, California, the Pacific Northwest, and other parts of the country, they set tremendous changes in motion. Local and regional politics, economics, and culture were all forever altered by the infusion of African-American perspectives, talents, and beliefs. The Great Migrations also inaugurated new conversations about race relations and the nature of American citizenship that continue to this day. Finally, this massive demographic shift was a catalyst for important and lasting changes in African-American social identity.

Blacks Build a New Relationship with Their Country

When African Americans undertook their exodus from the Jim Crow South to the factories and crowded cities of the North, they quickly discovered that Chicago, Detroit, Newark, Cleveland, Pittsburgh, New York, and other industrial centers were not the Promised Lands of their dreams. Discrimination and segregation still limited their housing and employment choices, and the homes, neighborhoods, and schools available to many black families all too often bore the grim hallmarks of poverty and neglect.

Despite these disappointments and challenges, however, millions of African Americans *were* able to build better lives for themselves and their families in northern cities and towns. Good-paying jobs in the North *were* more plentiful, educational opportunities for black children *were* greater, and blacks *were* better able to build and sustain stable middle-class neighborhoods of their own. And over time, the unfamiliar streets and skylines and weather of Chicago and Detroit and New York gradually came to feel like home.

The growing importance of African Americans to the economic, social, and artistic vitality of American communities in the North and West also gradually paved the way for them to attain new levels of political power and influence. The Great Migration itself was a "leaderless" movement. The decision to move was an individual one, made by millions of African Americans contemplating their futures. But once they arrived in New York or Detroit or San Francisco, they realized that fighting racial discrimination and providing for their families would be much easier if they presented a unified, national front.

Migration Fuels the Development of Black Political Leadership

One of the most important organizations dedicated to that fight was the National Association for the Advancement of Colored People (NAACP), which remains one of the nation's premier African-American civil rights organizations today. Founded in 1909 in response to the continuing problems of racial injustice in America, the NAACP sought relief from discrimination for blacks by focusing on legislative and legal advocacy. Its early leaders included W. E. B. Du Bois and Charles Hamilton Houston, the mentor of Thurgood Marshall. From the 1930s through the 1960s civil rights giants of the NAACP such as Walter F. White, Roy Wilkins, and Marshall played pivotal roles in securing landmark legal victories (such as *Brown v. Board of Education* in 1954). The organization also worked with civil rights icons such as Martin Luther King Jr. to organize historic protests against racial violence and discrimination.

Another trailblazer in the fight against discrimination was A. Philip Randolph, the most powerful black union leader of the mid-twentieth century. As head of the influential and respected Brotherhood of Sleeping Car Porters and

Carl B. Stokes taking the oath of office as mayor of Cleveland, Ohio, on November 13, 1967.

a champion of equal opportunity for blacks, Randolph challenged the common practice of discrimination in employment in the defense industries during World War II. Randolph convinced President Franklin D. Roosevelt to sign the Fair Employment Act of 1941, which banned racial discrimination in defense industry employment. This legislation set an important legal precedent, for it established the federal government's right—and obligation—to seek racial equality on a national basis, rather than leaving the issue to individual states. Randolph was also active in the effort to integrate unions. He fought tirelessly to open membership in national labor organizations to black workers. This goal, which was also pursued by countless local black organizers (and white supporters), eventually secured important gains in wages and working conditions for tens of thousands of African-American workers.

103

The Great Migration also laid the groundwork for the rise of black political leadership in America. Northern urban areas that experienced regular infusions of blacks from the South gradually coalesced into centers of black political power. As the number of African-American residents of these cities soared, so too did their capacity to elect fellow blacks to lead and guide their communities.

During the late 1960s and early 1970s, for example, several of the nation's leading "receivers" of black migrants elected black mayors for the first time. The first African-American mayor of a major U.S. city was Carl Stokes, who won Cleveland's mayoral election in November 1967 and took office on January 1, 1968. Stokes was a Cleveland native whose parents had fled Georgia as part of the Great Migration. In Los Angeles, a former police officer turned political activist named Tom Bradley became mayor in 1973. The son of sharecroppers and the grandson of slaves, Bradley led the city of Los Angeles for twenty years before retiring. The people of Detroit elected another son of sharecroppers, Coleman Young, as their mayor in 1973. Young held that office for twenty years before retiring from public life. The first black mayor of a major southern city was also elected to office in 1973. Maynard Jackson, who was a Democrat just like the other black mayors of his era, served three successful terms as mayor of Atlanta. Since these pioneering figures took the reins in the early 1970s, nearly every major American city has had a black mayor.

The rising political influence of African Americans has also been evident in Washington, especially since the civil rights gains of the 1960s. The first black congressmen in U.S. history came after the Civil War, when a small handful of African Americans represented the South in the U.S. Congress during Reconstruction. But the onset of Jim Crow gradually smothered all African-American representation in Washington (and in most state legislatures as well). From 1901 to 1929, not a single African American served in the U.S. House of Representatives or the U.S. Senate.

As the populations of northern cities swelled with black migrants from the rural South, however, this state of affairs began to change. African Americans became a majority in some urban congressional districts, and since they did not face the same voting restrictions in the North that they had confronted in the South, they were able to elect fellow African Americans to represent them in Washington. In 1929 Oscar De Priest of Chicago, a Republican,

President Barack Obama and First Lady Michelle Obama wave to the crowd during the Inaugural Parade that followed his January 20, 2009, inauguration as America's first black president.

became the first African American elected to Congress in the twentieth century. Other African-American politicians followed in his wake over the next several decades, including Shirley Chisholm, who in 1968 became the first American-American woman elected to the U.S. House of Representatives.

Chisholm and almost all other black members of Congress in the twentieth century were Democrats. African-American voters and politicians became loyal supporters of the Democratic Party from the 1930s through the 1960s, when Democratic presidents Franklin D. Roosevelt, Harry S. Truman, John F. Kennedy, and Lyndon B. Johnson pushed for various policies that bolstered black economic fortunes, attacked segregation, and supported African-American civil rights.

In 2011 the U.S. House of Representatives included forty-two black members of Congress (forty Democrats and two Republicans). The U.S. Senate included no African-American members for the 112th Congress (the session of Congress that runs from 2011 to 2013). The absence of black senators in the 112th Congress, however, has been largely obscured by the fact that in November 2008, the lone African-American senator of the 110th Congress—Barack Obama—was elected to be the forty-fourth president of the United States.

When former Democratic senator Barack Obama of Illinois took the presidential oath of office on January 20, 2009, millions of African Americans saw the event as confirmation that they had finally achieved full and equal membership in the American republic. "This moment has happened because black Americans have always believed that this is our country, too," wrote black diplomat and businessman Vernon Jordan. "And because other Americans from different backgrounds and all walks of life believed that as well.... At that singular moment when Barack Obama laid his hand upon the Bible Abraham Lincoln used at his first inaugural, I thought, with a profound amazement and pride, that, despite the bigotry and discrimination that still exists in American society, what was once not possible, or allowed, or permissible, and what was once unacceptable, preposterous, and unbelievable has become the reality of our existence."[1]

The Cultural Legacy of the Great Migration

The Great Migration's cultural legacy, which includes important contributions to American music, art, and literature, also built up over the course of decades. One of its greatest legacies is the Harlem Renaissance, founded in New York City by a remarkable group of African-American artists who had migrated to the city in the 1910s and 1920s. It was in Harlem that African-American life was actually *celebrated* in music, literature, and the arts for the first time. Since then, themes first explored in Harlem—the meaning of the Great Migration and the search for African-American identity—have inspired some of the greatest artists of the past century.

Richard Wright, Ralph Ellison, and James Baldwin all explored the theme of racial identity among northern migrants in their novels of the 1950s and 1960s. More recently, Toni Morrison, the first African-American woman to win the Nobel Prize in Literature, explored the meaning of black identity in a hostile, racist culture. In novels like *Beloved*, she pays tribute to the millions who lived and died in bondage and explores how the legacy of slavery continues to haunt America.

Motown founder Berry Gordy meets in his recording studio with members of the Jackson Five in 1971.

The black migrant experience has also been explored by some of America's finest playwrights. Dramatist Lorraine Hansberry grew up in Chicago with her parents, who were northern migrants. Her parents became prominent civil rights activists in Chicago, and Hansberry grew up surrounded by talented and ambitious African Americans who were committed to fighting racial discrimination. That theme inspired her greatest work, *A Raisin in the Sun* (1959), which takes its title from a poem by Langston Hughes, who is considered by many to be the greatest writer of the Harlem Renaissance. The play tells the story of a poor, struggling African-American family in Chicago that aspires to achieve "the American dream" of a good home, financial security, and the opportunity to develop one's talents. A very different interpretation of the Great Migration is found in the plays of prominent African-American playwright August Wilson. In such works as *Joe Turner's Come and Gone*, Wilson framed the Migration as a great mistake for African Americans. Wilson believed that migrants were lured from their southern homes with false promises of jobs and better lives, only to confront poverty, discrimination, and hopelessness.

Artist Romare Bearden, born in North Carolina, was also a child of the Great Migration. After moving to New York City with his family in 1914, he was inspired by the artists of the Harlem Renaissance. He devoted his own career to celebrating the African-American experience—and especially life in Harlem—on canvas. He also paid tribute to the successes of the civil rights movement in works such as *The Lamp*, which was created to celebrate the thirtieth anniversary of the landmark *Brown v. Board of Education* decision. Another major artist of the Great Migration, Jacob Lawrence, moved to New York in the 1930s. He studied under African-American artist Charles Alston, through whom he met several members of the Harlem Renaissance. Lawrence celebrated the African-American experience in his paintings, and his best-known work, a sixty-panel series called *The Migration*, documents the hopes, dreams, and experiences of the migrants.

The course of American music was changed forever by the contributions of black musicians who created and popularized musical forms like jazz and the blues. In the 1920s, Louis Armstrong brought the new rhythms and tonalities of jazz from New Orleans to New York, where it was further developed by musical giants like Duke Ellington. The work of these and other African-American jazz legends profoundly influenced the careers of generations of musicians, black and white. In the 1940s Muddy Waters and other African-American musicians brought the blues music of the Mississippi Delta to Chicago, where its structures and rhythms went on to influence a new generation of musicians, including the Beatles, the Rolling Stones, Eric Clapton, and other rock-and-roll artists. It formed the basis of rhythm and blues, as well as soul music, which reached new artistic heights and mass-market appeal in the 1960s under Berry Gordy's Motown record label, based in Detroit.

Improvements in Economics and Education

African Americans saw their economic situations improve significantly as a result of the political and social changes generated by the Great Migration. After discriminatory working conditions were struck down through Supreme Court rulings and civil rights legislation, the average income levels of African Americans improved dramatically. In 1940, for example, 87 percent of African-American families lived in poverty. By 1960, that figure had

African-American children play behind their home in Dumfries, Virginia, in 2006.

fallen to 47 percent, and by 2000, the poverty level for African Americans had fallen even further, to 22 percent.[2] U.S. Census figures from 2008-2009 indicate that the poverty rate for blacks increased to 25.8 percent during those two years, when the country as a whole experienced an economic recession.

Despite steady economic improvement for blacks, however, income disparities between whites and blacks remain significant. Since 1970 the average percentage of white families living in poverty has hovered around 8 to 9 percent, but the percentage of black households living in poverty has never fallen below 22 percent. This divide is even more pronounced among black and white children under the age of 18. In 2008, for instance, the proportion of black children living in poverty was 35.4 percent. In the white population, by contrast, 11.9 percent of white children lived in impoverished households.[3]

In the area of education, African Americans made great strides in levels of attainment during and after the Great Migration. As scholar Isabel Wilkerson notes, the improvement in academic performance for blacks in public schools became evident in the 1920s and 1930s. Citing the work of psychologist Otto Klineberg, Wilkerson reported that "studies conducted in the early 1930s found that, after four years in the North, the children of black migrants to New York were scoring nearly as well as northern-born blacks, who were 'almost exactly at the norm for white children.'"[4]

A recent study in *The Black Collegian* notes that as the Second Great Migration drew to a close in 1970, only 34 percent of blacks over age 25 had a high school degree. By 2000, however, that rate had jumped to 80 percent. In 1970, only 5 percent of blacks had bachelor's degrees. By 2000, though, improved academic performance, black income growth, civil rights gains, and increased scholarship opportunities had combined to bring the number of African Americans with a four-year college degree to 17 percent.[5] Despite these welcome trends, however, a racial gap is evident here as well. A significantly higher percentage of white adults—28 percent—possessed bachelor's degrees in 2000.[6] In addition, the high school dropout rate of African-American (and Hispanic) students far exceeds that of white students. According to a 2006 report from the U.S. Department of Education, the difference between white and minority graduation rates is as high as 40 to 50 percent in many states. This same study indicates that the greatest number of failing schools are in northern and western inner cities that serve primarily minority student bodies.[7]

The Persistence and Pathology of the Ghetto

Many social scientists who study the gap between the employment and educational levels of black and white Americans believe that the source of the problem lies with the plight of the poorest segment of the black population. Black inner-city neighborhoods, which first took root during the Great Migration, are today characterized by high concentrations of poverty, violence, and crime, crumbling infrastructure, and poor access to quality education and health care. The urban ghettos of America have thus been cited by some scholars as one of the most persistent and negative legacies of the Great Migration, though they also grant that the political, economic, and social contributors to these deplorable conditions are many and complex.

The grim conditions in many inner-city neighborhoods baffle and distress many African Americans who participated in the Great Migration. "We're the ones that's killing ourselves," said one resident of Harlem, which has grappled with serious drug and crime problems over the last half-century.

"I don't see one white person in this block selling drugs."[7] In some urban locales, writes Wilkerson, African-American neighborhoods are, "in fact, two neighborhoods—one, hard-working and striving to be middle class, the other, transient, jobless, and underclass; one, owners of property, the other, tenants and squatters; one, churchgoing and law-abiding, the other, drug-dealing and criminal—both coexisting on the same streets, one at odds with the other."[8]

In 2007 the Pew Research Center explored these divisions within the black community in a study titled "Blacks See Growing Values Gap between Poor and Middle Class." According to the study, the African-American community is becoming divided by ever-increasing disparities in income and class. The differences are so great, according to the report, that "nearly four-in-ten [African Americans] say that because of the diversity within their community, blacks can no longer be thought of as a single race."[9]

In 1970, only 5 percent of blacks had bachelor's degrees. By 2000, improved academic performance, black income growth, civil rights gains, and increased scholarship opportunities had combined to bring the number of African Americans with a four-year college degree to 17 percent.

Some analysts of the social and economic problems that beleaguer America's inner cities claim that participants in the Great Migration brought with them a negative family culture from the South, as reflected in low rates of marriage and childbirth within marriage. But sociologists such as Stewart Tolnay strongly challenge these claims. Tolnay's interpretation of the data indicates that "black southern migrants were actually more likely than native northerners to be married, and, if married, to reside with their spouse." Also, according to Tolnay, "migrants had lower levels of nonmarital childbearing, and migrant children were more likely than were their nonmigrant counterparts to reside with two parents." On the issue of employment and income, "southern migrants had higher rates of participation in the labor force, lower levels of unemployment, higher incomes, [and] lower levels of poverty and welfare dependency."[10]

Creating a New and Better America

In some ways, then, the impact of the Great Migration on African Americans in particular and the United States in general continues to be a subject of intense debate. Overall, though, Americans agree that the Great Migration

Affirmative Action

Affirmative action policies rank among the most significant and controversial legacies of the Civil Rights Act. Affirmative action is a set of initiatives designed to help eliminate past and present discrimination against people because of their race, color, religion, sex, or national origin. Under these programs, which have been carried out over the years by private employers, federal and state and local governments, and educational institutions, racial minorities and women have received special consideration for job openings, workplace promotions, or college admission—all areas in which they had historically suffered from discriminatory practices carried out by white males.

Affirmative action has both champions and detractors. Critics of affirmative action believe that such practices amount to "reverse discrimination" against whites and men. They claim that affirmative action gives minorities and women unfair advantages in getting an education or a job, and that it pays too little attention to the actual abilities of applicants.

Arguments over the legality of issue have led to several lawsuits that were argued before the U.S. Supreme Court, notably the *Bakke* decision of 1978, which challenged affirmative action programs in medical school admissions. In *Regents of the University of California v. Bakke*, the Court determined that the University of California Davis Medical School's racial quota system, which allowed minority candidates' admission with lower

was a profound event that symbolized much of what U.S. citizens love about their country. The Great Migration marked the first time that millions of African Americans took command of their own lives and futures. And as they moved into the cities of the North and West, the migrants forced the rest of the country to make choices as well. The migrants compelled each citizen to reexamine the meaning of freedom, opportunity, and what it means to be an American. They challenged the nation's white population to exhibit the strength and spirit to change its stereotypical ways of thinking about black Americans. "Over the decades," wrote Wilkerson, perhaps the wrong ques-

grades and test scores than white candidates, was a violation of the Four-teenth Amendment's equal protection clause.

Another landmark case concerning affirmative action was heard by the Supreme Court in 2005, after the University of Michigan faced two law-suits challenging its undergraduate and law school admissions policies. In the undergraduate case, *Gratz v. Bollinger*, the Court found that the uni-versity's admissions policies, which granted admission to virtually all quali-fied applicants who were also members of three select minorities (African Americans, Hispanics, and Native Americans) violated the equal protection clause of the Fourteenth Amendment and Title VI of the Civil Rights Act of 1964. However, in the law school case, *Grutter v. Bollinger*, the Court ruled in favor of the school's admissions policy, citing that neither acceptance nor rejection is based on race. Writing for the Court, Justice Sandra Day O'Con-nor noted that the original purpose of affirmative action—to overcome the prejudice that had kept women and minorities from equal access to educa-tion, employment, and other aspects of life—had not yet been fulfilled. "We expect that 25 years from now, the use of racial preferences will no longer be necessary to further the interest approved today," she wrote.

Sources:

The Oyez Project, *Gratz v. Bollinger*, 539 U.S. 244 (2003). Available online at http://www.oyez.org/cases/2000-2009/2002/2002_02_516.

The Oyez Project, *Grutter v. Bollinger*, 539 U.S. 306 (2003). Available online at http://oyez.org/cases/2000-2009/2002/2002_02_241.

The Oyez Project, *Regents of the University of California v. Bakke*, 438 U.S. 265 (1978). Available online at http://oyez.org/cases/1970-1979/1977/1977_76_811.

tions have been asked about the Great Migration. Perhaps it is not a question of whether the migrants brought good or ill to the cities they fled to or were pushed or pulled to their destinations, but a question of how they summoned the courage to leave in the first place or how they found the will to press beyond the forces against them and the faith in a country that had rejected them for so long. By their actions, they did not dream the American Dream, they willed it into being by a definition of their own choosing. They did not ask to be accepted but declared themselves the Americans that perhaps few others recognized but that they had always been deep within their hearts.[11]

The Great Migration became a defining moment in American history in part because it became the vehicle by which an oppressed people claimed their rightful place in the country. But the event also provided the nation itself with an opportunity to prove that its stated ideals of liberty and justice and opportunity for all were more than just words.

Notes

[1] Jordan, Vernon E., Jr. "Living with Jim Crow." *Newsweek*, January 27, 2009 (special commemorative inaugural edition), p. 88.

[2] Thernstrom, Stephen, and Abigail Thernstrom. *America in Black and White*. New York: Touchstone, 1999, p. 7.

[3] U.S. Bureau of the Census, *Income, Poverty, and Health Insurance Coverage in the United States: 2009*, Report P60, no. 238, Table B-2, pp. 62-7.

[4] Wilkerson, Isabel. *The Warmth of Other Suns: The Epic Story of America's Great Migration*. New York: Random House, 2010, p. 536.

[5] Jones, Nicholas B., and James S. Jackson. "The Demographic Profile of African Americans, 1970-71 to 2000-01," *The Black Collegian Online*, 2005. Available online at http://www.black-collegian.com/issues/30thAnn/demographic2001-30th.shtml.

[6] Jones and Jackson, "Demographic Profile."

[7] U.S. Department of Education, National Center for Education Statistics, *Digest of Education Statistics 2006* (NCES 2007-017). Washington, DC: U.S. Government Printing Office, 2007.

[8] Wilkerson, p. 506.

[9] "Optimism about Black Progress Declines: Blacks See Growing Values Gap Between Poor and Middle Class." Washington, DC: Pew Research Center, November 13, 2007, p. 1.

[10] Tolnay, Stewart E. "The African 'Great Migration' and Beyond." *Annual Review of Sociology 29*, 2003, p. 209.

[11] Wilkerson, p. 538.

BIOGRAPHIES

Robert S. Abbott (1870-1940)
Newspaper Publisher, Founder, and Editor of the
Chicago Defender

Robert Sengstacke Abbott was born on November 24, 1870, in Frederick, a small town on St. Simon's Island, Georgia. His parents, Thomas and Flora Butler Abbott, were born as slaves. Thomas had been a butler on a local plantation on St. Simon's. After the Civil War he moved to Savannah, Georgia, where he met Flora, who worked as a hairdresser. After they married, they returned to St. Simon's, where Robert was born. Thomas died shortly after Robert's birth, and Flora and Robert returned to Savannah to live.

In Savannah Flora met and married John Sengstacke, a minister and teacher, and Robert became known as Robert Sengstacke. As Robert grew older he attended Beach Institute, a prep school in Savannah. He went on to study at the Hampton Institute, a vocational and academic college that had been founded to educate former slaves. Robert studied printing as well as liberal arts, and when he graduated from Hampton in 1896, he moved to Chicago. Unable to find regular work as a printer because of racial prejudice, he decided to attend law school in the city. He received his degree from Kent College of Law in 1899, around the same time that he changed his name to Robert Sengstacke Abbott.

Abbott worked very hard to establish himself as a lawyer, but he was unable to find a firm that would hire him. He reluctantly fell back on his training as a printer to support himself. After several years of setting type for railroad timetables, Abbott made a decision that led him to a play a pivotal role in the Great Migration: he started his own newspaper.

Launching the *Chicago Defender*

On May 5, 1905, Abbott published the first issue of his new paper, the *Chicago Defender*. A one-man dynamo, he wrote, edited, arranged, printed, and distributed the handbill-size newspaper, which was devoted to publishing stories for and about the city's black community. During the next few years he struggled to keep his paper afloat against three other black newspapers in the city. He was greatly aided during this time by his landlady, Henrietta Plumer Lee, who let him use her dining room table as his home office (years later, after the *Chicago Defender* had become a financial success, Abbott bought Lee a house and turned his old apartment building into the paper's offices).

In 1909 Abbott changed the focus of the paper. Taking heed of the hard-hitting "muckraking" journalism of the times, he concentrated on printing investigative stories about the corruption of white officials and the impact of their actions on the black community. His African-American readers responded by buying the paper in the thousands. Abbott had found the key to his success: from that point onward, the *Defender* became Chicago's leading crusader against racial injustice, segregation, and corruption.

One of Abbott's first campaigns was for racial justice for African Americans in the armed services. He printed stories that outlined how blacks in military training camps during World War I (1914-1918) had been subjected to mistreatment and denied promotions to the officer ranks, based solely on their race. This coverage garnered a national readership for the paper and prompted other black newspapers to cover the issue. President Woodrow Wilson, though, was outraged at the *Defender's* embarrassing articles. Wilson and Congress were determined to stifle any opposition to the war or criticism of wartime activities undertaken by the United States. As a result, the Wilson administration tried to intimidate Abbott and other black newspaper publishers by launching investigations into their operations. The black newspapers did not oppose the war; they focused on the injustice of African-American soldiers fighting to secure rights for Europeans that they themselves did not have back at home. But any criticism was enough to anger Wilson and congressional supporters of the war.

Abbott was the central target of these investigations, but he refused to be silent. Instead, he hired new staff to expand the paper's size. Crusading managing editor J. Hockley Smiley was a particularly crucial hire. Working together, Abbott and Smiley transformed the *Defender* into an eight-page, eight-column publication that was just as substantial as the city's "white" newspapers. It even included sections devoted to Sports, Theater, Society, and Editorial, the first time those sections appeared in a black newspaper anywhere in the nation. Under Smiley, Abbott also began to publish large, sensational headlines such as "Lynching—A National Disgrace."

Perhaps most importantly, Abbott arranged to distribute his paper in the South, where 90 percent of the black population lived in 1910. Using black Pullman Car porters on major railroad lines to deliver the paper throughout the South, including the small towns along the Illinois Central line, Abbott made the *Defender* the most-read and most-influential African-American newspaper in the country.

The *Defender* and the Great Migration

Unlike most other newspapers of the time, the *Defender* fearlessly covered the racial violence that was being perpetrated against blacks in the South under the discriminatory system of laws and policies known as "Jim Crow." Abbott devoted particular attention to the murderous behavior of vigilante gangs like the Ku Klux Klan, who were terrorizing African Americans across the South without any fear of legal prosecution. Outraged by conditions in the South, Abbott decided to use his newspaper to urge long-suffering African Americans to migrate to the North, where they could escape the horrors of Jim Crow and build better lives for themselves.

By 1914, when World War I began in Europe, America's industrial centers of the North were experiencing labor shortages brought about by the high demand for manufactured goods and the sharp decline in the number of European immigrants available for work. Using banner headlines like "The Great Northern Drive," Abbott announced that the North—and Chicago in particular—was a "Promised Land" for blacks seeking good factory jobs and freedom from Jim Crow bondage. In addition, he introduced features in the *Defender* to help new migrants find transportation, housing, and job-seeking assistance once they reached the northern cities.

The results of the *Defender's* crusade were astounding. The paper's daily circulation during the peak years of the First Great Migration (1917 to 1919) reached 250,000 copies, with the overwhelming majority of them sold in the South. In addition, many of these papers were shared with family members, co-workers, or fellow churchgoers. Abbott's nephew, John Sengstacke, who took over the paper after Abbott's death, stated that "for every one *Defender* purchased, five to seven others either read or heard it aloud."[1]

119

White southerners were furious with the *Defender*, and the paper was banned throughout the region. In Arkansas, a judge issued an injunction banning its circulation. In Alabama, two *Defender* distributors were killed by an angry mob. But the Pullman porters who had distributed the paper continued to smuggle it into African-American neighborhoods throughout the South, getting the word out about the Migration and its promise.

According to the U.S. Department of Labor, the *Defender* was even more successful in spurring African-American migration than the labor agents for northern industrial firms, who had been sent to the South specifically to encourage black workers to take jobs in the North. Abbott's newspaper, explained the report's authors, "sums up the Negro's troubles and keeps them constantly before him, and it points out in terms he can understand the way to escape."[2] Indeed, one of the most crucial elements of the *Defender*'s appeal was that it was written for working-class African Americans.

The *Defender* Ends Its Great Migration Campaign

Abbott's migration drive was wildly successful. The black population in Chicago grew by 110,000 between 1916 and 1918 alone. After the end of the war in 1918, however, the North became less welcoming to black migrants. Hundreds of thousands of white military veterans returned to Chicago and other northern cities to find that their jobs and their neighborhoods were now occupied by African Americans. The resulting competition for jobs and housing sparked race riots across the country, including a deadly uprising in Chicago that left 23 blacks and 15 whites dead, and more than 500 people wounded.

The riots led to the end of the *Defender*'s campaign promoting migration and Chicago as the Promised Land. The combination of the return of military veterans, the competition for jobs, and the ensuing racial tensions ended Abbott's vision of the Great Migration as the sure cure for racism. Yet he continued to be an unabashed advocate for civil rights for African Americans, and his paper continued to be one of the most important and influential black newspapers in the country. He remained one of the most respected African-American leaders in the country, as well as one of the first self-made millionaires from the black community. When Abbott died on February 29, 1940, the *Defender* came under the editorial control of his nephew, John Sengstacke, who continued to advocate for racial equality, championing equal treatment for blacks in the military and throughout American society.

Today, the name of Robert S. Abbott is not widely recognized. But he is regarded by historians as one of the most influential and innovative voices in twentieth-century black journalism. Indeed, his early advocacy for civil rights—and for the Great Migration as a means to obtaining those rights for black Americans—have established him as an enduring figure in African-American history.

Sources

DeSantis, Alan. "A Forgotten Leader: Robert S. Abbott and the *Chicago Defender* from 1910-1920." *Journalism History*, Summer 1997, pp. 63-71.

Grossman, James R. *Land of Hope: Chicago, Black Southerners, and the Great Migration*. Chicago: University of Chicago Press, 1989.

"Robert Sengstacke Abbott." *Contemporary Black Biography*, Vol. 27. Detroit: Gale, 2001.

Notes

[1] DeSantis, Alan. "A Forgotten Leader: Robert S. Abbott and the *Chicago Defender* from 1910-1920." *Journalism History*, Summer 1997, p. 66.

[2] DeSantis, p. 66.

Mary McLeod Bethune (1875-1955)
Educator and Civil Rights Activist

Mary Jane McLeod was born on July 10, 1875, in Mayesville, South Carolina. Her parents were Samuel and Patsy McIntosh McLeod, who had been born into slavery. After the Civil War, they became tenant farmers on the same land they had worked as slaves. Mary was their fifteenth child, and the first who was born free. Her brothers and sisters had been sold off as infants, but they were able to return to their family after the war.

Mary grew up in the South at a time when discriminatory "Jim Crow" laws greatly limited the lives of all African Americans. When Mary was small, she went with her mother to the home of her parents' former owner to deliver laundry. Mary saw a white child with a book. When she reached for it she was told, "Put that down. You can't read." The incident, though, did not discourage Mary. Instead, it inspired her to pursue the best education she could possibly get.

Beginning a Life in Education

Mary first went to school at a Presbyterian mission school in Mayesville. She learned to read at the one-room schoolhouse, and this skill quickly proved helpful to her father at cotton auctions. Since Mary could read the scale accurately, she could tell when a buyer was trying to cheat her father. Around age eleven Mary received a scholarship to continue her education at a Presbyterian school in Concord, North Carolina, where she was an outstanding student. Determined to become a teacher and a Presbyterian missionary to Africa, she continued her studies at Chicago's Moody Bible Institute, where she was the institution's only black student.

Mary graduated in 1895 and applied to become a missionary in Africa, but she was told there were no positions available for blacks. She returned to Mayesville and worked as an assistant teacher in her former one-room Presbyterian school, then took a position teaching at the Haines Normal and Industrial Institute, a school for African Americans in Augusta, Georgia.

While teaching at Haines, she also volunteered to help poor families in the surrounding community. These experiences deepened her determination to devote her life to the education of African-American girls.

In 1897 Mary accepted a job at the Kindell Institute in Sumter, South Carolina, where she met Albertus Bethune, whom she married in 1898. Six months after the birth of their first child, Albertus Jr., Bethune accepted a teaching job in Palatka, Florida.

Daytona Normal and Industrial Institute for Negro Girls

In 1904 Bethune realized a longtime dream of establishing a school devoted to the education of African-American girls. The Daytona Normal and Industrial Institute for Negro Girls was originally housed in a two-story cottage near the city of Daytona's railroad tracks. Bethune's first pupils were five black girls, ages eight to twelve, who each paid 50 cents a month in tuition. They had no supplies, so Bethune used crates for desks, scavenged for other items, and raised money however she could. She and her students also grew vegetables, baked pies and cakes, and sold them to local workers to fund the school's operations.

Enrollment at the school gradually increased, mostly on the strength of girls who were the daughters of African-American laborers working on the nearby Florida East Coast Railway. Since these families could only afford modest tuition payments, however, the school continued to struggle financially. Bethune responded to this challenge by approaching several wealthy white vacationers who spent their winters in Florida. James Gamble, whose family owned Proctor & Gamble, and Thomas White, owner of White Sewing Machine Company, provided financial gifts that enabled Bethune to buy school supplies and expand the school. They also bought a house for Bethune. She called the house "The Retreat," and she lived there for the rest of her life.

As the number of students continued to grow, Bethune expanded her educational outreach to the wider black community of Daytona Beach. She initiated programs to teach the children of local turpentine workers to read and write and give them basic instruction in personal hygiene.

In 1923 Bethune agreed to merge Daytona Normal and Industrial Institute for Negro Girls with the Cookman Institute, a school for African-American boys, so as to give her school increased financial stability. She served as president of the school, which was renamed Bethune-Cookman Collegiate

Institute, from 1923 to 1943. Today the school continues to operate in Daytona Beach under the name of Bethune-Cookman University.

Champion of Civil Rights

Throughout her career as an educator, Bethune also advocated for equal rights for African Americans. She became involved with such national civil rights organizations as the National Association for the Advancement of Colored People (NAACP) and the National Association of Colored Women, one of the most important black women's groups in the country. During World War I, she helped to integrate the American Red Cross, and she participated in civil rights campaigns to integrate the military as well. In 1935 she founded the National Council for Negro Women, which worked as an advocacy organization to fight discrimination in housing, employment, and welfare.

In the 1930s Bethune became a friend and ally to First Lady Eleanor Roosevelt, who shared her interest in education and civil rights. In 1936 President Franklin D. Roosevelt appointed Bethune to the post of Director of African American Affairs within the National Youth Administration. Three years later, Roosevelt named Bethune to the post of Director of Negro Affairs, the highest political appointment yet achieved by an African-American woman.

In 1941 A. Philip Randolph announced his March on Washington to force the Roosevelt administration to address widespread discrimination against blacks in the defense industry. Bethune was an active supporter of Randolph's efforts, and after Roosevelt signed the Fair Employment Act in 1941, she worked to find defense employment for black women and young people. After the United States entered World War II in December 1941, Bethune was made a special assistant to the secretary of war. She selected the very first women to be trained as officers (generally in medical or administrative capacities), making sure that a certain percentage of those positions were filled by African-American women.

In 1945 Bethune was chosen as the NAACP's representative to the first meeting of the United Nations. When President Roosevelt died during the conference, Bethune returned to Washington and spoke at his memorial service as a representative of America's minorities. Eleanor Roosevelt gave Bethune the president's cane as a token of his esteem for her.

Bethune officially retired in 1950, but she continued to write and speak on education and civil rights issues. She also received numerous awards for her life's work. She died on May 18, 1955, and was commemorated with a statue in Washington, D.C., in 1974. This monument was the first one in the nation's capital ever dedicated to an African American or a woman. It is inscribed with Bethune's own words from her last will and testament: "I leave you love. I leave you hope. I leave you the challenge of developing confidence in one another. I leave you a thirst for education. I leave you respect for the use of power. I leave you faith. I leave you racial dignity. I leave you a desire to live harmoniously with your fellow man. I leave you finally a responsibility to our young people."[1]

Sources

Height, Dorothy I. "Remembering Mary McLeod Bethune." *Essence*, February 1994.

"Mary McLeod Bethune." *Women in World History: A Biographical Encyclopedia*, Vol. 2. Farmington Hills, MI: Gale, 2000, pp. 527-32.

McCluskey, Audrey Thomas, and Elaine M. Smith, eds. *Mary McLeod Bethune: Building a Better World, Essays and Selected Documents.* Bloomington: Indiana University Press, 2002.

Norment, Lynn. "10 Most Unforgettable Black Women." *Ebony*, February 1990.

Notes

[1] Bethune, Mary McLeod. Quoted from "Dr. Bethune's Last Will and Testament," Bethune-Cookman University. Available online at http://www.cookman.edu/about_bcu/history/lastwill_testament.html.

Tom Bradley (1917-1998)
Politician and First Black Mayor of Los Angeles

Thomas Bradley was born on December 29, 1917, in Calvert, Texas. His parents, Lee Thomas and Crenner Bradley, were sharecroppers, and his grandparents had been slaves. Bradley's family was part of the first Great Migration that took millions of African Americans out of the South. The family left Texas when Bradley was a small boy. After a brief stay in Arizona, the family settled in California, where Bradley's father found work with a railroad company and his mother worked as a maid. Bradley's father abandoned the family soon after they arrived in Los Angeles, however, and his mother struggled to support Tom and his four siblings.

Bradley attended Lafayette Junior High School and Los Angeles Polytechnic High School, where he thrived as both a student and athlete. He graduated from high school in 1937 and went to the University of California at Los Angeles (UCLA) on an athletic scholarship. Bradley became a captain of the school's track team and set a number of school records in various track events, but he left college after his junior year to join the Los Angeles Police Department (LAPD).

Bradley served in the city's police department for the next twenty years, rising to the rank of lieutenant (the highest rank available to African Americans at that time). While working as a police officer during the day, Bradley attended law school at night. After earning a law degree from Southwestern Law School in 1961, he left the police department and joined a Los Angeles-area law firm.

Rising to Mayor of Los Angeles

During his early career as an attorney, Bradley also became active in the local Democratic Party. In 1963 he won election to the Los Angeles City Council, representing a district that included whites, blacks, and Asians. He thus became one of the first black councilmen in the city's history—and proved that an African-American candidate could appeal to a wide range of voters.

During Bradley's first term on the city council, the Watts section of Los Angeles erupted into riots. Bradley was harshly critical of the way that the city's police department handled the incident. He accused the department, which consisted primarily of white administrators and officers, of brutality in its treatment of the African-American community. After winning re-election in 1965 and 1967, Bradley decided to run for mayor in 1969 against incumbent Sam Yorty, a conservative Democrat. Yorty's campaign tried to paint Bradley as an "anti-police" radical whose primary support came from black militants and subversive communists. He warned voters that many city police officers would quit if Bradley were elected. These ugly tactics paid off for Yorty, who narrowly won re-election. Bradley kept his seat on the city council, however, and served the city in that capacity for another two years.

In 1973 Bradley decided to challenge Yorty again. This time he was able to build a formidable coalition of black, white, Asian, and Hispanic supporters who lifted him to victory. Bradley thus became the first African-American mayor of a major city with a white majority. His victory made headlines worldwide, and he was heralded as a politician who could bridge the racial gap among his constituency.

Bradley served as mayor of Los Angeles for the next twenty years, winning re-election four times. His successes included revitalization of the city's downtown area and healthy growth in the finance, real estate, business, and international trade sectors. He also encouraged the hiring and promotion of blacks, Hispanics, and women in city jobs. During Bradley's tenure, Los Angeles grew to become the second-largest city in the country after New York, eclipsing Chicago.

In 1982 Bradley ran for governor of California against the incumbent, Republican George Deukmejian. Bradley entered Election Day with a lead in public-opinion polls, but when the election results were tallied Deukmejian came out ahead. Political analysts later attributed the surprise result to white voters who told pollsters that they were willing to vote for the black candidate, only to vote for the white candidate when they actually entered the voting booth. This political phenomenon, which can still be seen in some political elections, is known today as the "Bradley Effect."

An Olympic Triumph and a Police Scandal

Unbowed by this disappointment, Bradley spearheaded a successful campaign to bring the Summer Olympics Games to Los Angeles in 1984. The

Games had never before made a profit, but the 1984 edition was a big financial success thanks to the efforts of Bradley and organizer Peter Ueberroth. Bolstered by the success of the Olympics, Bradley made his second attempt to win the governorship of California. Once again, however, he lost to Deukmejian.

Bradley's darkest days as mayor came in 1991, when the city was rocked by one of the most notorious police brutality scandals of the era. That year, an African-American man named Rodney King was pulled over by the Los Angeles police and subjected to a ferocious beating while he lay on the ground. A videotape of the incident was broadcast all over the world. When the officers involved in the beating were later acquitted of the charges, some of the city's African-American neighborhoods were engulfed in rioting. The violence left 50 people dead. It also revealed a city torn by racial strife, poverty, and distrust of law enforcement.

Bradley decided not to seek re-election in 1993. He joined a law firm in Los Angeles after he left public office. Three years later he suffered a serious stroke that left him unable to speak. Bradley died of a heart attack in 1998, at the age of 80. Despite the problems that plagued the later years of his administration, Tom Bradley is considered one of the most successful African-American political leaders of his era, and he is still remembered as one of the first black mayors to come of age at the end of the Great Migration.

Sources

"Bridging the Divide: Tom Bradley and the Politics of Race," n.d. Available online at www.mayortom bradley.com.

Fritsch, Jane. "Tom Bradley, Mayor in Era of Los Angeles Growth, Dies," *New York Times*, Sept. 30, 1998, p. A15.

"Tom Bradley." *Encyclopedia of African-American Culture and History*. Farmington Hills, MI: Gale, 2006, pp. 323-24.

W. E. B. Du Bois (1868-1963)
Historian and Civil Rights Leader

William Edward Burghardt Du Bois (pronounced do-BOYS) was born on February 23, 1868, in Great Barrington, Massachusetts. His parents, Mary and Alfred Du Bois, were descended from African, Dutch, and French ancestors. Alfred, who was a barber, left the family when Du Bois was an infant. Mary worked as a domestic servant during Du Bois's childhood. His mother's extended family helped to raise him.

Du Bois was an outstanding student, but as one of the only black children in his rural Massachusetts hometown, he experienced racism at a young age, too. When a female classmate refused to accept a greeting card from him, "It dawned upon me with a certain suddenness that I was different from the others," he recalled, "shut out from their world by a vast veil." But Du Bois reacted to this insult with defiance: "The worlds I longed for, and all their dazzling opportunities, were theirs, not mine. But they should not keep these prizes, I said: some, all, I would wrest from them."[1] His determination to succeed—as well as his righteous anger—informed Du Bois's scholarship and writing throughout his life.

Educated at Prestigious Universities

While still in high school, Du Bois began to write for newspapers in Massachusetts and New York. He graduated from high school at age sixteen, finishing first in his class. He then continued his schooling by securing a scholarship to Fisk University in Nashville, Tennessee, one of the finest traditional black schools in the country.

Du Bois was an outstanding student at Fisk. Surrounded by other African Americans for the first time, he felt invigorated and alive. His years at Fisk, though, also gave him his first taste of life as a black man in the South. During his summers at Fisk, for example, he provided teaching instruction to black students from Nashville. He saw first-hand how they were denied basic civil rights. He also absorbed the ways in which the South's two-tier racial

129

class system forced African Americans to endure poor schools, jobs, housing, and the constant threat of violence against them. These experiences made Du Bois even more committed to the causes of equal rights and social justice for African Americans.

Du Bois graduated from Fisk in just three years and went on to Harvard University in Cambridge, Massachusetts, for graduate school. The school's administration did not consider a bachelor's degree from Fisk adequate preparation for graduate study, however, so Du Bois was required to earn a bachelor's degree from Harvard before tackling graduate-level studies. Du Bois finished his second bachelor's degree, then completed a master's degree in 1891. He then began working toward his doctoral degree at Harvard, which included two years of study in Germany. He greatly enjoyed his time in Germany, where he was fully accepted as a scholar and the equal of whites. In 1896 Du Bois became the first African American to receive a Ph.D. in history from Harvard. The topic of his doctoral thesis was a history of the African slave trade in the United States.

Scholar and Professor

After receiving his Ph.D., Du Bois began a career as a scholar and college professor. In 1894 he accepted a teaching post at Wilberforce College, a school founded by abolitionists in Ohio in 1856. He taught Greek and Latin there for two years, then went on to the University of Pennsylvania, where he began the country's first demographic study of African Americans, collecting data on the social, economic, and educational history of blacks in Philadelphia. He later published his findings as *The Philadelphia Negro* (1899), which is still considered a landmark work of scholarship.

In 1899 Du Bois and Daniel Murray of the Library of Congress prepared a presentation, titled "The Negro Exhibition," that was displayed at the 1900 Paris Exhibition. Their collection of charts, maps, graphs, and photographs documented the successes of African Americans in the thirty-five years since the conclusion of the Civil War, focusing especially on their achievements in economics and literacy. In addition to highlighting black achievement, however, Du Bois and Murray used their presentation to emphasize the continued discriminatory treatment of African Americans in the United States.

Du Bois's next academic post was at Atlanta University, also a traditional black college. He joined Atlanta's faculty in 1897 and directed demographic studies of African Americans. He also continued to publish penetrating analyses of the plight of blacks in the United States. One of his most famous books, *The Souls of Black Folk* (1903), contained a prophetic statement: "The problem of the twentieth century is the problem of the color line."[2]

In 1903 Du Bois also published a famous essay called "The Talented Tenth," in which he outlined his philosophy for African-American success in a racist world: "The Negro Race, like all races, is going to be saved by its exceptional men," he wrote. "The problem of education, then, among Negroes must first of all deal with the Talented Tenth; it is the problem of developing the best of this race that they may guide the Mass away from the contamination and death of the Worst."[3]

"The Talented Tenth" included criticisms of the most influential African-American leader of the time, Booker T. Washington. Washington was the founder of the Tuskegee Institute, a school for black youth that focused on vocational training rather than academics. Washington had also made a famous speech in 1895 in which he stated that blacks should not fight for equality with whites, but should accept segregation. Du Bois denounced Washington for his position on segregation and insisted that the future of African Americans depended on higher learning that would train men of "intelligence, broad sympathy, knowledge of the world that was and is."[4]

Du Bois further distanced himself from Washington in the pursuit of civil rights over the next few years. In 1905 he founded a new group, the Niagara Movement, which was the first all-African-American protest group. The organization met in Niagara, New York, and outlined a platform calling for equal rights in all aspects of life, including education, jobs, and the right to vote.

The NAACP, the *Crisis*, and the Great Migration

In 1909 Du Bois helped found the most influential civil rights organization of the twentieth century, the National Association for the Advancement of Colored People (NAACP). Formed in response to the continuing problems of racial discrimination and injustice, the NAACP expanded into an organization with its own arm for publishing and research. Du Bois headed this division, and he also served as the founding editor of the NAACP's magazine, the *Crisis*, first published in 1910. The magazine quickly became the voice of the organization—and of countless African-American readers thirsting for racial pride.

The *Crisis* also documented the First Great Migration. Beginning in 1917, Du Bois included information about the numbers of migrants from each state. He also explained the economic and social reasons for their journeys north, including the brutality of white violence against blacks across the South during the discriminatory "Jim Crow" era. "We face here a social change among American Negroes of great moment," he commented, "and one which needs to be watched with intelligent interest."[5]

Another focus for Du Bois and the *Crisis* was the treatment of black soldiers in the military. When African-American soldiers returned from World War I and were confronted with racism and violence in the land they had fought to defend, Du Bois demanded justice for them in the pages of *Crisis*. "Make way for Democracy!" he wrote. "We saved it in France, and by the Great Jehovah, we will save it in the United States of America, or know the reason why."[6]

Breaking with Black Leaders

In the 1920s many migrants who had moved to the North were drawn to the philosophy of black nationalist Marcus Garvey and his Universal Negro Improvement Association. Garvey attacked the NAACP's quest for equal rights in his publication *Negro World*. In Garvey's view, equal rights were unattainable for blacks in America. He advocated policies of segregation and separatism in the United States, as well as the establishment of a nation in Africa for blacks of all nationalities. Du Bois and other African-American leaders, including A. Philip Randolph and Robert S. Abbott, condemned Garvey, who was eventually imprisoned and deported for mail fraud.

By the early 1930s, though, Du Bois was also becoming discouraged with the lack of progress that African Americans were experiencing in their fight for equal rights. He left the NAACP in 1934 and increasingly voiced support for the idea of separate black schools and businesses. He also became involved with Pan-African organizations, which advocated for the common cause of people of African descent all over the world. In the mid-1940s he retired from teaching and research positions that he had long held at Atlanta University, Morehouse College, and Spelman College, three of the nation's leading black educational institutions.

In the late 1940s Du Bois participated in the formation of the Commission on Human Rights for the United Nations. Beginning in 1949, he served on the Council on African Affairs and the Peace Information Center, an anti-nuclear organization. Du Bois undertook these activities at the height of the so-called "Cold War," when the United States and the Soviet Union were locked in an escalating battle for political, economic, and military influence in the world. Du Bois's affiliation with the Peace Information Center aroused the suspicion of some U.S. officials, who considered the group to be a communist front for the Soviet Union. In 1951 Du Bois was indicted by American authorities for failing to register as an agent of a foreign government. He was furious with the charges. "I was not a criminal. I had broken no law, consciously or unwittingly," he declared. The case went to trial, but Du Bois was acquitted of all charges.

After his acquittal, Du Bois made plans to leave the United States. The U.S. State Department, however, refused to release his passport on the grounds that it was not in the best interests of the United States for him to journey abroad. State Department officials told him they would not return his passport unless he swore that he was not a member of the Communist Party. Du Bois fought back in court, and in 1958 the Supreme Court ruled in his favor. With passport in hand, Du Bois promptly left the country. But he did so with a diminished reputation in the eyes of many of his former supporters. Du Bois had lost the backing of many people in the black community who found that his political positions had become too extreme.

Joining the Communist Party

From 1958 until his death five years later, Du Bois traveled the world, writing and lecturing. His interest in communism continued to grow, and in 1961 he formally joined the Communist Party. That same year, at the age of 93, Du Bois became a resident of the African nation of Ghana. In 1963 he renounced his U.S. citizenship. Du Bois died in Ghana on August 27, 1963, the day before the historic March on Washington led by civil rights champion Martin Luther King Jr.

Du Bois is remembered today as one of the most important figures in the fight for equal rights for African Americans. He was the most influential intellectual of the movement for civil rights and a founder of the most important organization in the movement. Although he was a controversial figure at the time of his death, he remains a giant in the history of the struggle for equality.

Sources

Du Bois, W. E. B. *The Autobiography of W. E. B. Du Bois*. New York: International Publishers, 1968.
Du Bois, W. E. B. *The Souls of Black Folk: Essays and Sketches*. Chicago: McClurg, 1903.

Katz, Michael B., and Thomas J. Sugrue. *W. E. B. Du Bois, Race, and the City: The Philadelphia Negro and Its Legacy*. Philadelphia: University of Pennsylvania Press, 1998.

Lewis, David Levering. *W. E. B. Du Bois: Biography of a Race*, and *W. E. B Du Bois: The Fight for Equality in the American Century*. 2 volumes. New York: Holt, 1994, 2001.

Notes

[1] Du Bois, W. E. B. *The Souls of Black Folk: Essays and Sketches*. Chicago: McClurg, 1903, p. 2.

[2] Du Bois, *The Souls of Black Folk*, p. 17.

[3] Du Bois, W. E. B. "The Talented Tenth." *The Negro Problem: A Series of Articles by Representative Negroes of Today*. New York: J. Pott and Company, 1903, p. 33.

[4] Du Bois, "The Talented Tenth," p. 33.

[5] Du Bois, W. E. B. "The Migration of Negroes." The *Crisis*, June 1917, p. 66.

[6] Du Bois, W. E. B. "Returning Soldiers." The *Crisis*, May 1919, p. 13.

[7] Du Bois, W. E. B. *The Autobiography of W. E. B. Du Bois*. New York: International Publishers, 1968, p. 375.

[8] Du Bois, *Autobiography*, p. 57.

Marcus Garvey (1887-1940)
Jamaican Black Nationalist and Founder of the Universal Negro Improvement Association

Marcus Mosiah Garvey was born on August 17, 1887, in St. Ann's Bay, Jamaica, the youngest of eleven children in an impoverished family. Although he received little formal education, Garvey was an avid reader, a habit he continued after he became an apprentice to a printer. He worked as a journalist and became a labor leader as a young man. When he tried to organize a local printer's union, though, he lost his job. At that point Garvey traveled to Costa Rica and Panama before landing in London, England, where he worked for the *Africa Times and Orient Review*. The *Review* was a journal that advocated Pan-Africanism, the philosophy that blacks from every nation should work together for independence, self-government, and unity.

In 1914 Garvey returned to Jamaica, where he read *Up from Slavery*, the autobiography of influential African-American educator Booker T. Washington. Garvey was drawn to Washington's message of racial progress through self-improvement and hard work, but whereas Washington promoted racial harmony between blacks and whites, Garvey believed in the separation of the races. Acting on these beliefs, Garvey created the separatist Universal Negro Improvement Association (UNIA) in 1914. In March 1916 he moved UNIA headquarters from Jamaica to Harlem, New York, which was fast emerging as the most famous black community in the United States.

Garvey Attracts New Followers

Garvey arrived in Harlem at the height of the First Great Migration, when over one million African Americans were moving to the North to escape the discriminatory "Jim Crow" laws in the South and find new economic opportunities. Garvey's message of racial pride, self-sufficiency, and entrepreneurship resonated with many black migrants, as did his calls for

African Americans to return to Africa and establish a new, all-black nation. The goal of the UNIA, he said, was "to organize the 400,000,000 Negroes of the world into a vast organization to plant the banner of freedom on the great continent of Africa."[1]

Support for Garvey became especially strong among working-class blacks. During World War I, many black migrants who had come to the North looking for the freedoms they had been denied in the South became discouraged. Some of them even came to feel that the racial discrimination in employment, education, housing, and other aspects of life in the North was nearly as bad as it was in the Deep South. Garvey's message of self-sufficiency and separateness struck a chord with many of these disillusioned migrants.

In 1918 Garvey launched a publication, *Negro World*, to further spread the word about his philosophy. *Negro World* featured the writing of some of the finest African-American journalists, as well as aspiring writers associated with the Harlem Renaissance. Before long, it was the world's most widely read black newspaper, selling 50,000 copies per issue.

In 1919 Garvey purchased a Harlem auditorium, renamed it Liberty Hall, and began using it on a regular basis to deliver rousing speeches about black self-determination and the glorious possibilities about a return to Africa. Garvey also preached a message of pride in one's African heritage, in both mind and body. He claimed that God, Jesus Christ, and Jesus's mother Mary were black. He also asserted that it was an insult to God for anyone to be made to feel inferior based on the color of his or her skin.

Garvey's addresses drew such enthusiastic capacity crowds that he decided to embark on a national lecture tour. His travels took him all over the country, including to the migration cities of Detroit, Chicago, Cleveland, and Los Angeles. During this time his speeches became increasingly peppered with criticisms of the National Association for the Advancement of Colored People (NAACP) and liberal white civil rights activists who believed in integration and racial harmony.

The Success of UNIA

Garvey's UNIA grew at a tremendous pace during the early 1920s. More than 1,200 UNIA branches were founded in cities all over the world, with more than 700 individual chapters in the United States alone. Many of these chapters were in small southern towns, the original homes of many migrants.

Louisiana alone contained almost 80 branches, which amounted to the heaviest concentration of UNIA membership in the world. And unlike the NAACP, the UNIA limited its membership to blacks; whites were not allowed.

In 1920 Garvey made headlines around the world as he held the UNIA's first convention, a month-long conference that brought 25,000 followers to New York City. He published a manifesto entitled the "Declaration of Rights for the Negro People of the World," in which he declared that blacks would only answer to the name "Negro." This term was soon adopted by most white publications to refer to African-American people and communities.

Throughout this period Garvey encouraged blacks to start their own businesses and schools and buy their own property. He also established a shipping company, the Black Star Line, to promote the return to Africa among his followers. These initiatives gained Garvey even more followers.

Some African-American leaders, though, expressed great concerns about the influence of Garvey and the UNIA on black communities. Important leaders such as NAACP founder W. E. B. Du Bois, *Chicago Defender* publisher Robert S. Abbott, and labor organizer A. Philip Randolph all publicly opposed Garvey. They criticized Garvey's racial theories and viewed his "back to Africa" concept as an unrealistic one that would just end in disappointment for his followers. Their opposition to Garvey further intensified after he held a closed-door meeting in 1922 with leaders of the white supremacist group the Ku Klux Klan, who applauded his plan to solve America's racial problems by taking blacks back to Africa.

Randolph, Du Bois, and other civil rights leaders subsequently launched a campaign against Garvey. Their feelings about the Jamaican were summarized by a headline that Randolph used in his journal, the *Messenger*: "Garvey Must Go." Garvey's enemies also urged the U.S. Department of Justice to look into his financial dealings regarding his Black Star Line. Justice Department officials complied, and after conducting an investigation of UNIA operations they arrested Garvey on charges of mail fraud.

Garvey was convicted and sentenced to a five-year prison term in 1925. Two years later, however, his sentence was commuted by President Calvin Coolidge. Garvey was then deported to Jamaica, where he spent the next several years trying to keep his dream of an all-black African nation alive. He moved to England in 1935 and died there five years later, on June 10, 1940.

Sources

Anderson, Michael. "Self-Styled Moses." *Wilson Quarterly*, Summer 2008, pp. 89-92.

Grant, Colin. *Negro with a Hat: The Rise and Fall of Marcus Garvey*. Oxford, UK: Oxford University Press, 2008.

Hahn, Steven. "On History: A Rebellious Take on African-American History." The *Chronicle of Higher Education*, August 3, 2009.

Watson, Elwood D. "Marcus Garvey and the Rise of Black Nationalism." *USA Today*, November 2000, pp. 64-66.

Notes

[1] Quoted in Anderson, Michael. "Self-Styled Moses." *Wilson Quarterly*, Summer 2008, p. 89.

Lorraine Hansberry (1930-1965)
Playwright and Author of A Raisin in the Sun

Lorraine Vivian Hansberry was born on May 19, 1930, in Chicago, Illinois. Her parents, Carl A. and Nannie Perry Hansberry, ran a successful real estate business. They were also prominent members of the Chicago chapters of the National Association for the Advancement of Colored People (NAACP) and the Urban League. The political activism of Hansberry's parents gave her opportunities to converse with several of the most important black thinkers and artists of the day, including scholar W. E. B. Du Bois, poet Langston Hughes, singer and activist Paul Robeson, and African scholar William Leo Hansberry, who was also her uncle. Hansberry's exposure to these leaders helped her gain an early appreciation for her racial heritage.

Although Hansberry's family was wealthy and could afford private school, she attended the local public school because her parents wanted her to be educated with other African-American children. She later described Betsy Ross Elementary, an all-black, segregated school, as "a ghetto school … and, therefore, one in which as many things as possible might be safely thought of as 'expendable.' That, after all, was why it existed: not to give education, but to withhold as much as possible, just as the ghetto itself exists not to give people homes, but to cheat them out of as much decent housing as possible."[1]

Firsthand Experience with Racial Violence

Chicago was one of the main receiving cities of the Great Migration. Hansberry grew up at a time when the South Side, the black section of Chicago, was teeming with new residents who had to put up with inferior, overcrowded housing because they were unable to move into non-white neighborhoods. Early in his real estate career, Carl Hansberry had built a lucrative business by purchasing houses in formerly white neighborhoods that had been abandoned as blacks moved into new areas. He then divided these units into apartments to rent to black families. But he was staunchly opposed to the racist "restrictive covenants" that allowed legal segregation in housing. When Lorraine was seven, her father challenged these covenants by buying a house for his own family in Hyde Park, a wealthy, white section of the city that surrounded the University of Chicago.

Shortly after they moved in, an angry mob of whites appeared in front of the house. One member of the mob threw a brick through a window, narrowly missing young Lorraine. Other harassment followed, including death threats, but the Hansberrys refused to leave. Finally, white members of the community filed a lawsuit that successfully pushed the family out of Hyde Park. But Carl Hansberry fought back. He countersued, and the case was finally decided in his favor by the U.S. Supreme Court in 1940. Although the Court determined that restrictive covenants were unconstitutional, they continued to be used to discriminate against blacks in housing in Chicago and many other cities.

Angry and disillusioned, Carl Hansberry decided to find a place outside of the United States to live. He bought a house in Mexico in 1946, but suffered a stroke and died at the age of 51 before the family completed the move. His daughter was convinced that her father's battles with racism caused his death. In a letter published in the *New York Times*, Hansberry wrote that "the cost, in emotional turmoil, time, and money, led to my father's early death as a permanently embittered exile in a foreign country when he saw that after such sacrificial efforts the Negroes of Chicago were as ghetto-locked as ever."[2]

Making a Living as a Writer

After graduating from high school in 1947, Hansberry attended the University of Wisconsin. She found the classes at the predominantly white college to be rather conventional and boring, but she enjoyed her studies in theater. She left school after two years and moved to New York in 1950, where she took a job working on *Freedom*, the radical African-American journal created and edited by Paul Robeson. Hansberry reviewed books and wrote and edited articles. In 1952 she even represented Robeson at an Intercontinental Peace Congress when he was forbidden to leave the United States because of his controversial political activities.

In 1953 Hansberry married Robert Nemiroff, a white Jewish writer and student at New York University. Over the next few years she devoted increasing time and energy to creative writing projects. In 1956 her husband co-wrote the hit song "Cindy, Oh Cindy," and the money from the royalties allowed Hansberry to write full-time. She was working on several pieces, including several plays and an opera, when she and her husband attended a play that featured extremely stereotypical depictions of African Americans. The portrayals offended Hansberry deeply, but they also became the catalyst for her first and most famous play, *A Raisin in the Sun*.

A Raisin in the Sun

Hansberry took the play's title from the famous Langston Hughes poem "Harlem," which contains the stirring lines: "What happens to a dream deferred/Does it dry up like a raisin in the sun?" Initially, Hansberry wondered whether *A Raisin in the Sun* would ever see the stage. Members of New York's theatre community expressed doubts that white audiences would have any interest in her play, which centered on a black family. But the play's fortunes changed when Nemiroff gave a copy of the script to Sidney Poitier, a widely respected and popular black actor. Poitier agreed to play one of the leads and helped Hansberry find other investors to produce the play.

A Raisin in the Sun debuted on March 11, 1959, at Broadway's Ethel Barrymore Theater. The production starred Poitier, Claudia McNeil, Ruby Dee, and Louis Gossett Jr. It represented a number of firsts: it was the first play by a black playwright produced on Broadway, as well as the first with an all-black cast, black director, and black themes. And it created a sensation.

Hansberry's work focused on the Younger family, African Americans who live in an overcrowded apartment on Chicago's South Side. As the play opens, the father of the family has died and left an insurance policy worth $10,000. Each surviving member of the family—mother Lena, son Walter, and daughter Beneatha—sees the money as the key to their dreams. But all those dreams are different: Lena wants a house in the white suburbs, Walter wants to buy his own liquor store, and Beneatha wants to go to medical school. As the play unfolds, Hansberry not only examines their dreams, but also their torments and fears.

A Raisin in the Sun won the prestigious New York Drama Critics' Circle Award for best play in 1959. Hansberry thus became the youngest person and the only African-American playwright to have a work so honored. The drama was praised by both white and black critics, but it had special resonance for

African-American audiences. In the words of author James Baldwin, "Never before in the entire history of the American theater had so much of the truth of black people's lives been seen on the stage."[3] Hansberry also wrote a film version of the play that was released in 1961. The movie, which again starred Poitier, brought the work to a much larger audience.

Hansberry's Later Works

Hansberry's second play represented a radical departure from her first. *The Sign in Sidney Brustein's Window* features a Jewish protagonist who is involved in local politics. It opened in New York on October 15, 1964, but it ran for only 101 performances before closing.

While preparing for the play's opening, Hansberry's health suddenly declined. She was subsequently diagnosed with intestinal cancer, and she died on January 12, 1965, at the age of 34. She left behind several unfinished works, including a play, *Les Blancs*, that was completed by her husband. He also collected her writings and published them as an informal autobiography titled *To Be Young, Gifted and Black*. The title was taken from Hansberry's final speech, to the United Negro College Fund, in which she told her audience that "to be young, gifted and black" was something to celebrate, and not to waste. A revised version of the work became a successful play and television drama, and Hansberry's friend Nina Simone used the title in a popular song.

Today, Hansberry is remembered as an outstanding playwright whose gifts were cut short by illness. *A Raisin in the Sun*, meanwhile, remains a powerful evocation of African Americans facing discrimination during the years of the Great Migration. A timeless classic, the play has been performed continuously since Hansberry's death in the United States and around the world.

Sources

Concise Dictionary of American Literary Biography: The New Consciousness, 1941-1968. Detroit: Gale, 1987.

Hansberry, Lorraine. *Lorraine Hansberry in Her Own Words: To Be Young, Gifted and Black*, adapted by Robert Nemiroff. New York: Vintage Books, 1995.

"Lorraine Hansberry." *Afro-American Writers after 1955: Dramatists and Prose Writers*, Vol. 38. Detroit: Gale, 1985.

"Lorraine Hansberry." *Dictionary of Literary Biography, Volume 7: Twentieth-Century American Dramatists*. Detroit: Gale, 1981.

McKissack, Patricia C., and Fredrick L. McKissack. *Young, Black, and Determined: A Biography of Lorraine Hansberry*. New York: Holiday House, 1997.

Notes

[1] Hansberry, Lorraine. *Lorraine Hansberry in Her Own Words: To Be Young, Gifted and Black*, adapted by Robert Nemiroff. New York: Vintage Books, 1995, p. 3.

[2] Hansberry, p. 9.

[3] Quoted in Hansberry, p. xviii.

Langston Hughes (1902-1967)
Poet, Short Story Writer, and Playwright of the Harlem Renaissance

Langston Hughes was born on February 1, 1902, in Joplin, Missouri, to James and Carrie Langston Hughes. His parents were of mixed racial heritage, including African American, Native American, and French ancestry, but they identified themselves as black. They divorced when Langston was young, and James Hughes moved to Mexico. His mother was forced to travel extensively to find work, so she left her son in Lawrence, Kansas, with his maternal grandmother, Mary Patterson Langston.

Mary Langston raised her grandson to revere his cultural heritage, but she also taught him all about the sad chapters of African-American history, including the corrosive influence of slavery and racial discrimination. When Hughes was twelve years old, his grandmother died. At that point he reunited with his mother, who had remarried. They lived in Lincoln, Illinois, then moved to Cleveland, Ohio, where Hughes attended high school. An excellent student, he worked on the school literary magazine and yearbook and exhibited an early talent for writing poetry. Hughes also immersed himself in the religious spirituals and blues music of the surrounding black community.

Going to Harlem

After graduating from high school, Hughes went to Mexico to visit his father. This journey inspired one of his first major poems, "The Negro Speaks of Rivers," which reflects on the meaning of rivers to African and African-American history. The poem, which Hughes dedicated to black scholar and activist W. E. B. Du Bois, was published in the *Crisis* in 1921.

That year Hughes enrolled at Columbia University in New York City. He spent much of his time, though, in Harlem, a black section of the city that was one of the prime destinations of the First Great Migration. Harlem's rich musical life and vibrant energy enchanted Hughes, but in 1923 he took employment as a ship's cook in order to see the world. After extensive travels through Europe he returned to Harlem in 1924, which by then had become a haven for black artists of all kinds. Their work, which celebrated the African-American experience by showcasing black life and black themes, led people to call this era of the community's existence the Harlem Renaissance.

Hughes penned a number of important poems and essays upon returning to Harlem, but in 1926 he decided to resume his academic studies at Lincoln University, a historically black college in Pennsylvania. After graduating in 1929, he returned to Harlem and tried to find a job in publishing. But despite his growing status as the "poet laureate" of the Harlem Renaissance, Hughes found most doors closed to him because of his skin color. He also observed that for all the bountiful black talent in Harlem, the owners of the clubs and the stores were white. Hughes expressed his anger and frustration with these circumstances in works such as "My Early Days in Harlem." In 1931 Hughes left Harlem, certain that the glory days of the Renaissance were over.

A Nationally Recognized Poet

In 1932 Hughes and several other African Americans accepted an invitation to tour the Soviet Union, the leading communist power in the world at that time. Hughes found the nation to be more free of racial prejudice than his own country. Upon returning to the United States, Hughes praised the Soviet Union as less oppressive to blacks and minorities. He also spoke positively about its free and accessible education and health care systems.

During the 1930s and 1940s Hughes wrote numerous critically acclaimed poems, plays, novels, short stories, essays, and children's books. He also founded a series of theaters for working-class African Americans, with plays featuring the lives of regular people like themselves. One of his most memorable creations of this period was Jesse B. Simple, a fictional character who became a fixture in a column the poet wrote for the *Chicago Defender*, one of the most successful black newspapers in the country. Simple is a Harlem-based storyteller who relates his tales of everyday life in black America to a writer named Boyd. Simple thus became a vehicle for Hughes to offer his own opinions on life in America. Simple appeared in the *Defender*, as well as in several short stories and a play, from 1940 to 1965.

Hughes's explorations of the African-American experience led him to pen several works about the Great Migration, including "Bound No'th Blues" and "One-Way Ticket." But much of his poetry, such as 1951's "Harlem," focused more on the triumphs and tragedies experienced by black migrants in their new homes in the North.

During the 1950s Hughes became ensnared in the anti-communist fervor that gripped the United States at that time. Because he had spoken positively about the Soviet Union when he visited there in the 1930s, Hughes was called before the House Committee on Un-American Activities in 1953. He defended himself by saying that he no longer held his former pro-Soviet opinions. Hughes's testimony saved him from censure, but his remarks were condemned by some members of the African-American community who thought he was trying to save his writing career—and avoid possible imprisonment—by abandoning his principles.

Hughes spent his later years living and writing in Harlem. During the 1960s, as the movement for civil rights grew more militant, some black activists questioned whether he was truly committed to the cause. Yet Hughes continued to write poetry and other works that celebrated African-American life, condemned injustice, and championed the goals of freedom and equality. He died of cancer on May 22, 1967, in Harlem. In 1981 his Harlem home was declared a historic landmark by the city of New York.

Sources

De Santis, Christopher. *Dictionary of Literary Biography, Volume 315: Langston Hughes, a Documentary Volume*. Farmington Hills, MI: Gale, 2005

Hughes, Langston. *The Big Sea: An Autobiography*. New York: Knopf, 1940.

Meltzer, Milton. *Langston Hughes*. Brookfield, CT: Millbrook Press, 1997.

Rampersad, Arnold. *The Life of Langston Hughes*. 2 vols. New York: Oxford University Press, 1986 and 1988.

Martin Luther King Jr. (1929-1968)
Civil Rights Leader and President of the Southern Christian Leadership Conference (SCLC)

Martin Luther King Jr. was born in Atlanta, Georgia, on January 15, 1929, to Alberta Williams King and Martin Luther King Sr. He was given the name Michael when he was born. When he was about six years old, however, his father changed his own name and that of his son to "Martin Luther" to honor the sixteenth-century German theologian and founder of the Reformation in the Christian church. Martin's father and grandfather were both Baptist ministers, and he and his two siblings were raised in a home that instilled a deep love of religion and learning.

King attended the local segregated schools in Atlanta. An outstanding student, he graduated from high school at age fifteen and enrolled at Atlanta's Morehouse College, one of the finest traditional black colleges in the country. He studied sociology and received his bachelor's degree from Morehouse in 1948.

King decided to follow his father and grandfather into the ministry. He spent the next three years studying for a bachelor of divinity degree at Crozer Theological Seminary in Chester, Pennsylvania. After graduating from Crozer in 1951, King moved on to Boston University, where he began studies for a doctoral degree in theology. He also met his future wife, Coretta Scott, at Boston University (they married in 1953 and eventually had four children). King received his doctorate in 1955.

Early Civil Rights Activity

King's career as a minister began in September 1954, when he accepted an appointment at the Dexter Avenue Baptist Church in Montgomery, Alabama. He also joined the local chapter of the National Association for the Advancement of Colored People (NAACP), which was a leading voice for African-American civil rights.

King undertook his ministry in Montgomery at a time when the Civil Rights Movement was gaining strength and momentum. A key event in this regard took place in Montgomery on December 1, 1955, when Rosa Parks, a Montgomery seamstress and the secretary of the local NAACP, was arrested for refusing to give up her seat on a public bus to a white person, as required by city law. The arrest outraged Montgomery's black community. King and the NAACP called on African Americans across the city to boycott Montgomery's segregated bus system. They also convinced Parks to file a lawsuit against the city for its discriminatory policies.

The bus boycott was a tremendous success. The city's revenue from bus fares dropped dramatically, and white-owned businesses complained that they were suffering from the downturn in African-American customers. King and other protestors were arrested for their role in organizing and maintaining the protest, but the boycott remained in place. It lasted until December 1956, when the U.S. Supreme Court ruled that the public bus system laws of Montgomery—and other segregation laws across the state of Alabama—were unconstitutional and had to be changed.

New Organizations and Demonstrations

This victory inspired King and other black religious leaders across the South to found the Southern Christian Leadership Conference (SCLC). King took a leadership role in the SCLC from the very outset. The organization's activities were imbued with the deep Christian faith that King shared with the other ministers. The SCLC also was greatly influenced by the pacifist philosophy of Indian leader Mohandas Gandhi, who had effectively used nonviolent protests to secure his country's independence from Great Britain in 1947. In 1959 King even traveled to India to study Gandhi's teachings and methods.

One of the first campaigns crafted by King and the SCLC was the Crusade for Citizenship, which began in 1958. The crusade was a direct challenge to racist voting laws enacted throughout the South to keep African Americans from voting. The SCLC was aided in this effort by another new civil rights group, the Student Nonviolent Coordinating Committee (SNCC), a coalition of black and white college students who embraced King's nonviolent approach. Members of the SNCC staged "sit-ins"—efforts to integrate segregated restaurants throughout the South by protesting discriminatory seating policies. They also organized "freedom rides," in which black and white civil rights activists rode together in defiance of the South's segregated interstate bus system.

In 1963 King went to Birmingham, Alabama, a notorious stronghold of segregation enforced by police chief Eugene "Bull" Connor. King led marches and sit-ins to desegregate the city's schools, stores, and restaurants. When King and other demonstrators were arrested and put in jail for their "unlawful" activities, the civil rights leader penned one of his most famous and eloquent essays, "Letter from a Birmingham Jail." "I am in Birmingham because injustice is here," he wrote. "Injustice anywhere is a threat to justice everywhere."[1]

The events in Birmingham marked a turning point in American attitudes about the Civil Rights Movement. King's eloquence moved many white and black Americans to actively support the civil rights cause. In addition, millions of Americans were horrified by television footage of Birmingham police using high-pressure fire hoses and attack dogs on unarmed and peaceful demonstrators. The images from Birmingham shocked President John F. Kennedy as well. He responded with a televised address urging the U.S. Congress to develop civil rights legislation, which had long been a goal of King and the Civil Rights Movement.

The March on Washington

Sensing that public opinion was swinging in their favor, King and other civil rights leaders—including A. Philip Randolph (president of the Brotherhood of Sleeping Car Porters), John Lewis (president of the SNCC), Roy Wilkins (leader of the NAACP), and Whitney Young (president of the National Urban League)—organized a March on Washington to bring attention to the cause of civil rights, jobs, and poverty. The march, which took place on August 28, 1963, was another defining moment in the history of the Civil Rights Movement. The rally at the Lincoln Memorial was attended by nearly 250,000 black and white Americans who came from widely diverse political, social, and religious backgrounds.

The historical highlight of the March on Washington was King's "I Have a Dream" speech, which stands as one of the most famous addresses in modern history. "We will not be satisfied," he declared to his spellbound audience, "until justice rolls down like water and righteousness like a mighty stream."[2] King concluded his famous speech by presenting a vision of an

America in which people of every color and background are able to live at peace and in harmony.

Outbursts of Violence and Moments of Triumph

The next few years were rewarding ones for the Civil Rights Movement and King, who was universally recognized as its most influential and eloquent leader. On July 2, 1964, the Civil Rights Act of 1964 was signed into law by President Lyndon B. Johnson. The legislation prohibited discrimination in public facilities, employment, and education and ended federal aid to segregated institutions. During this same period, thousands of civil rights workers poured into the South for an African-American voter registration campaign known as "Freedom Summer." And in the fall of 1964, King received the Nobel Peace Prize. In accepting the prestigious award, King emphasized that he had "an abiding faith in America and an audacious faith in the future of mankind. I refuse to accept the view that mankind is so tragically bound to the starless midnight of racism and war that the bright daybreak of peace and brotherhood can never become a reality."[3]

Other victories followed in 1965. On March 7 civil rights demonstrators were savagely attacked by city police and state troopers in Selma, Alabama. The ugly assault injured John Lewis and many other civil rights activists, but news footage of the event also boosted public support for their cause—and increased public disgust with the racist whites who were perpetrating such violence. A second march was organized in Selma, and President Johnson made sure that this one was protected by federal authorities. King led this successful march, which brought 25,000 protestors to the steps of the state capital in Birmingham on March 25. Five months later, the Voting Rights Act of 1965 was signed into law. This landmark law prohibited the denial or abridgement of a person's right to vote based upon race or color. It thus put an end to the discriminatory Jim Crow voting laws that had held sway across the South for generations.

King continued his civil rights crusade into 1966 and 1967, but he also became increasingly known for his criticism of the Vietnam War and his efforts to address urban poverty. He believed that the violent race riots that had erupted in Watts (a neighborhood in Los Angeles), Detroit, Newark, and other cities during this period could be directly traced to the feelings of hopelessness and anger that dominated poor minority neighborhoods in the inner cities.

Struck Down in Memphis

King responded to the turmoil in America's cities with a pledge to address the riots and the social problems that had caused them. He traveled across the country, bringing his message of nonviolence to urban areas that had been scarred by the unrest. One of his destinations was Chicago, one of the greatest receiving cities of the Great Migration. He was saddened by the poverty he encountered there. "Negroes have continued to flee from behind the Cotton Curtain," he said, "but now they find that after years of indifference and exploitation, Chicago has not turned out to be the New Jerusalem."[4] King was also astonished at the level of anger and hatred that his visit elicited from whites in the city. "I have seen many demonstrations in the South," he said after a particularly ugly demonstration from white opponents. "But I have never seen anything so hostile and so hateful as I've seen here today."[5]

In late 1967 King and the SCLC launched a Poor People's Campaign to highlight the issues of hunger, substandard housing, and limited educational opportunities in America's poorest communities. He was still working on this campaign on April 3, 1968, when he arrived in Memphis, Tennessee, to support sanitation workers who were striking for better pay and working conditions. The following day, King was shot and killed by an assassin while standing on the balcony of a downtown hotel.

The news of King's tragic death sent the nation reeling. A new round of riots broke out in black communities across the country. After King's death, the movement for civil rights became less cohesive and more diffuse, and black activists who preached more militant messages assumed new prominence. But King's role in bringing new civil rights to African Americans and other minorities has never been forgotten. He has become an iconic figure in American history since his death, revered as a voice for freedom, equality, and dignity for all people.

Sources

Branch, Taylor. *Parting the Waters: America in the King Years, 1954-63*. New York: Simon & Schuster, 1988.

Branch, Taylor. *Pillar of Fire: America in the King Years, 1963-65*. New York: Simon & Schuster, 1998.

Branch, Taylor. *At Canaan's Edge: America in the King Years, 1965-68*. New York: Simon & Schuster, 2006.

King, Coretta Scott. *My Life with Martin Luther King*. New York: Holt, Rinehart, & Winston, 1969.

King, Martin Luther, Jr. *A Testament of Hope: The Essential Writings and Speeches of Martin Luther King, Jr.*, edited by James Melvin Washington. San Francisco: Harper & Row, 1986.

King, Martin Luther, Jr. *The Autobiography of Martin Luther King Jr.*, edited by Clayborne Carson. New York: Warner Books, 1998.

Lewis, David Levering. *King: A Biography*. Urbana: University of Illinois Press, 1978.

Notes

[1] King, Martin Luther, Jr. "Letter from a Birmingham Jail." Available online at http://mlk-kpp01. stanford.edu/index.php/resources/article/annotated_letter_from_birmingham/.

[2] King, Martin Luther, Jr. "I Have a Dream." Available online at http://www.mlkonline.

[3] King, Martin Luther, Jr. "The Nobel Prize in 1964." Available online at http://nobelprize.org /nobel_prizes/peace/laureates/1964/.

[4] Quoted in Ralph, James R., Jr. *Northern Protest: Martin Luther King Jr., Chicago, and the Civil Rights Movement*. Cambridge, MA: Harvard University Press, 1993, p. 35.

[5] Quoted in "Dr. King Is Felled by Rock: 30 Injured as He Leads Protesters; Many Arrested in Race Clash." *Chicago Tribune*, August 6, 1966, p. 1.

Jacob Lawrence (1917 2000)
Creator of The Migration *and Other Artistic Works about the African-American Experience*

Jacob Armstead Lawrence was born on September 7, 1917, in Atlantic City, New Jersey, to Jacob and Rosalee Lawrence. They were both migrants from the South who had moved north as part of the Great Migration. Their search for better jobs for themselves and better opportunities for their children became "a part of my life," Lawrence later wrote. "I grew up knowing about people on the move from the time I could understand what words meant."[1]

Lawrence's family moved frequently during his childhood. He spent several years in Easton, Pennsylvania, where his father worked in the local mines. After his father lost his job, however, his parents' marriage was broken by the financial strain. Lawrence and his younger sister and brother moved with their mother to Philadelphia, where she found work as a domestic servant. But Rosalee Lawrence could not make enough money on her own to support her children. When Jacob was ten, he and his siblings were placed in foster care. Their mother, meanwhile, moved to the Harlem section of New York City to find work.

The Lawrence children spent the next three years in foster care, but they were finally reunited with their mother after she found work that enabled her to bring them to New York. Jacob attended public school in Harlem, and his mother enrolled him in an after-school art program at the Utopia Children's House. Lawrence studied at Utopia with African-American painter and artist Charles Alston. Under Alston's tutelage, Lawrence blossomed into a remarkable artist who particularly enjoyed painting murals that featured scenes of everyday life on the streets of Harlem.

Lawrence entered school at the New York High School of Commerce, a vocational school that offered courses in commercial art, in 1932. But he lost interest in school and dropped out after two years. He thus entered the workforce during the Great Depression, when up to one-quarter of the country's workers were unemployed—and a much greater percentage of African Americans had trouble finding work. Rosalee Lawrence lost her job as a domestic worker during this horrible economic downturn, and the family was forced to rely on public assistance for basic food and shelter. Jacob helped out as best he could, working as a paper boy and a delivery boy. In 1936 he was able to enroll in the Civilian Conservation Corps, a federal program that put unemployed men to work on conservation, roadbuilding, and park creation projects.

Becoming Part of the Harlem Renaissance

Throughout these years of hardship, Lawrence never lost his love of art. He rented a studio from his mentor, Charles Alston, for eight dollars a month and continued to paint. Alston also introduced Lawrence to his circle of friends and fellow artists, including Langston Hughes, Romare Bearden, and other prominent members of the Harlem Renaissance. Alston also introduced him to painter and sculptor Gwendolyn Knight, whom he married in 1941.

Lawrence continued to paint works set in Harlem throughout the 1930s. Late in that decade he met artist Augusta Savage, who helped him to win a grant from the Works Progress Administration (WPA), another federal program that provided support to artists and writers during the Depression. In 1938 Lawrence's work was featured for the first time in a one-man exhibition in a Harlem gallery. His paintings were widely praised, and before long his name was known throughout New York City's artistic community.

Painting the African-American Experience

From his earliest efforts to his most mature works, Lawrence celebrated African-American life. His first major expression of this subject was a series of panels that depicted the life and achievements of Haitian revolutionary hero Toussaint L'Ouverture, which he completed in 1937. He continued his commemoration of African-American heroes in series that featured abolitionists Frederick Douglass (completed in 1938) and Harriet Tubman (finished in 1939).

Lawrence is best known, however, for *The Migration,* a series of paintings that depicts the Great Migration. He began the work around 1940 after studying the history of the migration at the Schomberg Library in Harlem.

Drawing on that history, as well as his own family's memories, he began to create what would become a series of sixty panels that traces the migration in all its aspects. Taken in their entirety, the panels express the hopes, fears, and challenges faced by the migrants.

Early panels in the series depict African Americans in their impoverished homes in the South. Lawrence portrays the backbreaking work of the sharecroppers, cotton crops withered by infestations of boll weevils, and ominous threats of white violence that regularly lurked under the Jim Crow laws of the segregated South.

The subject matter of the paintings then shifts to the theme of escaping the South. Some panels recount how the migrants heard about the promise of the North from local church leaders or the pages of black newspapers. Subsequent panels depict the migrants' northward journeys, featuring images of train stations overflowing with crowds of African Americans. Lawrence then uses his brushes to document the positive aspects—and dispiriting elements—of black life in the North. His panels feature northern factories where African Americans found work, for instance, but he also includes images of crowded housing and racial discrimination in the cities of the North. Ultimately, however, Lawrence's masterwork provides a proud, hopeful, and stirring depiction of the Great Migration.

The Migration was first shown in New York in 1942, to great acclaim. It became part of an exhibition of his art that toured the country for two years. In 1942 Lawrence was drafted into the U.S. Coast Guard, where he served during World War II. He continued to work as an artist during the war, creating a series of murals depicting the lives of U.S. servicemen.

When the war was over in 1945, Lawrence returned to New York. He expanded his themes of African-American life to include music and musicians, and many of these works evoked the distinct rhythms and tonal colorings of jazz music. He and his wife, Gwendolyn Knight, moved to Seattle in 1971, where he taught at the University of Washington. He continued to paint as well, but he also wrote and illustrated children's books as well as biographies of such noted African Americans as Harriet Tubman. He was also the recipient of numerous awards, including the National Medal of Arts and the Spingarn Medal from the National Association for the Advancement of Colored People (NAACP).

Publishes Children's Book on the Great Migration

In 1992 Lawrence published a children's book that featured reproductions of his famous Great Migration panels. This work, titled *The Great Migration: An American Story*, included extensive commentary from Lawrence on his paintings. The narrative features the recurring phrase "And the migrants kept coming."

The artist concluded his book with an homage to the African Americans who took part in the Great Migration and a tribute to all people who journey in search of a better life. "Theirs is a story of African-American strength and courage," he said. "I share it now as my parents told it to me, because their struggles and triumphs ring true today. People all over the world are still on the move, trying to build better lives for themselves and their families."[2]

Lawrence died in Seattle on June 9, 2000, but his paintings—and especially *The Migration*—remain well-known celebrations of African-American struggles and triumphs. The sixty-panel series is now divided into two exhibits. One is on permanent display at the Phillips Collection in Washington, D.C., and the other is featured at the Museum of Modern Art in New York.

Sources

Bearden, Romare, and Harry Henderson. *Six Black Masters of American Art*. Garden City, NY: Zenith, 1972.

"Jacob Lawrence." *Encyclopedia of African-American Culture and History*, Vol. 3, 2nd ed. Farmington Hills, MI: Gale, 2006, pp. 1268-70.

"Jacob Lawrence." *Scribner's Encyclopedia of American Lives*, Vol. 6. Farmington Hills, MI: Gale, 2002, pp. 296-98.

Nesbitt, Peter, and Michelle DuBois. *The Complete Jacob Lawrence: Paintings, Drawings, and Murals (1935-1999)*. Seattle: University of Washington Press, 2000.

Notes

[1] Lawrence, Jacob. *The Great Migration: An American Story*. New York: HarperCollins, 1993, p. 2.

[2] Lawrence, p. 59.

A. Philip Randolph (1889-1979)
Labor and Civil Rights Leader

Asa Philip Randolph was born on April 15, 1889, in Crescent City, Florida, to James William and Elizabeth Robinson Randolph. His father was a minister in the African Methodist Episcopal (AME) Church in Jacksonville and often worked odd jobs as well. Even though the family was poor and had little money for books, his parents valued education and reading, and they raised Asa and his brother to take pride in their African-American heritage. James Randolph took his sons to the library every week until 1896, when the *Plessy v. Ferguson* decision handed down by the U.S. Supreme Court allowed segregation in all public facilities. He was so outraged by the decision that he refused to let his children ride segregated streetcars or visit the newly segregated public library.

Randolph attended the Cookman Institute, Florida's first all-black high school, and graduated in 1907 as valedictorian. His family had no money for college, so he worked for several years as a waiter and at other jobs before moving to New York City in 1911. Randolph lived in Harlem, where he met many other African-American migrants who had left the discriminatory "Jim Crow" South. He had a fine speaking and singing voice and began taking acting classes. When a career in theater failed to materialize, however, he started studying at City College, which offered free tuition. Randolph was especially interested in politics and sociology, particularly as these subjects related to equal rights for blacks. Before long he had become an outspoken advocate for African-American civil rights.

In 1914 Randolph married Lucille Green. Two years later he joined the Socialist Party, and in 1917 he joined with Green and fellow political activist Chandler Owen to found a new publication called the *Messenger*. The magazine gave them a platform to publicize their socialist political beliefs, but it put them at odds with mainstream American politics. It also made them the targets of law enforcement officials during World War I (1914-1918), when

Congress approved a variety of laws that criminalized anti-war writings and speeches. The U.S. attorney general tried to block the antiwar *Messenger* from being distributed, and in 1917 Randolph was arrested for voicing opposition to the war in a speech. The charges were later dropped.

Randolph remained active in socialist politics for the next several years. He helped run the election campaigns of several New York socialists, and he even made an unsuccessful bid for the office of state comptroller himself. Randolph also became involved in the campaign waged by African-American civil rights leaders against African nationalist Marcus Garvey, who wanted black Americans to voluntarily return to Africa and establish a new nation there.

Organizing the Brotherhood of Sleeping Car Porters

Randolph gained national prominence in 1925 when he was asked by black porters who worked for the Pullman Company, which made luxury railroad sleeping cars, to help them form a labor union. The all-black Pullman porters were responsible for handling baggage and preparing the sleeping cars for patrons. They were among the most highly respected members of the black community, but they had been denied representation by the existing railroad workers union because they were black.

Randolph agreed to help, and in 1925 he began twelve years of negotiations to create the Brotherhood of Sleeping Car Porters union that would be formally recognized by the Pullman Company. During this period he also worked tirelessly to address the great discrepancy in hours, wages, and working conditions that existed between white and black railroad workers at that time. For example, Pullman porters were required to work 400 hours per month for an average wage of $67, while their white counterparts worked only 240 hours per month for an average wage of $150.

In 1937 the Brotherhood of Sleeping Car Porters finally signed a landmark contract agreement with Pullman. This contract, for which Randolph was largely responsible, guaranteed them decent wages, hours, and working conditions. It was the first labor contract between a white-owned business and a black union, and it marked the arrival of the first major African-American union in the history of the United States.

Randolph next took on the American Federation of Labor (AFL), the largest labor organization in the nation. The AFL had originally banned racial discrimination in its affiliate unions, but by the 1930s segregated union chapters dotted its ranks. In a fiery address to the AFL national convention in 1936, Randolph warned its membership about the consequences of continued discrimination against black workers. He alluded to Booker T. Washington's famous declaration that "in all things purely social" white and black Americans "can be as separate fingers, yet one as the hand in all things essential to mutual progress." Randolph rejected Washington's stance, saying that "white and black workers ... cannot be organized separately as the fingers on my hand. They must be organized altogether, as the fingers on my hand when they are doubled up in the form of a fist.... If they are organized separately, they will not understand each other. They will fight each other, and if they fight each other, they will hate each other. And the employing class will profit from that condition."[1]

Pushing for Passage of the Fair Employment Act

In 1941 Randolph took up the issue of discrimination against African Americans working in the defense industry during World War II. Migrants by the millions had left the South and moved to the cities of the North and West in search of decent jobs in the defense industry and other economic sectors that were enjoying tremendous wartime growth. However, some businesses armed with federal defense contracts refused to hire blacks. Randolph wanted the administration of President Franklin D. Roosevelt to ban the federal government from giving contracts to any company that discriminated against blacks in their hiring practices.

Determined to press the issue, Randolph announced his intention to lead a march of 100,000 African-American laborers in Washington, D.C., on July 1, 1941, to bring attention to the problem. "We loyal Negro American citizens demand the right to work and fight for our country,"[2] Randolph declared. The march was also promoted by the National Association for the Advancement of Colored People (NAACP) and the nation's leading black newspapers.

President Roosevelt at first tried to put Randolph off. He sent his wife, Eleanor, to meet with Randolph instead. Roosevelt believed that the march would embarrass the United States among its wartime allies. In addition, Roosevelt was concerned about how the effort would affect his political fortunes. He wanted to keep the allegiance of African-American voters, but he also wanted to appease white business owners who did not want to be forced to integrate their workforces.

Randolph refused to back down and insisted on meeting the president face to face. Afterward, Roosevelt finally took measures to satisfy Randolph and thus keep the march from going forward. On June 25, 1941, Roosevelt signed Executive Order 8802, known as the Fair Employment Act, which prohibited discrimination in the defense industry. It stated that any company with a contract with the federal government could not discriminate against potential employees on the basis of race. The anti-discrimination laws also extended to labor unions working in companies with federal contracts. Randolph was delighted with Roosevelt's move, and he called off the march.

Roosevelt's executive order created a commission to implement the law, called the Fair Employment Practice Committee (FEPC). The FEPC was supposed to investigate allegations of discrimination in the defense industry, but it had little power and authority. When confronted with a backlash from white business owners who refused to implement the new policies, the FEPC backed down. The FEPC's weak performance greatly frustrated Randolph. But even though they are generally considered failures, the Fair Employment Act and the FEPC marked the first real efforts on the part of the federal government to address the problem of racial discrimination on a national level. For that reason, the Fair Employment Act is regarded as one of Randolph's most significant achievements.

Throughout World War II (1939-1945) and in the years that followed, Randolph also fought to integrate the U.S. armed forces. When black veterans came home from the war, they took part in a movement called the "Double V." This phrase signified America's victory in defeating fascism and tyranny in Europe and the Pacific, but it also referred to the goal of achieving victory at home against the discrimination that trapped black Americans as second-class citizens of their own country.

In early 1948 President Harry S. Truman invited Randolph and other civil rights leaders to the White House to discuss the issue of integration of the military. Randolph was outspoken in his efforts on behalf of black soldiers. He told Truman and members of Congress that if the military remained segregated, African Americans would become increasingly resistant to military service. He pointed out that black men had little incentive to put their lives at risk for a country that treated them so poorly. These arguments, which were echoed by other civil rights leaders, made a big impression on the president. On July 28, 1948, Truman issued Executive Order 9981, which ended segregation in the armed forces.

Randolph and the Civil Rights Movement

As the most prominent African American in the labor movement, Randolph continued to fight for equal rights and representation for blacks in all aspects of American life. He became an important figure in the Civil Rights Movement of the 1950s and 1960s. In 1951 he helped create the Negro American Labor Council to fight racial discrimination in American labor unions, and he also served on the executive council of the AFL-CIO from 1955 to 1974.

Randolph also organized one of the most celebrated civil rights demonstrations ever held in Washington, D.C. He was the original planner of the August 1963 March on Washington, which was highlighted by Martin Luther King Jr.'s "I Have a Dream" speech. Randolph organized the event, formally known as the March on Washington for Jobs and Freedom, as a labor and civil rights forum. He also provided the introduction for King, telling the hundreds of thousands of people gathered in front of the Lincoln Memorial that "we are the advance guard of a massive moral revolution for jobs and freedom. This revolution reverberates throughout the land, touching every village where black men are segregated, oppressed, and exploited."[3]

Randolph's health declined in the mid-1960s, and he retired as president of the Brotherhood of Sleeping Car Porters in 1968. But he continued to write and speak out on social issues through his organization, the A. Philip Randolph Institute, until his death in 1979. His funeral procession was led by President Jimmy Carter. Randolph is still remembered today as a devoted champion of civil rights and social justice and as one of the most important African-American political and social leaders of the twentieth century.

Sources

Hill, Norman. "Forging a Partnership between Blacks and Unions." *Monthly Labor Review*, August 1987, p. 38.

Miller, Calvin Craig. *A. Philip Randolph and the African-American Labor Movement*. Greensboro, NC: Morgan Reynolds, 2005.

Schlager, Neil, ed. "Brotherhood of Sleeping Car Porters." *St. James Encyclopedia of Labor History Worldwide*. Farmington Hills, MI: Gale, 2006, pp. 106-11.

Notes

[1] Quoted in Hill, Norman. "Forging a Partnership between Blacks and Unions." *Monthly Labor Review*, August 1987, p. 38.

[2] Quoted in Arensen, Eric. "A Victory for Fair Employment?" *Footsteps*, January-February 2002, p. 36.

[3] Quoted in the *Crisis*, August-September 1973, p. 228.

Malcolm X (1925-1965)
Political and Religious Leader and Civil Rights Activist

Malcolm Little, who later became known as Malcolm X, was born on May 19, 1925, in Omaha, Nebraska. His parents, Louise and Earl Little, had a total of eight children. Louise was a homemaker, and Earl was a minister in the Baptist church. He was also a follower and advocate of Marcus Garvey, a black nationalist and the founder of the Universal Negro Improvement Association (UNIA).

Terrorized by White Supremacists

When Louise Little was pregnant with Malcolm, their home in Omaha was stormed by the Ku Klux Klan, a white supremacist organization that frequently terrorized and attacked African Americans. Earl and Louise Little knew their family was in danger, so they left Omaha in 1926 and moved first to Milwaukee, then to Lansing, Michigan, where Earl Little found work as a Baptist preacher. He also continued to give speeches in support of Garvey and black nationalism.

One night in 1929, the family home was burned to the ground. Malcolm X later recalled "that nightmare night in 1929, my earliest memory. I remember being suddenly snatched awake into a frightening confusion of pistol shots and shouting and smoke and flames."[1] Police investigators claimed that the fire was an accident, but the Little family always suspected that a local white racist group known as the Black Legion had committed the crime.

Two years later, Earl Little was found murdered. Once again, the family suspected that the Black Legion was responsible, but no one was ever arrested for the crime. After her husband's death, Louise Little struggled to bring in enough income to feed her eight children. After several years, she suffered a nervous breakdown and was put in a mental hospital, where she remained for twenty-six years. Her children were placed in different foster homes, and Malcolm spent his adolescence being shuffled from one to another.

Despite the disruption of living in various foster homes growing up, Malcolm was an excellent student and loved school. He attended mostly white public schools in the Lansing area and thought about going to college and becoming a lawyer. But his teachers belittled his dreams, telling him that blacks simply could not achieve those kinds of goals. Malcolm subsequently lost interest in his school work. He also had an early run-in with police at age thirteen, when he placed a thumbtack on a teacher's chair. Malcolm was expelled from school, and when the teacher pressed charges against him, he spent almost a year in detention centers and reform school.

Malcolm dropped out of school for good at age sixteen and moved to Boston. Over the next few years he divided his time between Boston and Harlem. He became heavily involved in gambling, drugs, and other criminal activities in both cities, and in 1946 he was arrested in Boston on robbery charges. Malcolm was convicted of the charges later that year and sentenced to ten years in prison.

A Religious Conversion

When Malcolm Little entered prison he was both a drug addict and an angry young man. During his incarceration, however, he began to study the Black Muslim faith, the religion of the Nation of Islam. The Nation of Islam was founded in Detroit in 1930 by Wallace D. Fard (later known as Wali Fard Muhammad). The religion's major tenets were developed by Fard's successor, Elijah Muhammad, who claimed to be the messenger of God. He preached that blacks were superior to whites, who were to blame for the economic and political inequality of blacks. Elijah Muhammad asserted that whites were doomed to be swept from the face of the earth by a vengeful God.

Muhammad also promoted the same ideals of black nationalism that had been espoused by Marcus Garvey. The Black Muslims called for African Americans to create and maintain a separate existence from white Americans. The keys to this existence were the encouragement of black-owned business-es and high standards of personal behavior, including complete rejection of alcohol and tobacco. Like Garvey, they also promoted the idea of blacks form-ing their own country.

Little struck up a correspondence with Elijah Muhammad, and he became a devout Black Muslim. Following his conversion to the faith in 1948, he renamed himself "Malcolm X," discarding the "Little" surname as a relic of slavery. The "X" symbolized the freedom conferred on him by his new faith. When Malcolm X was released from prison in 1952, he moved to Chicago, which was not only one of the biggest receiving cities of the Great Migration but also the headquarters of the Nation of Islam. Working closely with Elijah Muhammad, Malcolm X moved up in the organization's ranks. As an assistant minister, he helped open new Black Muslim temples in Detroit, Philadelphia, New York, and other receiving cities of the Great Migration.

A Fiery Spokesman

From the time of his release from prison in the early 1950s, Malcolm X was a dynamic and charismatic speaker, and he drew many new adherents to the Nation of Islam. Like Marcus Garvey, he held a particular appeal to poor and working-class people who had been victimized by discrimination in the North. He denounced racism and police brutality and promoted the social, economic, and political benefits to be found in the separatism advocated by the Black Muslim faith. He also preached that African Americans should be proud of their racial heritage and history, and that they should arm themselves and seize their full rights "by any means necessary."

The confrontational, racially charged rhetoric employed by Malcolm X was a direct challenge to the nonviolent approach of civil rights leaders like Martin Luther King Jr. Malcolm believed that the quest for racial equality and integration was foolish, and he openly criticized King and his followers. For his part, King understood Malcolm X's anger. "He, like so many of our number, was a victim of the despair inevitably deriving from the conditions of oppression, poverty, and injustice which engulf the masses of our race,"[2] he said. King, however, thought that Malcolm's rhetoric was irresponsible and counterproductive. "I have often wished that he would talk less of violence, because violence is not going to solve our problem,"[3] King said.

Despite the attention that Malcolm X received, however, his influence in America's black communities remained limited. Most African Americans supported King's steadfast but nonviolent approach to civil rights over the more confrontational one championed by Malcolm X and other leaders of the Nation of Islam. According to a national survey conducted by *Newsweek* magazine in 1963, 88 percent of African Americans polled had a positive opinion of King, while only 15 percent held a positive view of Malcolm X.

Many white Americans, meanwhile, feared Malcolm X for his radical views. Their negative impressions of him became particularly strong after he was featured on a 1959 five part television news report, "The Hate That Hate Produced," hosted by CBS newsman Mike Wallace. The program featured extensive footage of Malcolm X delivering passionate speeches about the Nation of Islam and its controversial doctrines. By this point, Malcolm had also been identified by the FBI and New York law enforcement as a political subversive. Investigators began to follow him and monitor his activities. At one point his home was broken into, and he was subjected to wiretapping and other surveillance by the government. Malcolm X was one of several high-profile African-American political figures who were followed by the FBI; the agency's surveillance file on Malcolm X, begun in 1953, eventually bulged to more than 11,000 pages.

The Nation of Islam's dogged adherence to separatism also led Malcolm X to form questionable alliances. In 1961 he served as Elijah Muhammad's emissary to a secret meeting with Ku Klux Klan leaders, whose support Muhammad was seeking for his plan to create an all-black nation. Two years later, however, the Nation of Islam leader abruptly suspended Malcolm from his post. This decision stemmed from Muhammad's jealousy over his lieutenant's growing influence and popularity within the church and the wider black community.

This betrayal by his mentor shocked Malcolm, who undertook a closer study of Muhammad's teachings and behavior. He learned that the leader had carried on numerous affairs with female members of the faith in direct violation of the teachings of the Nation of Islam. In March 1964 Malcolm X broke with the Nation of Islam and founded his own religious organization within the Islamic faith, called the Muslim Mosque. This new organization adhered much more closely to traditional Islam than to the tenets of the Black Muslims.

A New Perspective on Race Relations

Shortly after breaking with Elijah Muhammad, Malcolm X traveled to the Middle East to take part in the *hajj* (pilgrimage) to Mecca, the holiest city in Islam. The *hajj* is one of the fundamental precepts of the Muslim faith, and in completing the journey, Malcolm X experienced profound changes in his beliefs. He met Muslims from all over the world, of every race and nationality. As he shared his religious experiences with them, he began to see beyond separatism to a belief in the oneness of all humankind.

When he returned to the United States in May 1964, Malcolm X reached out to other African-American leaders, including Martin Luther King Jr., to try to build a coalition of like-minded political leaders to fight for civil rights. "It's time for us to submerge our differences and realize that it is best for us to first see that we have the same problem,"[4] he said. Yet even this olive branch to the mainstream Civil Rights Movement was couched in a speech entitled "The Ballot or the Bullet." Malcolm warned in this address that if the federal government failed to pass major civil rights legislation, frustrated African Americans might need to seize their rights through violence.

The Nation of Islam was outraged by Malcolm X's new message of harmony. In addition, Elijah Muhammad felt threatened by Malcolm's continued popularity among African Americans. In February 1965 his home in Queens, where his wife and four daughters also lived, was firebombed. Malcolm knew that Elijah Muhammad was responsible for the attack, and he realized that he was a marked man. On February 21, 1965, Malcolm was giving a speech in Harlem when three men entered the hall and assassinated him; all three were members of the Nation of Islam.

The Autobiography of Malcolm X, which Malcolm had authored with Alex Haley, was published a few months later. The book brought the life story and evolving political and religious beliefs of this pivotal figure in American history to a much wider audience. In 1992 film director Spike Lee made a critically acclaimed biographical movie about Malcolm X that recounted the story of his life, his teachings, and his belief—found late in life—that whites and blacks were capable of coexisting peacefully.

Sources

Malcolm X, and Alex Haley. *The Autobiography of Malcolm X*. New York: Grove Press, 1965.

Moore, John, ed. "Malcolm X." *Encyclopedia of Race and Racism*. Farmington Hills, MI: Gale/Cengage, 2009, pp. 276-80.

Muhammad, E. Najee. "The Educational Development of Malcolm X." *Western Journal of Black Studies*, Winter 2002, pp. 240-49.

Myers, Walter Dean. *Malcolm X: By Any Means Necessary*. New York: Scholastic, 1993.

Notes

[1] Malcolm X, and Alex Haley. *The Autobiography of Malcolm X*. New York: Grove Press, 1965, p. 5.

[2] King, Martin Luther, Jr. *The Autobiography of Martin Luther King Jr.*, edited by Carson Clayborne. New York: Warner Books, 1998, p. 265.

[3] King, p. 265.

[4] Malcolm X. "The Ballot or the Bullet." *Great Speeches by African Americans*. Mineola, NY: Dover Publications, 2006, p. 116.

PRIMARY SOURCES

The *Chicago Defender* Reports on Lynchings in the Jim Crow South

In 1905 Robert S. Abbott founded the Chicago Defender, *which became one of the most important African-American newspapers of the twentieth century. The* Defender *focused on news for and about the black community, and beginning around 1909 this coverage included numerous articles on the ways in which corrupt white officials were hurting African-American families and communities. African-American readers responded to this "muckraking"—a term for hard-hitting investigative journalism—by buying the paper by the thousands. Abbott had found the key to his success: from that point onward, the* Defender *became a leading voice against racial injustice, fighting segregation and corruption in Chicago and throughout the country.*

Abbott's paper even had a significant presence in the South, where 90 percent of the black population lived in 1910. Using black Pullman porters to deliver the paper throughout the South—including the small towns along the Illinois Central line, the main train artery from Chicago to the land of Jim Crow—Abbott made the Defender *the most widely read and influential African-American newspaper in the country.*

One of the crucial stories that the Defender *covered was violence against blacks in the South. Perpetuated under the Jim Crow laws, these acts of violence were carried out by vigilante gangs like the Ku Klux Klan, which were able to intimidate, beat, and murder African Americans in the South without fear of legal prosecution. Abbott published reports of lynchings in the South in all their grisly detail at a time when most other newspapers studiously avoided the issue. One such report from 1917 is reprinted below.*

The widespread incidence of lynching across the South also led the publisher to make the Defender *into a leading promoter of the Great Migration. In issue after issue, Abbott encouraged African Americans to leave Jim Crow behind and seek new opportunity in the North.*

In view of the widespread discussion of the causes ... of the migration of Negroes to the North it is timely to consider the lynchings for the year just closed. I find according to the records kept by Monroe N. Work, head of the Division of Records and Research of the Tuskegee Institute, that in 1916 there have been 54 lynchings. Of those lynched, 50 were Negroes and 4 were whites. This is 4 less Negroes and 9 less whites than were put to death in 1915 when the record was 54 Negroes and 13 whites. Included in the record are 3 women....

The charges for which Negroes were put to death were attempted rape, 9; killing officers of the law, 10; murder, 7; hog stealing and assisting another person to escape, 6; wounding officers of the law, 4; rape, 3; insult, 2; for each of the following offenses one person was put to death: slapping boy; robbing store; brushing against girl on street; assisting his son, accused of rape, to escape; entering a house for robbery or some purpose; defending her son, who in defense of mother, killed man; fatally wounding a man with whom he had quarreled; speaking against mob in act of putting a man to death; attacking a man and wife with club.

Lynchings occurred in the following states: Alabama, 1; Arkansas, 4; Florida, 8; Georgia, 14; Kansas, 1; Kentucky, 2; Louisiana, 2; Mississippi, 1; Missouri, 1; North Carolina, 2; Oklahoma, 4; South Carolina, 2; Tennessee, 3; Texas, 9.

Source

"Why They Leave the South: The Lynching Record for 1916." *Chicago Defender*, January 6, 1917. Available online at http://faculty.washington.edu/steptoe/afram%20270/Music%20and%20 Images/Defender%20Why%20Leave%20the%20South.pdf.

The Massacre of East St. Louis

By 1917 the Great Migration had brought nearly one million African Americans to the cities of the North. Many migrants found work in factories that were scrambling to fulfill orders for military goods from European allies fighting in World War I. One of the cities that attracted large numbers of Negro migrants (as they were then commonly called) was St. Louis, Missouri. In both St. Louis and neighboring East St. Louis, Illinois (which is located directly across from St. Louis on the east bank of the Mississippi River), thousands of black workers found jobs in factories and foundries. As time passed, however, area business owners became skilled at using African Americans as replacement workers when unions of white workers waged strikes for better wages and working conditions. Corporations thus were able to pit desperate blacks and equally desperate whites against each other to keep wages extremely low. The practice of hiring African-American strikebreakers infuriated white workers, and in July 1917, this anger exploded in East St. Louis into one of the first—and worst—race riots of the twentieth century.

The Crisis, which was the flagship publication of the National Association for the Advancement of Colored People (NAACP), reported extensively on the events in St. Louis. In the following excerpted article, co-written by legendary civil rights leader and historian W. E. B. Du Bois and journalist Martha Gruening, the Crisis details some of the horrors of what it called the "massacre of East St. Louis."

On the 2nd of July 1917, the city of East St. Louis in Illinois added a foul and revolting page to the history of all the massacres of the world. On that day a mob of white men, women, and children burned and destroyed at least $400,000 worth of property belonging to both whites and Negroes; drove 6,000 Negroes out of their homes; and deliberately murdered, by shooting, burning, and hanging, between one and two hundred human beings who were black....

What was their quarrel with the Negroes? In answering that question we get down to the real story. It is here we meet with the facts that lay directly back of the massacre, a combination of the jealousy of white labor unions and prejudice.

East St. Louis is a great industrial center, possessing huge packing and manufacturing houses, and is, therefore, one of the biggest markets in the country for common unskilled labor. The war, by the deportation of white foreign workers, caused a scarcity of labor and this brought about the beginning of a noticeable influx of Negroes from the South. Last summer 4,500

171

white men went on strike in the packing plants of Armour & Co., Morris & Col, and Swift & Co., and Negroes from the South were called into the plants as strike-breakers. When the strike ended the Negroes were still employed and … many white men failed to regain their positions.…

Evidently, the leaders of the labor unions thought something must be done, some measure sufficiently drastic must be taken to drive these interlopers away and to restore to these white Americans their privileges. The fact that the Negroes were also Americans meant nothing at such a time as this.…

"The Southern Negro," writes [Edward F. Mason, secretary of the Central and Trades Labor Union], "has come into our community. No less than ten thousand of undesirable Negroes," he continued, "have poured in and are being used to the detriment of our white citizens." There is the appeal direct to prejudice.…

When genuine mob law did finally reign on July 2, the scenes were indescribable.…

[*The article devotes several pages to gruesome eyewitness accounts and testimonials of brutality and murder against unarmed African Americans around the city.*]

These rioters combined business with pleasure. These Negroes were "butchered to make" an East St. Louis "holiday."

Carlos F. Hurd, an eye-witness, realizes this fact and speaks of it in the article which he publishes July 3 in the *St. Louis Post-Dispatch*:

> A mob is passionate, a mob follows one man or a few men blindly; a mob sometimes takes chances. The East St. Louis affair, as I saw it, was a man hunt, conducted on a sporting basis, though with anything but the fair play which is the principle of sport.…There was little leadership, and there was a horribly cool deliberateness and a spirit of fun about it.…

The damning statements go on and on. Among the Negroes one finds a note sometimes of blank stark despair. John T. Stewart in the *St. Louis Star* draws a pathetic picture:

> One aged Negro woman passed the police station carrying in her arms all that mob spirit and fire had left of her belongings. They consisted of a worn pair of shoes—she was barefooted—

an extra calico dress, an old shawl, and two puppies. Tears were streaming down her face and she saw neither soldiers nor her enemies as she passed beneath the lights of the City Hall, going she knew not where.

Saddest of all is Miss Gruening's account of the old woman whom she saw poking about in the desolate ruins of what had once been her home. Her family had escaped to St. Louis, but not a fraction of their possessions remained intact. The woman was old—sixty-five—not an easy age at which to begin life anew.

"What are we to do?" she asked Miss Gruening. "We can't live South and they don't want us North. Where are we to go?"

From the statements gathered by the investigators, many of these driven people seem to feel that the example of the South in dealing with Negroes is responsible for the methods of East St. Louis. Many of them express firmly their resolve, in spite of all, never to go back South. They will stay in St. Louis, they say, or push further North....

Prejudice is a bad thing. But prejudice in the hands of the Organized Labor of America! The Central Trades and Labor Union of East St. Louis has perpetuated a grim jest. Its motto is "Labor omnia vincit." Latin is apt to be a bit obscure, so we translate: "Labor conquers everything." It does. In East St. Louis it has conquered Liberty, Justice, Mercy, Law, and the Democracy which is a nation's vaunt....

Source

Gruening, Martha, and W. E. B. Du Bois. "The Massacre of East St. Louis," *Crisis*, September 1917, pp. 219-243. Available online at http://www.inmotionaame.org/texts/?migration=8&topic=99& type=text.

The Chicago Race Riot of 1919

After World War I ended in 1918, Chicago and many other U.S. cities experienced an economic downturn that intensified the competition between working-class whites and blacks for jobs and housing. In July 1919, the city became engulfed in racial violence that ultimately claimed the lives of 38 residents (23 blacks and 15 whites). The rioting also injured hundreds of people and resulted in heavy losses of homes and other property due to arson and vandalism.

Walter White was a journalist and prominent civil rights activist with the National Association for the Advancement of Colored People (NAACP). In this excerpt from an essay published in the NAACP's magazine, the Crisis, *he offers his personal analysis of the root causes of the Chicago Riot of 1919. He cites eight specific factors that contributed, in one way or another, to the bloodshed that raged across Chicago from July 27 to August 3. (White dates the unrest from July 27 to July 30, but historians generally agree that riot-related violence lasted until the third of August.) The causes identified by White include deep-seated racial prejudice, political corruption, intense competition among poor whites and blacks for scarce jobs and decent housing, and the increased willingness of blacks to strike back when confronted with mob violence.*

Many causes have been assigned for the three days of race rioting, from July 27 to 30 in Chicago, each touching some particular phase of the general condition that led up to the outbreak. Labor union officials attribute it to the action of the packers [meatpacking operations], while the packers are equally sure that the unions themselves are directly responsible. The city administration feels that the riots were brought on to discredit the [William Hale] Thompson forces, while leaders of the anti-Thompson forces, prominent among them being State's Attorney Maclay Hoyne, are sure that the administration is directly responsible. In this manner charges and counter-charges are made, but, as is usually the case, the Negro is made to bear the brunt of it all—to be "the scapegoat." A background of strained race relations brought to a head more rapidly through political corruption, economic competition and clashes due to the overflow of the greatly increased colored population into sections outside of the so-called "Black Belt," embracing the Second and Third Wards, all of these contributed, aided by magnifying of Negro crime by newspapers, to the formation of a situation where only a spark was needed to ignite the flames of racial antagonism. That spark was contributed by a white youth when he knocked a colored lad off a raft at the 29th Street bathing beach and the colored boy was drowned.

Four weeks spent in studying the situation in Chicago, immediately following the outbreaks, seem to show at least eight general causes for the riots, and the same conditions, to a greater or less degree, can be found in almost every large city with an appreciable Negro population. These causes, taken after a careful study in order of their prominence, are:

1. Race Prejudice
2. Economic Competition.
3. Political Corruption and Exploitation of Negro Voters.
4. Police Inefficiency.
5. Newspaper Lies about Negro Crime.
6. Unpunished Crimes Against Negroes.
7. Housing.
8. Reaction of Whites and Negroes from War.

Some of these can be grouped under the same headings, but due to the prominence of each they are listed as separate causes.

Prior to 1915, Chicago had been famous for its remarkably fair attitude toward colored citizens. Since that time, when the migratory movement from the South assumed large proportions, the situation has steadily grown more and more tense. This was due in part to the introduction of many Negroes who were unfamiliar with city ways and could not, naturally, adapt themselves immediately to their new environment. Outside of a few sporadic attempts, little was done to teach them the rudimentary principles of sanitation, of conduct or of their new status as citizens under a system different from that in the South. During their period of absorption into the new life, their care-free, at times irresponsible and sometimes even boisterous, conduct caused complications difficult to adjust. But equally important, though seldom considered, is the fact that many Southern whites have also come into the North, many of them to Chicago, drawn by the same economic advantages that attracted the colored workman. The exact figure is unknown, but it is estimated by men who should know that fully 20,000 of them are in Chicago. These have spread the virus of race hatred and evidences of it can be seen in Chicago on every hand. This same cause underlies each of the other seven causes.

With regard to economic competition, the age-long dispute between capital and labor enters. Large numbers of Negroes were brought from the South by the packers and there is little doubt that this was done in part so that the Negro might be used as a club over the heads of the unions. John

Fitzpatrick and Ed Nockels, president and secretary, respectively, of the Chicago Federation of Labor, and William Buck, editor of the *New Majority*, a labor organ, openly charge that the packers subsidized colored ministers, politicians, and Y.M.C.A. secretaries to prevent the colored workmen at the stockyards from entering the unions. On the other hand, the Negro workman is not at all sure as to the sincerity of the unions themselves. The Negro in Chicago yet remembers the waiters' strike some years ago, when colored union workers walked out at the command of the unions and when the strike was settled, the unions did not insist that Negro waiters be given their jobs back along with whites, and, as a result, colored men have never been able to get back into some of the hotels even to the present day. The Negro is between "the devil and the deep blue sea." He feels that if he goes into the unions, he will lose the friendship of the employers. He knows that if he does not, he is going to be met with the bitter antagonism of the unions. With the exception of statements made by organizers, who cannot be held to account-ability because of their minor official connection, no statements have been made by the local union leaders, outside of high sounding, but meaningless, protestations of friendship for the Negro worker. He feels that he has been given promises too long already. In fact, he is "fed up" on them. What he wants are binding statements and guarantees that cannot be broken at will.

With the possible exception of Philadelphia, there is probably no city in America with more of political trickery, chicanery, and exploitation than Chicago. Against the united and bitter opposition of every daily newspaper in Chicago, William Hale Thompson was elected again as mayor, due, as was claimed, to the Negro and German vote. While it is not possible to state that the anti-Thompson element deliberately brought on the riots, yet it is safe to say that they were not averse to its coming. The possibility of such a clash was seen many months before it actually occurred, yet no steps were taken to prevent it. The purpose of this was to secure a two-fold result. First, it would alienate the Negro set from Thompson through a belief that was expected to grow among the colored vote when it was seen that the police force under the direction of the mayor was unable or unwilling to protect the colored people from assault by mobs. Secondly, it would discourage the Negroes from regis-tering and voting and thus eliminate the powerful Negro vote in Chicago. Whether or not this results remains to be seen. In talking with a prominent colored citizen of Chicago, asking why the Negroes supported Thompson so unitedly, his very significant reply was:

The Negro in Chicago, as in every other part of America, is fighting for the fundamental rights of citizenship. If a candidate for office is wrong on every other public question except this, the Negroes are going to vote for that man, for that is their only way of securing the things they want and that are denied them.

The value of the Negro vote to Thompson can be seen in a glance at the recent election figures. His plurality was 28,000 votes. In the second ward it was 14,000 and in the third 10,000. The second and third wards constitute most of what is known as the "Black Belt."

The fourth contributing cause was the woeful inefficiency and criminal negligence of the police authorities of Chicago, both prior to and during the riots. Prostitution, gambling and the illicit sale of whisky flourish openly and apparently without any fear whatever of police interference. In a most dangerous statement, State's Attorney Maclay Hoyne, on August 25, declared that the riots were due solely to vice in the second ward. He seemed either to forget or to ignore the flagrant disregard of law and order and even of the common principles of decency in city management existing in many other sections of the city.

All of this tended to contribute to open disregard for law and almost contempt for it. Due either to political "pull" or to reciprocal arrangements, many notorious dives run and policemen are afraid to arrest the proprietors.

During the riots the conduct of the police force as a whole was equally open to criticism. State's Attorney Hoyne openly charged the police with arresting colored rioters and with an unwillingness to arrest white rioters. Those who were arrested were at once released. In one case a colored man who was fair enough to appear to be white was arrested for carrying concealed weapons, together with five white men and a number of colored men. All were taken to a police station; the light colored man and the five whites being put into one cell and the other colored men in another. In a few minutes the light colored man and the five whites were released and their ammunition given back to them with the remark, "You'll probably need this before the night is over."

Fifth on the list is the effect of newspaper publicity concerning Negro crime. With the exception of the *Daily News*, all of the papers of Chicago have played up in prominent style with glaring, prejudice-breeding headlines every crime or suspected crime committed by Negroes. Headlines such as

"Negro Brutally Murders Prominent Citizen," "Negro Robs House" and the like have appeared with alarming frequency and the news articles beneath such headlines have been of the same sort. During the rioting such headlines as "Negro Bandits Terrorize Town," "Rioters Burn 100 Homes—Negroes Suspected of Having Plotted Blaze" appeared. In the latter case a story was told of witnesses seeing Negroes in automobiles applying torches and fleeing. This was the story given to the press by Fire Attorney John R. McCabe after a casual and hasty survey. Later the office of State Fire Marshall Gamber proved conclusively that the fires were not caused by Negroes, but by whites. As can easily be seen such newspaper accounts did not tend to lessen the bitterness of feeling between the conflicting groups. Further, many wild and unfounded rumors were published in the press—incendiary and inflammatory to the highest degree, a few of them being given below in order to show their nature. Some are:

> Over 1,000 Negroes had been slain and their bodies thrown in "Bubbly Creek" and the Chicago River.
>
> A Negro had been lynched and hanged from a "Loop" building overlooking Madison Street.
>
> A white woman had been attacked and mutilated by a Negro on State Street.
>
> A Negro woman had been slain, her breasts cut off and her infant had been killed by having its brains dashed out against a wall.
>
> A white child had been outraged by a colored man.
>
> A white child had been kidnapped by a band of colored men and its body later found, badly mutilated and dismembered....

A long period of such publicity had inflamed the minds of many people against Negroes who otherwise would have been unprejudiced. Much of the blame for the riots can be laid to such sources.

For a long period prior to the riots, organized gangs of white hoodlums had been perpetrating crimes against Negroes for which no arrests had been made. These gangs in many instances masqueraded under the name of "Athletic and Social Clubs" and later direct connection was shown between them and incendiary fires started during the riots. Colored men, women, and children had been beaten in the parks, most of them in Jackson and Lincoln Parks. In one case a young colored girl was beaten and thrown into a lagoon. In other cases Negroes were beaten so severely that they had to be taken to hospitals. All of these cases had caused many colored people to wonder if they could expect any protection whatever from the authorities. Particularly vicious in their attacks was an organization known locally as "Regan's Colts."

Much has been written and said concerning the housing situation in Chicago and its effect on the racial situation. The problem is a simple one. Since 1915 the colored population of Chicago has more than doubled, increasing in four years from a little over 50,000 to what is now estimated to be between 125,000 and 150,000. Most of them lived in the area bounded by the railroad on the west, 30th Street on the north, 40th Street on the south and Ellis Avenue on east. Already overcrowded this so-called "Black Belt" could not possibly hold the doubled colored population. One cannot put ten gallons of water in a five-gallon pail. Although many Negroes had been living in "white" neighborhoods, the increased exodus from the old areas created an hysterical group of persons who formed "Property Owners' Associations" for the purpose of keeping intact white neighborhoods. Prominent among these was the Kenwood-Hyde Park Property Owner's Improvement Association, as well as the Park Manor Improvement Association. Early in June the writer, while in Chicago, attended a private meeting of the first named at the Kenwood Club House, at Lake Park Avenue and 47th Street. Various plans were discussed for keeping the Negroes in "their part of the town," such as securing the discharge of colored persons from positions they held when they attempted to move into "white" neighborhoods, purchasing mortgages of Negroes buying homes and ejecting them when mortgage notes fell due and were unpaid, and many more of the same calibre. The language of many speakers was vicious and strongly prejudicial and had the distinct effect of creating race bitterness.

In a number of cases during the period from January, 1918, to August, 1919, there were bombings of colored homes and houses occupied by Negroes outside of the "Black Belt." During this period no less than twenty bombings took place, yet only two persons have been arrested and neither of the two has been convicted, both cases being continued.

Finally, the new spirit aroused in Negroes by their war experiences enters into the problem. From Local Board No. 4, embracing the neighborhood in the vicinity of State and 35th Streets, containing over 30,000 inhabitants of which fully ninety per cent are colored, over 9,000 men registered and 1,850 went to camp. These men, with their new outlook on life, injected the same spirit of independence into their companions, a thing that is true of many other sections of America. One of the greatest surprises to many of those who came down to "clean out the niggers" is that these same "niggers" fought back. Colored men saw their own kind being killed, heard of many more and believed that their lives and liberty were at stake. In such a spirit most of the fighting was done.

Source

White, Walter. "N.A.A.C.P.—Chicago and Its Eight Reasons." *Crisis*, Oct. 1919, pp. 293-97. Available online at http://historymatters.gmu.edu/d/4978/.

African Americans Praise Life in the North

After the race riot of 1919, the Chicago Commission on Race Relations was formed to analyze the reasons why the riot had taken place and to make recommendations for the prevention of further violence. Its lengthy and exhaustive study, The Negro in Chicago: A Study of Race Relations and a Race Riot, *was published in 1922. In investigating the origins of the riot, the commission pointed to several factors, including the heightened competition for jobs between blacks and whites after World War I, overcrowded and inadequate housing in black neighborhoods, the prevalence of racial discrimination in both the public and the private sectors, and problems with inconsistent and inadequate police services to the black and white communities.*

Members of the commission also went into the black community and interviewed African-American migrants. The commission asked interviewees what had motivated them to migrate to Chicago and how they felt about their decision to relocate in the wake of the riot. Despite the riot, the commission found that most African-American migrants remained at peace with their decision. These findings from the report are excerpted here.

Migrants have been visited in their homes, and met in industry, in the schools, and in contacts on street cars and in parks. Efforts have been made to learn why they came to Chicago and with what success they were adjusting themselves to their new surroundings.

Some of the replies to questions asked are given:

Question: Why did you come to Chicago?

Answers:

> Looking for better wages.
> So I could support my family.
> Some of my people were here.
> Persuaded by friends.
> Wanted to make more money so I could go into business; couldn't do it in the South.
> To earn more money.
> For better wages.
> Wanted to change and come to the North.
> Came to get more money for work.
> To better my conditions.
> Better conditions.

Better conditions.

Better living.

More work; came on visit and stayed.

Tired of the South.

To get away from the South, and to earn more money.

Question: Do you feel greater freedom and independence in Chicago? In what ways?

Answers:

Yes. The chance to make a living; conditions on the street cars and in movies.

Going into places of amusement and living in good neighborhoods.

Yes. Educationally, and in the home conditions.

Yes. Go anywhere you want to go; voting; don't have to look up to the white man, get off the street for him, and go to the buzzard roost at shows.

Yes. Just seem to feel a general feeling of good-fellowship.

On the street cars and the way you are treated where you work.

Yes. Can go any place I like here. At home I was segregated and not treated like I had any rights.

Yes. Privilege to mingle with people; can go to the parks and places of amusement, not being segregated.

Yes. Feel free to do anything I please. Not dictated to by white people.

Yes. Had to take any treatment white people offered me there [in the South], compelled to say "yes ma'am" or "yes sir" to white people, whether you desired to or not. If you went to an ice cream parlor for anything you came outside to eat it. Got off sidewalk for white people.

Yes. Can vote; feel free; haven't any fear; make more money.

Yes. Voting; better opportunity for work; more respect from white people.

Yes. Can vote; no lynching; no fear of mobs; can express my opinion and defend myself.

Yes. Voting, more privileges; white people treat me better, not as much prejudice.

Yes. Feel more like a man. Same as slavery, in a way, at home. I don't have to give up the sidewalk here for white people as in my former home.

Yes. No restrictions as to shows, schools etc. More protection of law.

Yes. Have more privileges and more money.

Yes. More able to express views on all questions. No segregation or discrimination

Sure. Feel more freedom. Was not counted in the South; colored people allowed no freedom at all in the South.

Find things quite different to what they are at home. Haven't become accustomed to the place yet.

Question: In what respects is life harder or easier here than in the South?

Answers:

Easier. I don't have to work so hard and get more money.

Easier in that here my wife doesn't have to work. I just couldn't make it by myself in the South.

Living is much easier, chance to learn a trade. I make and save more money.

Easier, you can make more money and it means more to you.

Easier to make a living here.

Easier, I get more money for my work and have some spare time.

Have better home, but have to work harder. I make more money, but spend it all to live.

Have more time to rest here and don't work as hard.

Find it easier to live because I have more to live on.

Earn more money; the strain is not so great wondering from day to day how to make a little money do.

Work harder here than at home.

Easier. Work is hard, but hours are short. I make more money and can live better.

More money for work, though work is harder. Better able to buy the necessities of life.

Easier; more work and more money and shorter hours.

[Cost of] living higher, but would rather be here than in South. I have shorter hours here.

Don't have to work as hard here as at home. Have more time for rest and to spend with family.

Easier to live in St. Louis. More work here and better wages. Living higher here. Saved more there.

Must work very hard here, much harder than at home.

Harder because of increased cost of living.

The entire family feels that life is much easier here than at home. Do not find work as hard anywhere.

Question: What do you like about the North?

Answers:

Freedom in voting and conditions of colored people here. I mean you can live in good houses; men here get a chance to go with the best-looking girls in the race; some may do it in Memphis, but it ain't always safe.

Freedom and chance to make a living; privileges.

Freedom and opportunity to acquire something.

Freedom allowed in every way.

More money and more pleasure to be gotten from it; personal freedom Chicago affords, and voting.

Freedom and working conditions.

Work, can work any place, freedom.

The schools for the children, the better wages, and the privileges for colored people.

The chance colored people have to live; privileges allowed them and better homes.

The friendliness of the people, the climate which makes health better.

Like the privileges, the climate; have better health.

No discrimination; can express opinion and vote.

Freedom of speech, right to live and work as other races. Higher pay for labor.

Freedom; privileges; treatment of whites; ability to live in peace; not held down.

Freedom of speech and action. Can live without fear, no Jim Crow.

More enjoyment; more places of attraction; better treatment; better schools for children.

Liberty, better schools.

I like the North for wages earned and better homes colored people can live in and go more places than at home.

Privileges, freedom, industrial and educational facilities.

The people, the freedom and liberty colored people enjoy here that they never before experienced. Even the ways of the people are better than at home.

Haven't found anything yet to like, except wife thinks she will like the opportunity of earning more money than ever before.

Source

Chicago Commission on Race Relations. *The Negro in Chicago: A Study of Race Relations and a Race Riot*. Chicago: University of Chicago Press, 1922, pp. 98-101.

Langston Hughes Remembers the Harlem Renaissance

Langston Hughes was an African-American poet, short story writer, and playwright who became a leading figure in the movement known as the Harlem Renaissance. He came to New York City's Harlem neighborhood for the first time in 1921 to attend college at Columbia University. He was dazzled by the array of literary, artistic, and musical talent on display in Harlem, as well as the strong sense of African-American identity that coursed through the theatres, clubs, shops, and residential areas. He was particularly drawn to the celebrations of the black experience that formed the foundation for so much of the work of the Renaissance artists. Before long Hughes was exploring similar themes in his own literary efforts.

Hughes left Harlem after one year to travel and work abroad, but he returned in 1925. Once again, he was struck by the richness of the artistic environment of Harlem, and reveled in it. One year later he began studies at Lincoln University, a black college in Pennsylvania. After graduating in 1929, Hughes returned to Harlem. But despite being a published poet with a growing reputation, he could not find work in the publishing industry. Hughes further recognized that for all the bountiful black talent in Harlem, the owners of the clubs and the stores were white. The blacks of Harlem had to go downtown to work and often couldn't shop where they worked. In the following excerpt from his well-known essay "My Early Days in Harlem," Hughes makes his contempt for this exploitive, racist culture evident. But he also talks about his love for the vibrant atmosphere of 1920s Harlem, where scores of talented African-American writers, musicians, dancers, and painters from all around the world were building an enduring artistic legacy.

O n a bright September morning in 1921, I came out of the subway at 135th and Lenox into the beginnings of the Negro Renaissance. I headed for the Harlem Y.M.C.A. down the block, where so many new, young, dark, male arrivals in Harlem have spent early days. The next place I headed to that afternoon was the Harlem Branch Library just up the street. There, a warm and wonderful librarian, Miss Ernestine Rose, white, made newcomers feel welcome, as did her assistant in charge of the Schomburg Collection, Catherine Latimer, a luscious café au lait. That night I went to the Lincoln Theatre across Lenox Avenue where maybe one of the Smiths—Bessie, Carla, Trixie, or Mamie—was singing the blues. And as soon as I

Credit: Reprinted by permission of Harold Ober Associates Incorporated. Freedomways, 1963. © 1963 by Langston Hughes.

could, I made a beeline for *Shuffle Along*, the all-colored hit musical playing on 63rd Street in which Florence Mills came to fame.

I had come to New York to enter Columbia College as a freshman, but *really* why I had come to New York was to see Harlem. I found it hard a week or so later to tear myself away from Harlem when it came time to move up the hill to the dormitory at Columbia. That winter I spent as little time as possible on the campus. Instead, I spent as much time as I could in Harlem, and this I have done ever since. I was in love with Harlem long before I got there, and I still am in love with it. Everybody seemed to make me welcome. The sheer dark size of Harlem intrigued me. And the fact that at that time poets and writers like James Weldon Johnson and Jessie Fauset lived there, and Bert Williams, Duke Ellington, Ethel Waters, and Walter White, too....

When I came back to New York in 1925 the Negro Renaissance was in full swing. Countee Cullen was publishing his early poems, Aaron Douglas was painting, Zora Neale Hurston, Rudolph Fisher, Jean Toomer, and Wallace Thurman were writing, Louis Armstrong was playing, Cora La Redd was dancing, and the Savoy Ballroom was open with a specially built floor that rocked as the dancers swayed. Alain Locke was putting together *The New Negro*. Art took heart from Harlem creativity. Jazz filled the night air—but not everywhere—and people came from all around after dark to look upon our city within a city, Black Harlem. Had I not had to earn a living, I might have thought it even more wonderful than it was. But I could not eat the poems I wrote. Unlike the whites who came to spend their money in Harlem, only a few Harlemites seemed to live in even a modest degree of luxury. Most rode the subway downtown every morning to work or to look for work.

Downtown! I soon learned that it was seemingly impossible for black Harlem to live without white downtown. My youthful illusion that Harlem was a world unto itself did not last very long. It was not even an area that ran itself. The famous night clubs were owned by whites, as were the theaters. Almost all the stores were owned by whites, and many at times did not even (in the middle of Harlem) employ Negro clerks. The books of Harlem writers all had to be published downtown, if they were to be published at all. Downtown: *white*. Uptown: *black*. White downtown pulling all the strings in Harlem....

Harlem, like a Picasso painting in his cubistic period. Harlem—Southern Harlem—the Carolinas, Georgia, Florida—looking for the Promised Land—dressed in rhythmic words, painted in bright pictures, dancing to jazz—and ending up in the subway at morning rush time—*headed downtown*. West Indian Harlem—warm rambunctious sassy remembering Marcus Garvey. Haitian Harlem. Cuban Harlem, little pockets of tropical dreams in alien tongues. Magnet Harlem, pulling an Arthur Schomburg from Puerto Rico, pulling an Arna Bontemps all the way from California, a Nora Holt from way out West, and E. Simms Campbell from St. Louis, likewise a Josephine Baker, a Charles S. Johnson from Virginia, an A. Philip Randolph from Florida, a Roy Wilkins from Minnesota, an Alta Douglas from Kansas. Melting pot Harlem—Harlem of honey and chocolate and caramel and rum and vinegar and lemon and lime and gall. Dusky dream Harlem rumbling into a nightmare tunnel where the subway from the Bronx keeps right on downtown, where the money from the nightclubs goes right back downtown where the jazz is drained to Broadway, whence Josephine goes to Paris, Robeson to London, Jean Toomer to a Quaker Meeting House, Garvey to the Atlanta Federal Penitentiary, and Wallace Thurman to his grave; but Duke Ellington to fame and fortune, Lena Horne to Broadway, and Buck Clayton to China.

Source

Hughes, Langston. "My Early Days in Harlem," *Freedom Ways*, Summer 1963, pp. 312-14. Available online at http://www.inmotionaame.org/texts/index.cfn?migration=8&topic=107type=text.

President Roosevelt Signs the Fair Employment Act

During the Second Great Migration, African Americans migrated by the millions out of the South to the manufacturing cities of the North and West. Many of the migrants found jobs in factories that were producing materials for use in World War II. However, some defense industry contractors refused to hire African Americans, and those who did find employment were frequently given the most difficult, dangerous, and lowest-paying jobs. Many labor unions that represented factory workers closed their membership to African Americans as well.

In 1941 black labor leader A. Philip Randolph took up the issue of discrimination against African Americans working in the defense industry. He pressed for the federal government to ban discrimination against blacks in any defense industry employment, and he warned the Franklin D. Roosevelt administration that he intended to organize massive demonstrations in Washington, D.C., if this inequity was not addressed. Randolph's efforts paid off on June 25, 1941, when President Roosevelt signed Executive Order 8802, which is reprinted below. Popularly known as the Fair Employment Act, this executive order barred a wide range of discriminatory practices in the U.S. defense industry.

W HEREAS it is the policy of the United States to encourage full participation in the national defense program by all citizens of the United States, regardless of race, creed, color, or national origin, in the firm belief that the democratic way of life within the Nation can be defended successfully only with the help and support of all groups within its borders; and

WHEREAS there is evidence that available and needed workers have been barred from employment in industries engaged in defense production solely because of considerations of race, creed, color, or national origin, to the detriment of workers' morale and of national unity:

NOW, THEREFORE, by virtue of the authority vested in me by the Constitution and the statutes, and as a prerequisite to the successful conduct of our national defense production effort, I do hereby reaffirm the policy of the United States that there shall be no discrimination in the employment of workers in defense industries or government because of race, creed, color, or national origin, and I do hereby declare that it is the duty of employers and of labor organizations, in furtherance of said policy and of this order, to provide for the full and equitable participation of all workers in defense industries, without discrimination because of race, creed, color, or national origin;

And it is hereby ordered as follows:

1. All departments and agencies of the Government of the United States concerned with vocational and training programs for defense production shall take special measures appropriate to assure that such programs are administered without discrimination because of race, creed, color, or national origin;

2. All contracting agencies of the Government of the United States shall include in all defense contracts hereafter negotiated by them a provision obligating the contractor not to discriminate against any worker because of race, creed, color, or national origin;

3. There is established in the Office of Production Management a Committee on Fair Employment Practice, which shall consist of a chairman and four other members to be appointed by the President. The Chairman and members of the Committee shall serve as such without compensation but shall be entitled to actual and necessary transportation, subsistence and other expenses incidental to performance of their duties. The Committee shall receive and investigate complaints of discrimination in violation of the provisions of this order and shall take appropriate steps to redress grievances which it finds to be valid. The Committee shall also recommend to the several departments and agencies of the Government of the United States and to the President all measures which may be deemed by it necessary or proper to effectuate the provisions of this order.

Franklin D. Roosevelt
The White House,
June 25, 1941.

Source

Roosevelt, Franklin D. Executive Order 8802: Prohibition of Discrimination in the Defense Industry. June 27, 1941. Available online at http://www.ourdocuments.gov/doc.php?flashtrue&doc=72.

An Eyewitness Account of the 1943 Race Riot in Detroit

In 1943, at the height of the Second World War, one of the deadliest race riots of the twentieth century broke out in Detroit. It began on Belle Isle, a popular but segregated island park in the Detroit River, then spread throughout the city.

African-American civil rights activist and labor leader Simon P. Owens was an eyewitness to the racial violence that wracked Detroit in 1943. An Alabama native who had migrated to Detroit in 1924 and found work in the automobile industry, Owens offered a sorrowful account of these events in his book Indignant Heart: A Black Worker's Journal, *which was originally published in 1952. In the following excerpt from this memoir, written under the pseudonym Charles Denby, Owens describes the chaos and terror that enveloped the city during those grim days in 1943.*

The Detroit Riot broke out in June 1943, on a Sunday afternoon. The riot actually broke out two weeks before, in the Eastwood Amusement Park on Gratiot and Eight Mile Road. Both Negroes and whites attended the park but Negroes were not admitted to the swimming pool. Some jitterbug kids [young African Americans] had been drafted and were going into the army in a week. At the park, they were talking among themselves: "Why can't we swim in the pool with whites if we're going to fight a war and die with them?"

They pulled off their clothes and got in the pool. The manager and some other whites, rushed out and a big fight started. The police force came and closed off the area. They turned the streetcars back and sent away all the cars of people. The fight was quelled....

[The following Sunday] about three o'clock in the morning I heard a lot of shooting, cars running fast, and glass breaking....

Just as I dozed back to sleep [my roommate] ran in, jerked the covers off, "Get up. Get up at once. Get in the streets, there's a big race riot going on. Some white man just threw a Negro woman and her baby off the Belle Isle Bridge into the river." He said several Negroes and many whites had been shot and killed. "They just killed one white down on the corner."

Credit: Reprinted from excerpts of "Detroit Riots" from *Indignant Heart: A Black Worker's Journal* by Charles Denby. Copyright © 1978 Wayne State University Press. Reprinted with the permission of Wayne State University Press and The Raya Dunayevskaya Memorial Fund.

All the time he was talking he was getting his shotgun out of the closet and putting in shells....

[The next morning] the street was so crowded with Negroes that you couldn't see the sidewalk. Everyone was quiet, but every store that was white-owned, in that block, was completely smashed. Many things were in the street, groceries, druggist equipment, dry goods, everything. Nobody was touching the stuff.

With everything so quiet I thought the riot was all over. I went to one man and asked him about going to work.

He said, "You can go if you want to, I'm going to stay here. The Oakland streetcar isn't running, but you could catch the Russell bus."

I caught the Russell bus to the crosstown and went to the plant. Many Negroes were missing. It looked as if all the white workers were there. There was no tension in the plant between Negroes and whites. Mainly the Negroes got in groups themselves and talked about the riot. About eleven o-clock the company began to put up notices in the department telling the workers which route to take home and which streetcars were running.

On the streetcar that evening, there were very few Negroes. When the car got to Mount Elliott and Forest it was supposed to turn left, but instead it went out Mount Elliot.

I yelled at the conductor asking him where he was going. He said he was going to the West side and asked where I wanted to go.

"You won't get there on this car. There is a race riot going on and we can't cross Hastings at all."

He rang the emergency bell and stopped the car. He said he didn't know how I would get home but he gave me a transfer to the Gratiot car. When I got off the bus at Hastings there seemed to be more Negroes on the street than in the morning. I spoke to one or two people, saying that I thought the riot was about over.

"Hell, no, man, we're just beginning."

They told me about someone they knew who was shot and killed. They told about this white, or that one, who killed some Negro. One told about a friend of his who was an ex-prize fighter. The police were beating his sister and he rushed up, knocked one of the police down, took away his revolver and killed two policemen. Two other policemen came up and shot the fighter in the head. The blood was very fresh on the sidewalk....

[*The author then happens upon a verbal confrontation between a group of African-American rioters and four policemen—two white and two "Negro." The crowd retreats when a police riot wagon pulls up and fires tear gas into the crowd.*]

As I went toward home I saw two kids sitting in a park. A white man came through the park and they got up and walked towards him. One of the boys seemed to know him and the other boy didn't. One boy tried to tell his buddy to let the man go. His buddy knocked the man down and beat him in the face. The white man pulled a gun and killed the boy who was trying to protect him. His buddy tried to help his friend and the white man ran away. A man across the street fired, and followed him around the next block. Ten Negroes came back, walking slow, and said they had killed the white man. The pal of the dead boy just sat by his body. He sat on the stone with the body until the wagon came to pick it up. After the wagon took the boy's body his pal continued to sit on the stone and didn't move....

Everyone, everywhere I went, was asking who and what had started the riot. No one seemed to know. The riot seemed to spring up everywhere at once. The riots seemed like a dream to me. I was wondering if this was the way death felt. All the time I felt like I was tipping on thin ice and any minute I would fall through. I saw all the police passing and I'd see a group breaking up a store and the police would leave them alone. A little further on, another group would do the same and the police would shoot into the crowd and go away laughing. I was wondering if this was like the war. What struck me was how grim all the Negroes were. I've known my people all my life and when anyone would die they would moan and cry. The expression everybody carried on their face was forceful, solid, and firm. All during the riots there wasn't one tear—except for one time.

I'd say, "It's a riot, it's true. Why is it nobody seems to be bothered about it? How is it they're not nervous, or crying, when they tell about their brother or mother getting shot up?"

One time, I got to a crowd and some people were crying. Two policemen had just killed a little kid and his body was still lying in the store. An older woman had told the child to go in and throw some stuff out of the store. The police came and the kid ran and hid behind the icebox. He lay down, scared, on his face. The police shot him through the back as he lay there. That kinda got me too. If I had had my gun I would have shot every police I could see. After the crowd told me the story, and I could see the little kid lying there, I really got mad. I got a pistol that night. I was with them then.

There were mounted police everywhere. Everyone had to walk in the middle of the street because the pavement was so crowded. There were threats from the whites that they would burn us out. We decided we wouldn't wait for them to burn our families and our neighborhood. Every one of us went down and laid on John R [a major street in Detroit].

We said, "We won't wait. We'll make the battle-line at Woodward [Avenue]." Half an hour after that, the state troopers came and went to shooting in on us and we went home.

Some of the white businessmen tried to go back to their stores when the riot was over and many were killed. There was a drugstore on the corner of Hastings and Henrie Streets. When they opened up they lasted one week and were killed. The store was closed up and later sold to a Negro. Places where Negroes could never get jobs opened up with Negroes running them. The owners didn't ever come around.

Source
Denby, Charles. *Indignant Heart: A Black Worker's Journal*. Detroit: Wayne State University Press, 1978, pp. 110-20.

President Truman Integrates the American Military

On July 26, 1948, President Harry S. Truman signed Executive Order 9981 calling for integration of the U.S. military, which up until that time had been completely segregated by race. Truman's order, which is reprinted here, was hailed by civil rights activists, many of whom had made integration of the armed forces a special focus of their reform efforts. At first, efforts to craft a formal plan for desegregation were resisted by the U.S. Army. In 1951, however, America's entrance into the Korean War greatly increased the Army's need for soldiers. Since African-American enlistment rates were much higher than white rates of enlistment, U.S. military leaders had virtually no choice but to integrate previously all-white combat units. Subsequent studies revealed that integration of military units raised the morale of black soldiers without lessening white morale, and that integrated units actually reported improved fighting performances and reductions in racial tensions. By December 1951 all U.S. Army units serving overseas had been desegregated, and within another two years the Army reported that over 95 percent of African-American soldiers were serving in integrated units. White and African-American soldiers have served side-by-side ever since then.

Establishing the President's Committee on Equality of Treatment and Opportunity in the Armed Forces.

WHEREAS it is essential that there be maintained in the armed services of the United States the highest standards of democracy, with equality of treatment and opportunity for all those who serve in our country's defense:

NOW THEREFORE, by virtue of the authority vested in me as President of the United States, by the Constitution and the statutes of the United States, and as Commander in Chief of the armed services, it is hereby ordered as follows:

1. It is hereby declared to be the policy of the President that there shall be equality of treatment and opportunity for all persons in the armed services without regard to race, color, religion or national origin. This policy shall be put into effect as rapidly as possible, having due regard to the time required to effectuate any necessary changes without impairing efficiency or morale.

2. There shall be created in the National Military Establishment an advisory committee to be known as the President's Committee on Equality of Treatment and Opportunity in the Armed Services, which shall be composed of seven members to be designated by the President.

3. The Committee is authorized on behalf of the President to examine into the rules, procedures and practices of the Armed Services in order to determine in what respect such rules, procedures and practices may be altered or improved with a view to carrying out the policy of this order. The Committee shall confer and advise the Secretary of Defense, the Secretary of the Army, the Secretary of the Navy, and the Secretary of the Air Force, and shall make such recommendations to the President and to said Secretaries as in the judgment of the Committee will effectuate the policy hereof.

4. All executive departments and agencies of the Federal Government are authorized and directed to cooperate with the Committee in its work, and to furnish the Committee such information or the services of such persons as the Committee may require in the performance of its duties.

5. When requested by the Committee to do so, persons in the armed services or in any of the executive departments and agencies of the Federal Government shall testify before the Committee and shall make available for use of the Committee such documents and other information as the Committee may require.

6. The Committee shall continue to exist until such time as the President shall terminate its existence by Executive order.

Source

Truman, Harry S. Executive Order 9981: Establishing the President's Committee on Equality of Treatment and Opportunity In the Armed Forces, July 26, 1948. Available online at http://www.trumanlibrary.org/9981.htm.

An African-American Migrant Builds a New Life in the North

Sam Moore was born on April 1, 1932, in Texarkana, Texas. Raised in a small town outside of Texarkana, he became part of the Second Great Migration when he moved to Detroit, Michigan, in 1953. The following excerpted interview of Moore was conducted by Keena Arrington. It is part of Marygrove College's Novak Digital Interview Collection: Detroit Immigration Series. In the interview, which was conducted on March 6, 2008, Moore relates how he rose from a position of poverty to become a successful businessman and then a bishop at the Mt. Sinai House of Prayer in Detroit.

Moore: [Around 1953], I thought about migrating to a bigger city. At that time I was making about thirty-two dollars a week at this plant. Thought about where I would go and I thought about California, I thought about Georgia, I thought about Ohio, I thought about Detroit. I thought about lots of towns and states that I could go to, but I had a cousin come to Detroit. And he wrote me a letter and told me about how good things were in Detroit. Job[s] [were] plentiful, the factory was hiring....

[In 1953] I moved to Detroit.... I didn't know anything about it, but this is where I wanted to come. And when I got here and seen streetcars and buses and the train and a whole lot of people. I feel good because I feel kind of like I was ... in the Promised Land. I seen plenty of food. I seen birds, I seen people working had good job[s], taking their lunch kit to work and everything. So it made me feel good so I began to look around in the city to see where I could relocate myself....

[I left] to better myself. And to help my mother you know, because she and my stepfather were struggling with eight children there at home and they didn't have.... I was one of the breadwinners and I was the oldest boy so I was trying to take care. Keep my sisters and brothers in school and try to get them to be educated so I come to Detroit so I could get a better job so I could do that.

Now Detroit, when I got here, I never seen a city so big. I never seen a city in my life that was so big.... But in this city I didn't know how to survive

Credit: Arrington, K. (Interviewer) & Moore, S. (Interviewee). (2008). Sam Moore: Migration within U.S. [Interview transcript]. Retrieved from The John Novak Digital Interview Collection of the Marygrove College Library Web site: http://research.marygrove.edu/novakinterviews/index.html. Reprinted by permission.

so I began to question around. They told me about Black Bottom [a mostly African-American neighborhood in Detroit]. When I got to Black Bottom I felt a little more comfortable because I seen Negroes there. That's what we was called then, Negroes....

Yeah, when I got to Detroit I was a Negro. And that sounded good to me, that's better than what they was calling me [back in the South] I thought. And so I was a Negro, until after awhile they gave us another name. We were called a black. I'm black and proud, so I felt good about myself. I began to see I could feel proud, I'm black. Before I was kind of looking down on myself because I looked at the other race of people.... All the races seemed to be a prosperous race but the Negro was the one that had the dirty jobs, got the less pay, and lived in the slum areas and everything was down. When I was down there [in the South] we looked out for one another, we helped one another, we supported one another....

But when I come to the city, I found out we killed each other, we fought each other, we stole from each other, we robbed each other. Especially in Black Bottom....

Moving to the city of Detroit, at that time it was around in August, and they used to lay peoples off, they called it a changeover in the factory. I was here during that time and I was unable to find employment, unable to find work. I walked the streets in Detroit until I ran out.... When I come here I had sixteen dollars. I paid I think about two dollars a week for a room. So after about a month you know, I was ... no place to stay, so I become home-less and I walked the streets. I slept in the streets. I slept on the side of the streets. And to eat? Well I would get what I could get by walking, seeing stuff thrown away or something like that or something that they didn't want like some food or something. I was able to eat, but I was looking for a job and it was hard for me to locate a job. I got a letter from my mother and she said, she could always sense that when I was in trouble, she said, "Son, come on back home. We can make it here." So I told her, "No, I'm gonna stay on here cause I'm gonna get a job and I wanna help ya."

So what I did, I was sleeping in these places and one old gentleman came up and he seen me. No clothes on hardly, raggly, dirty, needed a bath because no place to clean myself up ... and he asked me did I want work and I told him yes. So that was about, I would say that was about twenty, thirty miles out of the city, so we caught a bus and we rolled out there. I got this job but I had to live on the job. I worked in the front of the place and I lived in the back of it. They used to have bowling alleys. When I come here people were doing lots of bowling. And I worked with this man, he was called a pin captain. Then he give me a job of setting pins....

It wasn't that much money. It was enough to survive. Some days I make a dollar fifty, some days I make two dollars, some days three dollars and good was four dollars a day. So that was really good money. So I stayed there, I didn't have to pay no rent or nothing. I just slept and stayed right in the back of this old building that I was working in. I stayed there and I would send my mother, every week I'd send my mother money back home. I was around twenty or twenty-one at that time. I thought since I come to the city, I seen in the paper, I seen how things were, it seemed like it was good and jobs were plentiful, but I stayed there and kept on being blessed over the little that I did get.

And so one guy came by that place-bowling alley and asked if I wanted a job, a landscape job. And he was going to pay me, I thought he was going to pay me a dollar and twenty-five cents an hour because that's what they was getting in the factory, but he only gave me seventy-five cent. Sixty or seventy-five cent an hour to work for him. So I take that job and I did landscape work for him. And I sent my money back [to family down South]. I wasn't keeping anything for myself....

The man now, he is deceased, but I learned so much from that man. He was a white man and I never had a white man that treat me like that white man did. That white man treat me like I was his son. I sit down, I ate with him. We worked side by side and he taught me landscape work, how to do job, how to name the plants and everything. And so I worked for him, but I always sent my money back home. And he said to me, he said, "Sam, don't send your money back home. You take the money and get yourself something." So I listened to him, but I was still sending money back to my parents. And I worked for this man for approximately nine years, so after I started working with him, about a year after I started working with him I was able to save up enough money at that point to buy me another car.

I had met this young lady while I was in Texas. We went to school together. And I met her and I thought that we would get married. And so we kept on writing each other. She was still in Texas and I was here so we decided, I proposed to her in a letter and she accepted my proposal. And that was one of the happiest things [in] my life....

So I went back and this beautiful lady … and I proposed to her and we got married. Brought her [back to Detroit], drove her up, and didn't even have a place to stay. So we slept in the car, you know. Which wasn't comfortable, but listen, we was together. We stayed in the car and somebody seen us sleeping in the car and they offered us their room, saying, "You all sleep in my room. I'll go some other place, find some place to sleep." So we slept in the room until I made a couple paychecks, because I worked with the landscape guy. Then we went and we rented a room and that's where we stayed there for awhile.

After we stayed there for awhile the Lord began to bless us. I learned how to survive. I learned how to be a father. I learned how to be a husband and I learned my responsibility, but I needed more money. I never had anything up to that point that mattered. I looked at other people, had cars. They had their own homes. So I told my wife, "We're gonna get us a place." So we moved out of that room into a three room, little bitty house….

[Over the next eight years they had three children.]

So now I'm looking for a house for us, and we found this house, we rented this place first. And I'm still working with this guy. I'm making now good money. I'm bringing home about thirty-seven, or thirty-eight dollars a week. From the landscaping company I'm working for. And this was good money, because when I get paid, I get home that thirty-two dollars everything was taken out. And we go to the grocery store our grocery, whole week's supply of groceries cost us sixteen dollars, so we go in and buy the groceries and we had enough groceries. We had extra money left over….

I was working with this guy—he had some choice accounts…. with big people. And I learned about a lot of these executives such as the president of General Motor[s], the president of Ford, some big doctors, some big lawyers. That's who he had, these big people, and these people sort of favored me, and they liked my work. I'd do extra work for them around there you know, and they favored me. This one gentleman named John Dykstra, he was the president of the Ford Motor Company at that time, lived out there in Bloomfield. And I worked for the Fishers [a famous family in the automotive industry] … and so I met all these people. But this one gentleman seemed that he favored me. He said to me, "Sam, why are you working for this man like you're working and he making all this money and you just getting a salary and you out here working?" And I told him, "I would like to go in business, but I don't have no money to go in business. I didn't have no money to buy the equipment, I didn't have no money—I didn't have no customers. I didn't know nobody." So he said, "I tell you what you do. You go out and get a price on everything that you would need, all your equipment and come back and let me know and I'll let you have the money."

This guy was a millionaire. You know. But he trusted me. So I went out, I applied me a good truck. I applied me some lawn equipment. I priced me all this stuff. I went and priced me some fertilizer and everything that I would need to start in the business. When I come back to his house, he was down in Florida, he had a home in Florida too. So his daughter said, "Daddy's out of town. When you come back to write him and let him know what you need, how much money you need. He will send it to you." So I did. I wrote him a letter and told him about the equipment I'd picked out and this is what it costs and this is the total amount. So about a few days later I got a check from Florida from John Dykstra. More money than I ever had in my life, you know. But he trusted me.… I taken this money and I did exactly what I planned to do. Went out and bought me a truck. He was my customer, my only first customer. And I bought me a truck, got all this equipment and stuff and started to work on his premises. And I looked at other's people's work and I tried to make my job look better than the next person. So by my job looking better than the next person's job looked, these people called me to do they job. And it was from mouth to mouth. I got the whole block, the whole village.…

I'm growing now financially. I'm making some money. But I realize I could make more money if I had more equipment. I learned that I could buy a bigger piece of equipment and make even more money. So this man was so nice to me, I thought he was one of the nicest [people] in the world. I went to him, I said to him, "I need to buy me some bigger equipment." This gentleman was so nice to me until he just disappointed me. He said, "Sam," he said, "You's a man. You got your own business. I'm trying to teach you." He said, "You go now and make your own arrangement. You go and buy your own equipment. You go and get your own job. You can't depend on me. I just help you to get started." And that was a letdown to me. But the first place I went to where they had this equipment, right away, boom, they let me have it. I went to the next place and got I don't know how much fertilizer. They just let me have it. But if he never pushed me out there, I never would have made it. I would have always been dependent on him.…

So, I got my business going and I was making money, dealing with these people. And I felt then I forgot about where I come from. I forgot about—I used to not have anything. I forgot about I had no clothes. I forgot about I had no food. I forgot about, you know, these things. But I was feeling fine in the city, making it. We bought us a nice home, a nice home. And I had another feeling in my life. A strange feeling that come over me that I didn't understand. And I fought it for years. And there was a calling on my life.

As far as reaching out, helping the needy, helping the less fortunate. I could look back and remember when I didn't have shoes, when I didn't have clothes, when I didn't have money. And I seen these people … and I wanted to do something to help the people. And the Lord called me into the ministry because I seen that they need teaching also.

And I taught people how to live. I taught people how to make money. Be honest…. Detroit was a big city, and Detroit was a wicked city.

Interviewer: Did you say wicked?

Moore: It was a city that you couldn't trust anybody. So I seen that we as Negroes needed some help, needed to be taught and need to go to school. So I began to teach them. Go to school, finish school, be educated. You know, learn something, be somebody. You're just as good as anybody. You don't have to take the low seat. You don't have to walk the streets. You don't have to become a bum—just because you can get all this knowledge, all this education and be somebody.

So this is what I began to teach and it led into my ministry as far as preaching.

Interviewer: And this is how you became where you are right now.

Moore: This is how I became what I am today.

Source
Moore, Sam. Interview with Keena Arrington. March 6, 2008. Marygrove College, Novak Digital Interview Collection: Detroit Immigration Series. Available online at http://research.marygrove.edu/novakinterviews/index.html.

The Kerner Report Analyzes the Root Causes of Racial Tensions in America

The Kerner Report was produced by the National Advisory Commission on Civil Disorders in 1968, during the administration of President Lyndon Johnson. The commission was created in response to the race riots that erupted in dozens of American communities in 1967. The commission was headed by Illinois governor Otto Kerner and included such high-profile figures as NAACP executive director Roy Wilkins, New York City mayor John Lindsay, and labor leader I.W. Abel.

The commission's final report was an exhaustive study of the social, political, and economic factors that contributed to the riots. In discussing widespread racial polarization and the complicity of white society in the creation and perpetuation of inner-city ghettos, the study's authors issued a famous warning that the nation was moving toward "two societies, one black, one white—separate and unequal." The so-called Kerner Commission then concluded with a series of policy recommendations designed to give African Americans "fuller participation in the social order and the material benefits enjoyed by the majority of all Americans."

When the Kerner Report was released in March 1968 it became a national bestseller, and more than two million copies were eventually sold (the introduction to the historic report is excerpted here). But the Johnson administration, which had already shepherded major civil rights legislation into law in the mid-1960s, did not craft any new policy initiatives in response to the report. The commission's findings were also harshly criticized by conservatives who charged that it relieved African Americans of any responsibility for the violence, educational failures, or economic struggles that afflicted their communities. One month after the publication of the Kerner Report, civil rights leader Martin Luther King Jr. was assassinated in Memphis, Tennessee. His violent death sparked another explosion of race riots in cities across the country.

The summer of 1967 again brought racial disorders to American cities, and with them shock, fear and bewilderment to the nation.

The worst came during a two-week period in July, first in Newark and then in Detroit.

Each set off a chain reaction in neighboring communities.

On July 28, 1967, the President of the United States established this Commission and directed us to answer three basic questions:

What happened?

Why did it happen?

What can be done to prevent it from happening again?

To respond to these questions, we have undertaken a broad range of studies and investigations. We have visited the riot cities; we have heard many witnesses; we have sought the counsel of experts across the country.

This is our basic conclusion: Our nation is moving toward two societies, one black, one white—separate and unequal.

Reaction to last summer's disorders has quickened the movement and deepened the division. Discrimination and segregation have long permeated much of American life; they now threaten the future of every American.

This deepening racial division is not inevitable. The movement apart can be reversed. Choice is still possible. Our principal task is to define that choice and to press for a national resolution.

To pursue our present course will involve the continuing polarization of the American community and, ultimately, the destruction of basic democratic values.

The alternative is not blind repression or capitulation to lawlessness. It is the realization of common opportunities for all within a single society.

This alternative will require a commitment to national action—compassionate, massive and sustained, backed by the resources of the most powerful and the richest nation on this earth. From every American it will require new attitudes, new understanding, and, above all, new will.

The vital needs of the nation must be met; hard choices must be made, and, if necessary, new taxes enacted.

Violence cannot build a better society. Disruption and disorder nourish repression, not justice. They strike at the freedom of every citizen. The community cannot—it will not—tolerate coercion and mob rule.

Violence and destruction must be ended—in the streets of the ghetto and in the lives of people.

Segregation and poverty have created in the racial ghetto a destructive environment totally unknown to most white Americans.

What white Americans have never fully understood but what the Negro can never forget—is that white society is deeply implicated in the ghetto.

White institutions created it, white institutions maintain it, and white society condones it.

It is time now to turn with all the purpose at our command to the major unfinished business of this nation. It is time to adopt strategies for action that will produce quick and visible progress. It is time to make good the promises of American democracy to all citizens—urban and rural, white and black, Spanish-surname, American Indian, and every minority group.

Our recommendations embrace three basic principles:

To mount programs on a scale equal to the dimension of the problems;

To aim these programs for high impact in the immediate future in order to close the gap between promise and performance;

To undertake new initiatives and experiments that can change the system of failure and frustration that now dominates the ghetto and weakens our society.

These programs will require unprecedented levels of funding and performance, but they neither probe deeper nor demand more than the problems which called them forth. There can be no higher priority for national action and no higher claim on the nation's conscience.

We issue this Report now, four months before the date called for by the President. Much remains that can be learned. Continued study is essential.

As Commissioners we have worked together with a sense of the greatest urgency and have sought to compose whatever differences exist among us. Some differences remain. But the gravity of the problem and the pressing need for action are too clear to allow further delay in the issuance of this Report....

PART II—WHY DID IT HAPPEN?

Chapter 4—The Basic Causes

In addressing the question "Why did it happen?" we shift our focus from the local to the national scene, from the particular events of the summer of 1967 to the factors within the society at large that created a mood of violence among many urban Negroes.

These factors are complex and interacting; they vary significantly in their effect from city to city and from year to year; and the consequences of one disorder, generating new grievances and new demands, become the causes of the next. Thus was created the "thicket of tension, conflicting evidence and extreme opinions" cited by the President.

Despite these complexities, certain fundamental matters are clear. Of these, the most fundamental is the racial attitude and behavior of white Americans toward black Americans.

Race prejudice has shaped our history decisively; it now threatens to affect our future.

White racism is essentially responsible for the explosive mixture which has been accumulating in our cities since the end of World War II. Among the ingredients of this mixture are:

Pervasive discrimination and segregation in employment, education and housing, which have resulted in the continuing exclusion of great numbers of Negroes from the benefits of economic progress.

Black in-migration and white exodus, which have produced the massive and growing concentrations of impoverished Negroes in our major cities, creating a growing crisis of deteriorating facilities and services and unmet human needs.

The black ghettos where segregation and poverty converge on the young to destroy opportunity and enforce failure. Crime, drug addiction, dependency on welfare, and bitterness and resentment against society in general and white society in particular are the result.

At the same time, most whites and some Negroes outside the ghetto have prospered to a degree unparalleled in the history of civilization. Through television and other media, this affluence has been flaunted before the eyes of the Negro poor and the jobless ghetto youth.

Yet these facts alone cannot be said to have caused the disorders. Recently, other powerful ingredients have begun to catalyze the mixture:

Frustrated hopes are the residue of the unfulfilled expectations aroused by the great judicial and legislative victories of the Civil Rights Movement and the dramatic struggle for equal rights in the South.

A climate that tends toward approval and encouragement of violence as a form of protest has been created by white terrorism directed against nonviolent protest; by the open defiance of law and federal authority by state and local officials resisting desegregation; and by some protest groups engaging in civil disobedience who turn their backs on nonviolence, go beyond the constitutionally protected rights of petition and free assembly, and resort to violence to attempt to compel alteration of laws and policies with which they disagree.

The frustrations of powerlessness have led some Negroes to the conviction that there is no effective alternative to violence as a means of achieving redress of grievances, and of "moving the system." These frustrations are reflected in alienation and hostility toward the institutions of law and government and the white society which controls them, and in the reach toward racial consciousness and solidarity reflected in the slogan "Black Power."

A new mood has sprung up among Negroes, particularly among the young, in which self-esteem and enhanced racial pride are replacing apathy and submission to "the system."

The police are not merely a "spark" factor. To some Negroes police have come to symbolize white power, white racism and white repression. And the fact is that many police do reflect and express these white attitudes. The atmosphere of hostility and cynicism is reinforced by a widespread belief among Negroes in the existence of police brutality and in a "double standard" of justice and protection—one for Negroes and one for whites.

To this point, we have attempted to identify the prime components of the "explosive mixture." In the chapters that follow we seek to analyze them in the perspective of history. Their meaning, however, is clear:

In the summer of 1967, we have seen in our cities a chain reaction of racial violence. If we are heedless, none of us shall escape the consequences.

Source

Kerner Commission. "Summary of Report: Introduction." *Report of the National Advisory Commission on Civil Disorders*. Washington, DC: U.S. Government Printing Office, 1968. Available online at http://www.eisenhowerfoundation.org/docs/kerner.pdf.

Reasons for the "Return Migration" to the South

African-American poet and author Maya Angelou was born in St. Louis, Missouri, and raised in Stamps, Arkansas. She migrated with her mother to San Francisco in the 1940s and eventually moved to New York, where she became a writer, singer, dancer, and civil rights activist. In 1960 she moved to Africa, where she lived and worked for several years. She returned to the United States in 1964 and worked with both Malcolm X and Martin Luther King Jr. In 1970 she published the memoir I Know Why the Caged Bird Sings, *which established her as one of America's leading literary voices. Since that time she has produced numerous works of fiction, nonfiction, poetry, and screenplays. In 1993 President Bill Clinton selected Angelou to write a poem for his inauguration.*

In the following excerpt from a 1990 essay, Angelou explores why she and many other African Americans decided to return to the South in the 1970s and 1980s. She devotes special attention to the ways in which the South, with all its "pain and pleasure," still calls to African Americans who fled their places of origin during the Great Migration.

Stamps, Arkansas, is a little larger than the page upon which its name is printed, yet it looms in my thoughts wider than the Steppes of Russia or Africa's Sahara Desert. Why does a small town, a whistle stop, a red dirt burg of 5,000 souls, a hamlet I left forever over 40 years ago, weigh so heavily on my present-day 1990, big-city, internationally wise, sophisticated mind? The answer to that multi-phased question is because Stamps is located in the American South and I am an African-American. The answer to the question "Why are so many young Black people moving South today?" is that the American South sings a siren song to all Black Americans. The melody may be ignored, despised or ridiculed, but we all hear it.

After generations of separation and decades of forgetfulness, the very name brings back to our memories ancient years of pain and pleasure.

At the turn of the century many African-Americans left the South, left the Southern soul-crushing prejudice and prohibition and moved North to Chicago and New York City, West to Los Angeles and San Diego. They were drawn by the ready promise of better lives, equality, fair play and good old American four-star freedom. Their expectations were at once fulfilled and at the same time dashed to the ground and broken into shards of disappointment.

The sense of fulfillment arose from the fact that there were chances to exchange the dull drudgery of sharecrop farming for protected work under unionized agreements. Sadly, for the last 30 years those jobs have been decreasing as industry became increasingly computerized. And the atmosphere which the immigrants imagined as free of racial prejudice was found to be discriminatory in ways different from the Southern modes and possibly even more humiliating. The great writer, John Oliver Killens, has said, "Macon, Georgia, is down South. New York City is up South."

A small percentage of highly skilled and fully educated Blacks found and clung to rungs on the success ladder, but most unskilled and undereducated Black workers were spit out by the system like so many un-digestible watermelon seeds.

They began to find their lives minimalized and their selves as persons trivialized. Many members of that early band of 20th century pilgrims must have yearned for the honesty of Southern landscapes; even if they were the targets of hatemongers who wanted them dead, they were at least credited with being alive. Northern Whites with their public smiles of liberal acceptance and their private behavior of utter rejection wearied and angered the immigrants.

They stayed, however, in big-city hovels, crowded into small tenements and flowing out to the mean and quickly criminal street. They bore and raised children who were sent South each summer to visit grandparents, third cousins, double-second cousins and extended families. Those children grew up mainly in the large Northern cities, with memories of now dead Southern summers and fish fry, Saturday barbecues and the gentle manners of Southern upbringing. These are the people who are coming to the South to live. They often find that their Southern relatives have died or have themselves been transplanted to Detroit or Cleveland, Ohio. Still they come to live in Atlanta ("Y'all like Hot Lanta?") and New Orleans, quickly learning to call the historic city by its rightful name of "N'Awlins." The returnees shop for churches with the same diligence they used to search for boutiques. What they find is the old-time religion made modern by young voices, young preachers, and young music. Surrounded by the ancient healing, they find that they can come home again.

They return and find or make their places in the land of their foreparents. They find and make friends under the shade of trees their ancestors left decades earlier. Many find themselves happy, without being able to explain the emotion. I think it is simply that they feel generally important.

Southern themes will range from a generous and luscious love to a cruel and bitter hate, but no one can ever claim that the South is petty. Even in little Stamps, Arkansas, Black people walk with an air which implies, "When I walk in, they may like me or dislike me, but everybody knows I'm here."

Source
Angelou, Maya. "Why Blacks Are Returning to Their Southern Roots," *Ebony*, April 1990, pp. 44-47.

The Great Migration and Its Enduring Impact on America

In 2010 Pulitzer Prize-winning journalist Isabel Wilkerson published The Warmth of Other Suns: The Epic Story of America's Great Migration. *Wilkerson's book chronicled the massive migration of African Americans from the Deep South to the industrial North between 1915 and 1970, paying particular attention to the life experiences of three migrants who were part of this exodus. In the following excerpt from a December 2010 interview with African-American author, political commentator, and television show host Tavis Smiley, Wilkerson explains why the book's subject matter was so important to her. She also provides an assessment of the historical importance of the Great Migration.*

Smiley: So why has this story been sitting untold for all this time?

Wilkerson: Well, one reason is that it began during World War I and it lasted until 1970, so it went on for a really long time. It went on for basically three generations. That meant for any of the journalists who might have been covering it, the ones who started covering it in the beginning weren't there at the end. So it was hard to grasp while it was going on.

Another thing is that during the waves of it people kept thinking it was going to end, but the people kept coming. So it was hard to grasp until really after it was over with.

Then finally, people didn't talk about it. That's one of the biggest losses, I think, to African American families, is that people, once they left, they turned away from the South. They didn't look back, and they often didn't tell their children about it. They didn't want to talk about it. It was too painful, what they'd gone through and the caste system of the South, which was Jim Crow.

Smiley: So we're really talking here about the migration of six million African Americans, although we were not African Americans at the time.

Wilkerson: No. (Laughs)

Smiley: Colored, Negro, whatever we were.

Wilkerson: (Laughs) Yeah, right.

Smiley: The migration of six million of us from the South to the North. What was the driver, the primary driver or drivers behind that massive migration from the South to the North?

Credit: Reprinted courtesy of The Smiley Group, Inc. © 2010.

Wilkerson: The primary driver was that for 80 years, in 1896 until after the civil rights movement, African Americans were living in a caste system that dictated their every move. They were bound by the laws of Jim Crow, which infiltrated every aspect of interaction between Blacks and Whites.

For example, it was against the law in Birmingham for a Black person and a White person to play checkers together. Someone actually sat down and wrote that down as a rule. They must have seen a Black person and a White person playing checkers, having too much fun, and said, "No, we can't have this."

There were Black and White ambulances. There were Black and White taxi cabs. There were even Black and White bibles. There was a Black bible and a White bible in many courthouses to swear to tell the truth on.

Smiley: Same bible, though?

Wilkerson: No, different bibles.

Smiley: I mean the same bible, one Black and one White.

Wilkerson: Correct.

Smiley: Yeah, I'm just making - okay. (Laughter) I was going to say, is there a Black bible? I missed that. I thought there was just one. They made it a Black bible.

Wilkerson: They made it a Black bible.

Smiley: Okay. (Laughter) So these six million Negroes were coming from where down South and going to where up North?

Wilkerson: Well, that's one of the things that I really wanted to get a grasp of for this book, is that it wasn't one migration, it was multiple migrations, and there were three main ones. One was up the East Coast from Florida, Georgia, the Carolinas, Virginia up to Washington, D.C., Philadelphia, Boston, New York.

Then there was a middle one, a middle migration stream from Mississippi, Alabama, western Georgia up to Chicago, Detroit, Cleveland, and so that was the middle one.

Then the one that's least known about and which I really enjoyed writing about was the one from Louisiana and Texas to California and the entire West Coast.

Smiley: What made you devote so much time and attention to this particular subject matter?

Wilkerson: Well, I'm a daughter of the great migration as, really, the majority of African Americans that you meet in the north and west are products of the great migration. It's that massive. Many of us owe our very existence to the fact that people migrated.

In my own family's case, my mother migrated from Georgia, from Rome, Georgia, to Washington, D.C., and my father migrated from southern Virginia to Washington, D.C., where they met, married and here I am. Had it not been for the great migration I wouldn't exist, and yet I felt that the story wasn't really being told from the perspective of the people who had lived this.

We didn't know why they left or how they made the decision to leave. What were their lives like before they left? How'd they get the courage to leave the only place they'd ever known for a place they'd never seen, for an uncertain future in a place that was often cold and forbidding, anonymous and not welcoming to them, and how did they make it once they got there?

Those were the kind of questions that I had, and those are the questions that really help to give us a sense of how the cities came to be and how so many African Americans ended up in these cities—Detroit, Chicago, Cleveland, Los Angeles, New York.

Smiley: After [Hurricane] Katrina I was on the air here and I railed every night on this program and on "Meet the Press" and everywhere where I appeared talking about Katrina.

I railed on the media. I couldn't stand the media picking up on this term of refugees to refer to these Black men and women in New Orleans who were, in fact, American citizens. They are not refugees. I said over and over and over again—these are American citizens.

I thought it was important to make that point so that we wouldn't lose sight of the fact that these people are us. They are us.

Wilkerson: I actually refer to them as immigrants. I refer to them as having the same kind of immigrant heart and motivations and desires and goals and dreams for themselves as any immigrant, as any person who might have crossed the Atlantic in steerage.

So what I'm looking at is the fact that what is it that propelled them is a human story, a classic American story, and how tragic is it that they ended up

213

having to go to far reaches of their own country in order to find the freedom that they really would have been born to.

So when I use it, I'm using that, in a way, as a provocative term to get us to think about this migration differently. They were doing what so many other groups of people are often lauded for doing. In other words, they came to these cities without really any backup at all.

They lived in neighborhoods where they were confined to. They doubled up and tripled up in homes or apartments or cold water flats. They took multiple jobs and ended up often making more money in the aggregate than the people who were there already.

In other words, they were working very hard in order to survive, which is the classic American story, a classic immigrant story, and yet they had to do that within their own country, within the borders of our own country, and yet they were not immigrants....

Smiley: Tell me about Ms. Ida Mae.

Wilkerson: She was a sharecropper's wife who was terrible at picking cotton. (Laughter) She could kill snakes—

Smiley: Sounds like me. (Laughter) I would have been terrible at it.

Wilkerson: (Laughter) You're right about that. She was terrible at picking cotton. She could kill snakes and wring the neck of a chicken for dinner, but she could not pick cotton, did not like picking cotton and her family ended up having to leave because a relative, a cousin, had been beaten to within an inch of his life because he had been accused of a theft that he had not committed.

The thing that they accused him of stealing turned up the next day, and so when her husband found out what had happened to his cousin he went home to his wife, Ida Mae, and he said, "This is the last crop we're making." So they ended up in Chicago from Mississippi, which was part of that Mississippi to Chicago migration.

Smiley: Robert Foster.

Wilkerson: He was a surgeon who had performed ably and with distinction in the army during the Korean War, but he got out of the army and found that he could not practice surgery in his own hometown of Monroe,

Louisiana, and so he set out on a course that ended up being far more treacherous than he'd anticipated to get to California.

Smiley: He ended up being somebody's doctor, who we all know.

Wilkerson: He ended up being somebody's doctor. Yes, he ended up being Ray Charles' doctor.

Smiley: (Laughter) Great story—Ray Charles' doctor. Does that say something, then, Isabel, about the folk who stayed behind, those who didn't go?

Wilkerson: I think that there's a way of looking at them that is also beautiful, and that is that they were the keepers of the culture. They were the keepers of the culture. In fact, some of them would say, "We need to stay here so that you'll have a place to come back to when you need to," and I thought that was beautiful.

So together, this migration was in some ways the precursor to the civil rights movement in many respects. In one way it was because it showed that this underpaid, lower level of the caste system of the South, the underpaid workers of the South, had an option and were willing to take that option. They were willing to act on that option, which was to leave.

When this migration began, 90 percent of all African Americans were living in the South—90 percent. By the time it was over, nearly half were living outside of the South. They were living in that great arc from Washington, D.C. up to Boston, then over to Cleveland and Chicago, Detroit, and then all the way over to Los Angeles. They were living anywhere but the South.

Smiley: One doesn't have to be a rocket scientist to know that the period you're talking about happens to be, as [historian] Taylor Branch might put it, America in the King years. It certainly covers a part of the King years.

One doesn't think of it in that way. When we think of Dr. [Martin Luther] King fighting for justice and equality and for the rights of Black folk, we think primarily of Black folk in the South, and that's of course where Dr. King was based.

But it's fascinating to think now, as I listen to you talk, that while King was leading this movement, Negroes were getting out of the South as fast as they could at this very time.

Wilkerson: At that very moment. In fact, he had, too. He went to Boston University and he had the exposure to the freedoms of the North. That was in the early '50s. He also met his wife, Coretta Scott, in the North. So that even had—there was a connection there between the great migration—you could say he was part of the great migration for a time, and then he went back to fight for that ultimate moment of truth in the South as well.

Smiley: To your point now, were there folk like King who escaped the South for whatever purpose, whatever reason, for whatever period of time, and then felt called back to the South?

Wilkerson: I must say most did not. Most in that original migration left, and they left for good. Some of them even changed their name when they left, and they didn't look back, which is why the story often was not told to the succeeding generations, and I think it needs to be told.

I think the entire country needs to be aware of the sacrifices made by the people and the ultimate impact that this had on the country.

Smiley: What's the abiding lesson—now that you've blessed us with this text, what's the abiding lesson for Black people of this migration in 2010?

Wilkerson: I would hope that it would encourage every African American family, North and South, to examine its history. This was a migration that had no leader. It was a leaderless migration. People made decisions on the basis of what was in their heart, and I think this is a story of inspiration that says that so much power is within us.

These individual people, one by one, multiplied by six million, ended up helping to change this country. That's an inspiration for anyone of any race, but particularly for Black families.

People need to go back and talk with the oldest people in their families and find out what are the stories, before it's too late. I felt a great urgency in working on this book because I knew that people were passing on and I didn't have but so much time to get to them. That would be the lesson I would be seeing in it.

Source

Wilkerson, Isabel. Interview with Tavis Smiley. *Tavis Smiley*, December 23, 2010. Los Angeles: The Smiley Group/TS Media, Inc., 2010. Available online at http://www.pbs.org/wnet/tavissmiley /archive/201012/20101223_wilkerson.html.

IMPORTANT PEOPLE, PLACES, AND TERMS

Abbott, Robert S. (1868-1940)
African-American newspaper publisher and founder of the *Chicago Defender*.

Black Nationalism
Political movement of the 1920s that promoted black separatism. It was very influential in the formation of the ideology of the Nation of Islam and other radical African-American political movements.

Boycott
The refusal to buy or use products or otherwise deal with businesses or other institutions as a way to protest the policies of those institutions.

Bradley, Tom (1917-1998)
African-American politician and first black mayor of Los Angeles.

Brown v. Board of Education
Landmark U.S. Supreme Court case from 1954 that ended legalized segregation in public schools and launched the Civil Rights Movement.

Chicago Defender
Newspaper founded in 1905 by Robert S. Abbott that advocated for civil rights and promoted the Great Migration to southern blacks.

Civil Rights Act of 1964
Signed into law by President Lyndon B. Johnson on July 2, 1964, this legislation prohibited discrimination in public facilities, employment, and education, and ended federal aid to segregated institutions.

Civil Rights Movement
General term for the political and social movement of the 1950s and 1960s to win equal rights for African Americans.

Du Bois, W. E. B. (1868-1963)
African-American historian and civil rights leader.

Emancipation Proclamation
Proclamation signed by President Abraham Lincoln in 1863 that freed all slaves living in the Confederate states.

Fair Employment Act
An executive order (number 8802) signed by President Franklin D. Roosevelt on June 25, 1941, prohibiting racial discrimination in the hiring practices of the defense industry.

Fifteenth Amendment
Constitutional amendment adopted in 1870 that guaranteed male citizens the right to vote, regardless of race.

Fourteenth Amendment
Constitutional amendment adopted in 1868 that granted full citizenship to all African Americans.

Freedom Rides
Peaceful civil rights protests in which black and white activists traveled together on interstate buses to challenge segregated transportation facilities and systems in the South.

Garvey, Marcus (1887-1940)
Jamaican black nationalist and founder of the Universal Negro Improvement Association.

Great Migration
Term used to describe two major migrations of more than six million African Americans out of the South; the first took place from 1910 to 1930, and the second from 1940 to 1970.

Harlem Renaissance
A movement in literature, music, and art that arose out of the Harlem section of New York City in the 1920s; the Harlem Renaissance celebrated African-American history, life, and culture.

Hughes, Langston (1902-1967)
African-American poet, short story writer, and playwright, who became a leading figure in the Harlem Renaissance.

Inner city

Inner regions of modern cities that are predominantly African American and have high levels of poverty, unemployment, and crime; also called ghettos.

Jim Crow

Post-Reconstruction laws and customs that established segregation and discrimination against blacks in virtually all aspects of daily life across the South.

Kerner Report

A 1968 report of the National Advisory Commission on Civil Disorders that found that the United States "is moving toward two societies, one black, one white—separate and unequal."

King, Martin Luther Jr. (1929-1968)

African-American civil rights and religious leader and winner of the Nobel Peace Prize.

Lawrence, Jacob (1917-2000)

African-American artist best known for his epic series "The Migration."

Lynching

Term used to describe the killing of someone outside of any legal process, usually by hanging; the practice was used by white supremacists to terrorize African Americans in the South throughout the Jim Crow era.

Malcolm X

See X, Malcolm.

Migration

The movement of people from one area of a country or region to another with the intention of establishing a new life.

Montgomery Bus Boycott

A year-long civil rights protest, launched in 1955, that succeeded in ending segregation of the public transportation system in Alabama's capital city.

Moynihan Report

Informal name given to "The Negro Family: The Case for National Action," a controversial report written by Senator Daniel Patrick Moynihan and published by the Department of Labor in 1965.

NAACP
See National Association for the Advancement of Colored People.

National Association for the Advancement of Colored People
A civil rights organization founded in 1909 by a multiracial group to lobby for political and social changes that would grant equal rights to African Americans.

Parks, Rosa (1913-2005)
African-American woman whose refusal to give up her seat to a white man on a segregated city bus launched the Montgomery Bus Boycott.

Plessy v. Ferguson
Decision handed down by the U.S. Supreme Court in 1896 that legalized segregation of the races by ruling that "separate but equal" public facilities were constitutional.

Randolph, A. Philip (1889-1979)
African-American labor and civil rights leader who organized the Brotherhood of Sleeping Car Porters and the 1963 March on Washington.

Reconstruction
The post-Civil War period during which the federal government aided in the rebuilding of the South following the Civil War. The term refers especially to new laws that re-established civil governments and guaranteed the rights of newly freed African Americans.

Return Migration
The trend in which African Americans move back to southern states from the cities of the North and West.

SCLC
See Southern Christian Leadership Conference.

Segregation
The forced separation of people by race.

Separate but equal
A doctrine stating that government-mandated segregation of the races is legal as long as the facilities provided for the different groups are equal.

SNCC
See Student Nonviolent Coordinating Committee.

Southern Christian Leadership Conference (SCLC)
A civil rights organization founded in 1957 by the Reverend Martin Luther King Jr. and other ministers in the South.

Student Nonviolent Coordinating Committee (SNCC)
A prominent civil rights organization founded by college activists in 1960.

Thirteenth Amendment
Constitutional amendment adopted in 1865 that abolished slavery throughout the United States.

Voting Rights Act
Signed into law by President Lyndon B. Johnson on August 6, 1965, this landmark legislation prohibits the denial or abridgement of a person's right to vote based upon race or color.

X, Malcolm (1925-1965)
Nation of Islam minister, advocate of black nationalism, and activist for African-American rights.

CHRONOLOGY

1607
> English settlers land in what is today Chesapeake Bay, Virginia, and establish the colony of Jamestown.

1619
> The first African slaves are transported to North America.

1641
> The Massachusetts Bay Colony legalizes slavery.

1776
> The thirteen colonies of the United States of America declare their independence from England.

1781
> The Revolutionary War ends with an American victory; in 1783, the Treaty of Paris is signed, officially ending the war and granting the United States new territories to the west as far as the Mississippi River.

1787
> The U.S. Congress ratifies the Constitution.

1820
> Congress passes the so-called Missouri Compromise in an effort to stem the rising animosity between the North and South regarding the extension of slavery into new states.

1850
> Congress enacts the Fugitive Slave Law, which requires the U.S. government to actively assist slave owners in recapturing their runaway slaves. The law also compels citizens of Northern states to assist in the capture of any fugitive in their midst.

1857
> The U.S. Supreme Court hands down the notorious *Dred Scott* decision. The Court rules that the Missouri Compromise is unconstitutional because the federal government does not have the power to prohibit slavery in its territories. In addition, the

Court rules that all people of African ancestry, whether slave or free, are ineligible for U.S. citizenship—and thus have no legal standing to file suit in federal courts.

1861

The American Civil War begins.

1863

Abraham Lincoln signs the Emancipation Proclamation, freeing all slaves living in the Confederate states.

1865

The American Civil War ends with a Union victory.

Abraham Lincoln is assassinated by John Wilkes Booth on April 14.

The Thirteenth Amendment is adopted, banning slavery throughout the United States.

Reconstruction begins as the federal government aids in the rebuilding of the South and federal laws re-establish civil governments and guarantee rights to newly freed African Americans.

1868

The Fourteenth Amendment is ratified, granting full citizenship to all African Americans.

1870

The Fifteenth Amendment is adopted, guaranteeing male citizens the right to vote regardless of race.

1877

Reconstruction ends and African Americans are stripped of their rights throughout the South. Jim Crow laws are instituted in every southern state.

1896

The *Plessy v. Ferguson* decision handed down by the U.S. Supreme Court creates legalized segregation of the races based on the concept of "separate but equal" public facilities.

1909

The National Association for the Advancement of Colored People (NAACP) is established in New York by a group of white and black activists (including W. E. B. Du Bois and Ida B. Wells-Barnett).

1910

The cotton industry collapses in the South, spurring the earliest stirrings of the First Great Migration.

1914

World War I begins in Europe.

A labor shortage in the North prompts companies to send labor agents to the South in search of new employees.

1916

Marcus Garvey founds the Universal Negro Improvement Association (UNIA).

The *Chicago Defender*, a prominent black-owned newspaper, begins promoting migration with stories of jobs, housing, and opportunities in the North.

1917

Race riots erupt in East St. Louis, Illinois.

The United States enters World War I.

1918

World War I ends with a victory by the United States, England, and other Allied powers in November.

1919

Race riots break out in Chicago, claiming the lives of 23 blacks and 15 whites. Similar race-related violence erupts in other cities as well during the so-called "Red Summer" of 1919.

1920s

The famous Harlem Renaissance movement in literature, music, and art evolves in New York City.

1929

The Great Depression begins after the stock market crashes in October.

1933

Franklin D. Roosevelt is inaugurated as president and promptly launches an array of new government employment and economic programs known collectively as the New Deal.

1939

World War II begins in Europe.

1940

The Second Great Migration begins as defense-related manufacturers in the North and West offer work opportunities for a new generation of southern blacks.

1941

President Franklin D. Roosevelt signs the Fair Employment Act to curtail discrimination in hiring practices in the national defense industry.

The United States enters World War II after the Japanese launch a surprise attack on America's Pearl Harbor naval base in Hawaii on December 7.

1943

Race riots in Detroit result in the deaths of 25 blacks and 9 whites.

1945

World War II ends.

1948

President Harry Truman signs Executive Order 9981, ending segregation in the armed forces.

1954

The *Brown v. Board of Education* ruling handed down by the U.S. Supreme Court ends segregation in all public facilities, including public schools and public transportation.

1955

Rosa Parks refuses to give up her seat to a white passenger on a Montgomery, Alabama, bus and is arrested. Dr. Martin Luther King Jr. organizes the Montgomery Bus Boycott in response.

1960

Student protesters begin lunch counter sit-ins in Greensboro, North Carolina, to protest segregationist practices at eating establishments.

The Student Nonviolent Coordinating Committee (SNCC) is founded at Shaw University in Raleigh, North Carolina, to coordinate student protests on behalf of racial integration initiatives.

1961

The Congress on Racial Equality (CORE) begins the first Freedom Rides throughout the South, following the U.S. Supreme Court decision banning segregation in interstate travel.

1963

Dr. Martin Luther King Jr. organizes civil rights demonstrations in Birmingham, Alabama, and is arrested and jailed.

A. Philip Randolph organizes a mass march on Washington, D.C., for racial justice and jobs. The August "March on Washington" is highlighted by Martin Luther King Jr.'s "I Have a Dream" speech.

The Sixteenth Street Baptist Church in Birmingham, Alabama, is bombed on September 15, killing four African-American girls.

President John F. Kennedy is assassinated in Dallas, Texas, on November 22.

1964

President Lyndon B. Johnson signs the Civil Rights Act of 1964, making it illegal to discriminate on the basis of race, national origin, religion, or gender in voting, employment, education, and other areas of American life.

1965

Religious and civil rights leader Malcolm X is assassinated on February 21.

Peaceful protestors taking part in a voting rights march from Selma to Montgomery, Alabama, on March 7 are savagely attacked by Alabama state troopers. The "Bloody Sunday" attack increases public demands for new voting rights legislation. A second Selma-to-Montgomery march takes place two weeks later under federal protection.

President Lyndon B. Johnson signs the Voting Rights Act of 1965 into law on August 6.

1967

Widespread race riots take place across the United States, the largest of which occur in Detroit, Michigan, and Newark, New Jersey.

1968

Shirley Chisholm of New York becomes the first African-American woman to be elected to Congress.

Martin Luther King Jr. is assassinated in Memphis on April 4. His murder triggers a new round of rioting in urban centers across the country.

1970

The Second Great Migration (1940-1970) ends, delivering an additional five million African Americans from the South to destinations across the North and West.

1973

Several large American cities, including Los Angeles and Detroit, elect their first black mayors.

2009

The U.S. Census reports that 3.25 million African Americans relocated to the South from homes in the North and West between 1970 and 2009.

Barack Obama becomes the first African-American president in U.S. history.

SOURCES FOR FURTHER STUDY

In Motion: The African-American Migration Experience. Available online at http://www
.inmotionaame.org. A monumental undertaking, created and maintained by the
Schomburg Center for Research in Black Culture at the New York Public Library, In
Motion includes more than 16,500 pages of text and 8,300 illustrations, as well as
maps and extensive bibliographies. It covers thirteen African-American migrations,
from the sixteenth century to the present, including the transatlantic slave trade, the
First and Second Great Migrations, the Return Migration, and the migrations of
African people to the Caribbean Islands.

Lemann, Nicholas. *The Promised Land: The Great Black Migration and How It Changed
America*. New York: Random House, 1991. This work constitutes one of the first historical appraisals of the Great Migration. Lemann concentrates on the years 1940 to
1970, and on the migrants who settled in Chicago. He focuses in particular on the
decline in living conditions in the ghettos of the North—and the reasons why federal
programs developed during the 1960s to address poverty, unemployment, and violence failed to eradicate these problems.

Mintz, S. *Digital History*, http://www.digitalhistory.uh.edu. This comprehensive database
includes primary sources, audio files, timelines, online image galleries, and extensive
reference materials on all eras of American history. A collaborative effort of the University of Houston, the Chicago Historical Society, the National Park Service, and
other history sites, Digital History offers materials on the Great Migration from a
variety of media.

Stack, Carol. *Call to Home: African Americans Reclaim the Rural South*. New York: Basic
Books, 1996. One of the first treatments of the Return Migration, Stack's book is
based on interviews with dozens of black migrants from the North who returned to
their ancestral homes in the rural South. Stack focuses on several communities in
eastern North and South Carolina where migrants returned in search of a sense of
place and belonging.

Tolnay, Stewart. "The African American 'Great Migration' and Beyond." *Annual Review of
Sociology*, 2003. Tolnay, a demographer, has devoted most of his career to studying
the Great Migration. This essay is an important overview of the social, economic,
demographic, and cultural changes that the Migration brought to the northern cities.

Wilkerson, Isabel. *The Warmth of Other Suns: The Epic Story of America's Great Migration.* New York: Random House, 2010. Wilkerson's book stands as the most comprehensive and definitive book about the Great Migration to date. The author interviewed more than 1,200 migrants from all over the country, but she focuses her narrative on three migrants in particular: Ida Mae Gladney of Chicago, George Starling of New York, and Robert Foster of Los Angeles. She weaves their stories into the larger saga of African-American migrations from 1915 to 1970 to create an enthralling overview of black American history.

BIBLIOGRAPHY

Books and Periodicals

Adero, Malaika, ed. *Up South: Stories, Studies, and Letters of this Century's Black Migrations*. New York: The New Press, 1993.

Branch, Taylor. *Parting the Waters: America in the King Years, 1954-63; Pillar of Fire: America in the King Years, 1963-65; At Canaan's Edge: America in the King Years, 1965-68*. New York: Simon & Schuster, 1988, 1998, and 2006.

Chicago Commission on Race Relations. *The Negro in Chicago*. Chicago: University of Chicago Press, 1922.

DeSantis, Alan D. "Selling the American Dream Myth to Black Southerners: The *Chicago Defender* and the Great Migration of 1915-1919." *Western Journal of Communication*, Fall 1998.

Frey, William H. "The New Great Migration: Black Americans' Return to the South, 1965-2000." Washington, DC: Center on Urban and Metropolitan Policy, The Brookings Institution. The Living Census Series, 2004.

Griffin, Farah Jasmine. *"Who Set You Flowin'?" The African-American Migration Narrative*. New York: Oxford University Press, 1996.

Hirsch, Arnold. *Making the Second Ghetto: Race and Housing in Chicago, 1940-60*. Chicago: University of Chicago Press, 1998.

Johnson, James. "Recent African-American Migration Trends in the U.S.," *Urban League Review*, 1990.

Lemann, Nicholas. *The Promised Land: The Great Black Migration and How It Changed America*. New York: Random House, 1991.

Locke, Alain, ed. *The New Negro*. New York: Albert and Charles Boni, 1925.

Marks, Carol. *Farewell, We're Good and Gone: The Great Black Migration*. Bloomington: Indiana University Press, 1989.

Robinson, Isaac. "Blacks Move Back to the South," *American Demographics*, June 1986.

Sanders, Joshunda. "Moving Up and Out: Three Generations Reflect Continuing Migration of Black Middle Class," *San Francisco Chronicle*, July 21, 2002.

Scott, Emmet J. "Letters of the Negro Migrants of 1916-1918," *Journal of Negro History*, July 1919.

Sernett, Milton C. *Bound for the Promised Land: African American Religion and the Great Migration*. Durham: Duke University Press, 1997.

Stack, Carol. *Call to Home: African Americans Reclaim the Rural South*. New York: Basic Books, 1996.

Sugrue, Thomas. *The Origins of the Urban Crisis: Race and Inequality in Postwar Detroit*. Princeton, NJ: Princeton University Press, 1996.

Tolnay, Stewart. "The Great Migration and Changes in the Northern Black Family, 1940 to 1990," *Social Forces*, June 1997.

Tolnay, Stewart. "The African American 'Great Migration' and Beyond," *Annual Review of Sociology*, 2003.

Trotter, Joe William, Jr., ed. *The Great Migration in Historical Perspective: New Dimensions of Race, Class, and Gender*. Bloomington: Indiana University Press, 1991.

Wilkerson, Isabel. *The Warmth of Other Suns: The Epic Story of America's Great Migration*. New York: Random House, 2010.

Web Sites

"Black Migration" in *Jazz: A Film by Ken Burns*. Available online at http://www.pbs.org/jazz/places/faces_migration.htm.

In Motion: The African-American Migration Experience. Available online at http://www.inmotionaame.org.

John Novak Digital Interview Collection. Available online at http://research.marygrove.edu/novakinterviews/index.html.

University of Illinois at Chicago Great Migration Resources. Available online at http://www.uic.edu/educ/bctpi/pt3/greatmigration.html.

DVDs

The Promised Land. Discovery Channel and British Broadcasting Corporation, 1995.

Up South: African-American Migration in the Era of the Great War. American Social History Productions, Inc., 1993.

PHOTO AND ILLUSTRATION CREDITS

Front Cover and Title Page: Photo by Jack Delano. FSA/OWI Collection, Prints & Photographs Division, Library of Congress, LC-USF34-040827-D

Chapter One: Library of Congress Prints & Photographs Division, LC-USZ62-15398 (p. 9); Yale Collection of American Literature, Beinecke Rare Book and Manuscript Library (p. 10); Library of Congress Prints & Photographs Division, LC-DIG-ppmsca-19211 (p. 12); General Research & Reference Division, Schomburg Center for Research in Black Culture, The New York Public Library, Astor, Lenox and Tilden Foundations (p. 17); General Research & Reference Division, Schomburg Center for Research in Black Culture, The New York Public Library, Astor, Lenox and Tilden Foundations (p. 19); Manuscripts, Archives and Rare Books Division, Schomburg Center for Research in Black Culture, The New York Public Library, Astor, Lenox and Tilden Foundations (p. 22).

Chapter Two: Map by Michael Siegel/Rutgers Cartography, 2011 © General Research & Reference Division, Schomburg Center for Research in Black Culture, The New York Public Library, Astor, Lenox and Tilden Foundations (p. 27); Courtesy, State Archives of Florida (p. 29); Science, Industry & Business Library, The New York Public Library, Astor, Lenox and Tilden Foundations (p. 31); General Research & Reference Division, Schomburg Center for Research in Black Culture, The New York Public Library, Astor, Lenox and Tilden Foundations (p. 33); Photographs and Prints Division, Schomburg Center for Research in Black Culture, The New York Public Library, Astor, Lenox and Tilden Foundations (p. 35); General Research & Reference Division, Schomburg Center for Research in Black Culture, The New York Public Library, Astor, Lenox and Tilden Foundations (p. 39); The Granger Collection, NYC—All rights reserved. (p. 41); Courtesy of Franklin D. Roosevelt Presidential Library and Museum, Hyde Park, New York (p. 45).

Chapter Three: FSA/OWI Photograph Collection, Library of Congress Prints & Photographs Division, LC-DIG-ppmsc-00199 (p. 51); Map by Michael Siegel/Rutgers Cartography, 2011 © General Research & Reference Division, Schomburg Center for Research in Black Culture, The New York Public Library, Astor, Lenox and Tilden Foundations (p. 53); Grand Rapids History & Special Collections, Archives, Grand Rapids Public Library, Grand Rapids, MI (p. 55); FSA/OWI Photograph Collection,

Library of Congress Prints & Photographs Division, LC-USW36-187 (p. 58); Walter P. Reuther Library, Wayne State University (p. 61); AP Photo (p. 65); U.S. News & World Report Magazine Photograph Collection, Library of Congress Prints & Photographs Division, LC-DIG-ppmsc-01271 (p. 67).

Chapter Four: AP Photo (p. 70); AP Photo/Gene Herrick (p. 73); Courtesy of Tennessean (p. 75); Photograph No. 306-SSM-4C(36)6; "Civil Rights March on Washington, D.C.: Leaders of March Leading Marchers Down the Street," 8/28/1963; Records of the U.S. Information Agency, 1900-2003, Record Group 306; National Archives and Records Administration—College Park (Maryland) (p. 77); William Lovelace/Express/Getty Images (p. 81); New York World-Telegram and the Sun Newspaper Photograph Collection, Library of Congress Prints & Photographs Division, LC-USZ62-111167 (p. 82); Walter P. Reuther Library, Wayne State University (p. 84); AP Photo (p. 86).

Chapter Five: AP Photo/James Crisp, file (p. 91); Walter P. Reuther Library, Wayne State University (p. 93); Cynthia Johnson/Time Life Pictures/Getty Images (p. 98).

Chapter Six: AP Photo/File (p. 103); DoD photo by Mass Communication Specialist 1st Class Chad J. McNeeley/Released (p. 105); Leroy Patton/Ebony Collection via AP Images (p. 107); Nikki Kahn/The Washington Post/Getty Images (p. 109).

Biographies: The Abbott Sengstacke Family Papers/Robert Abbott Sengstacke/Getty Images (p. 117); Chicago History Museum/Getty Images (p. 122); AP Photo (p. 126); Photo by Cornelius M. Battey, 1918. Library of Congress Prints & Photographs Division, LC-USZ62-16767 (p. 129); George Grantham Bain Collection, Library of Congress Prints & Photographs Division, LC-USZ61-1854 (p. 135); AP Photo (p. 139); Photograph by James L. Allen, Yale Collection of American Literature, Beinecke Rare Book and Manuscript Library (p. 144); AP Photo/Charles E. Kelly (p. 147); George Rose/Getty Images (p. 153); Photograph No. 306-SSM-4D(102)31; "Civil Rights March on Washington, D.C.: A. Philip Randolph," 8/28/1963; Records of the U.S. Information Agency, 1900-2003, Record Group 306; National Archives and Records Administration—College Park (Maryland) (p. 157); Photo by Herman Hiller, New York World-Telegram and the Sun Newspaper Photograph Collection, Library of Congress Prints & Photographs Division, LC-USZ62-119478 (p. 162).

INDEX